CW00515701

PUBLICATIONS OF THE SCOTTISH COUNCIL
FOR RESEARCH IN EDUCATION

63

THE SCHOOL BOARD OF GLASGOW
1873–1919

THE SCHOOL BOARD
OF GLASGOW
1873-1919

JAMES M ROXBURGH

UNIVERSITY OF LONDON PRESS LTD

ISBN 0 340 14928 0

University of London Press Ltd
St Paul's House, Warwick Lane, London EC4P 4AH

Printed in Great Britain by
Neill and Co Ltd, Edinburgh

CONTENTS

5

LIST OF TABLES

PREFACE

Scotland is approaching the centenary of her Public School System yet hardly anything has been written of its history in detail. Most histories of education in Scotland end where public schools begin, in 1872. It is my hope that this short study will contribute to a fuller and more comprehensive knowledge of this important period.

The area administered by the School Board of Glasgow was that of the municipality in 1872. The western boundary was the River Kelvin from the Clyde to Great Western Road, thence north to the Forth and Clyde Canal near Firhill. From there the line ran due east to Springburn, then south-east to Parkhead where it turned south-west back to the Clyde. South of the river only Tradeston, Gorbals and Hutchesontown lay within the City. Although many of the surrounding suburbs were incorporated in the City during the following fifty years, their own school boards retained control of education. Thus the area of the Glasgow Board remained unaltered, except for the addition in 1911 of Maryhill and Springburn whose Boards voluntarily amalgamated with Glasgow.

The choice of Glasgow as the area of study is readily justified. In size it was easily the largest of the Boards in Scotland, and as such was bound to influence the rest of the country either for good or for ill. Nowhere else did the new system face a greater test, for in 1872 two in every five of Glasgow's children of school age were not enrolled in a school of any kind and only about one in two attended a reasonably efficient school. Secondary education was confined to the High School and the Academy, and even there usually ended at the age of fourteen or fifteen. Both charged high fees which effectively excluded all but the sons of the well-to-do. Other boys had absolutely no hope of a secondary education, not even the most brilliant, for the High School had no scholarships or free places. So the challenge to the new School Board was great. It is worth seeing what it made of it.

As far as possible I have tried to avoid straying into educational issues which are more properly national in character rather than local, and I have often assumed in the reader a considerable knowledge of the broader history of education. At other times, however, I have thought it better to set the Glasgow scene within a wider canvas and to sketch in the background. Quite often references are made to particular Glasgow schools in the belief that, although of no value to the outsider, they will interest the native Glaswegian who will know them by sight or repute, or will himself perhaps have laboured there either as pupil or teacher.

This is not a full history of the School Board period which would have required a much longer book. Several very important aspects of the Board's work have been omitted: notably the introduction of social services through the education authority, the development of curricula, the growth of technical and industrial classes, of physical education and of special schools for the handicapped, and the integral part played by evening classes in Glasgow's school system. Little has been said of the internal life of the schools, nothing of such minutiae as holidays or discipline. I believe, however, that the topics which are dealt with are of major significance and that they serve to exemplify the work, the idealism, the limitations and achievements of the School Board of Glasgow.

I am very grateful to Professor Stanley Nisbet of the Education Department of Glasgow University, and to his colleagues, the late Mr John Clarke, Dr T R Bone and Dr H Hutchison, all of whom encouraged me to continue this study over a lengthy period of years.

Nearly all the research was carried out in the Mitchell Library and the Library of the University whose staffs were ever patient and helpful.

This work would have been impossible without the Records of the Glasgow School Board. In the beginning they could not be found, and they came to light only when I was given access to the inner recesses of 129 Bath Street through the kindness of Mr John T Bain, then Deputy Director of Education. Mr Bain also gave me a letter of introduction which enabled me to visit many of the old Board Schools.

I especially wish to thank the janitors of these schools for showing me round the buildings. They took me into basement cellars in quest of old relics or climbed into dusty belfries. Often they showed a strong pride in their schools and in their histories, and were able to add to what I already knew or to put me on to the track of something unknown. I am grateful also to the headmasters of these schools who allowed me to see Log Books and other documents.

Finally, I am glad to have this opportunity of thanking my cousin, Miss L C Wilson, for doing all my typing.

J M R

Bearsden 1970

Chapter 1
THE FIRST ELECTION

For a few months after the passing of the Education Act in 1872 little could be done locally until the Scotch Education Department had been given time to frame the procedure and rules for the forthcoming election. By February 1873 Glasgow City Council had chosen the Lord Provost as returning officer and he immediately set the date of the first school board election for 25 March.

Quite apart from the natural interest aroused by this first real step by government to guide and control education on a national basis in Scotland, there were other reasons why the pending election should be particularly intriguing. These were three: the secret ballot, the inclusion of women on the electors' roll, and the largely increased electorate. Since the passing of the Ballot Act only a few months earlier Glasgow had not yet had the opportunity to test its effects on the city's political life. It was widely held that the previous parliamentary election had been won for the Liberals by rushing last-minute reinforcements to the polling stations when it had become apparent that greater support was needed. Such astute management and, of course, other more doubtful devices would no longer be possible. No one knew what effect secrecy would have on similar occasions in the future, but in the voting for the School Board it was to have its first trial. The second of the new features gave women an equal say with men. The innovation itself seems to have aroused little comment and virtually no antagonism, but it did introduce a novel and unpredictable element into the election. About one fifth of the whole electorate proved to be women, though it was by no means certain that they would exercise their votes in large numbers for the climate of opinion of the day was still inclined to regard public affairs as the exclusive province of the menfolk. In the event, the female voters took almost as great a part proportionately as the men, for more than one third of those eligible exercised their vote while the proportion for the whole electorate was rather

13

less than one half. The last of the new factors, the low franchise qualification of £4, raised the municipal electorate to 101,871 compared with the parliamentary list of only 53,111. While Glasgow thus almost doubled its voters, still greater increases were met with in some other areas. In Govan, for example, the electorate was multiplied more than four times. These new voters were a completely unknown quantity, the more especially as they came from the poorer classes. Not only had they little education themselves but many hundreds were, indeed, wholly illiterate[1] and quite unable even to read the names of the candidates on the ballot paper. It is small wonder, then, that the newspapers of the day made little effort at any serious attempt to forecast the result of the election, and all the more so as the system of cumulative voting made the probable outcome even more perplexing.

Yet, in spite of the secrecy of the ballot and the other manifest steps which had been taken in the direction of greater democracy, many still thought it possible to "make an arrangement". Not that the election was to be rigged or the voters influenced in any way—there simply was to be no election. Nor was the motive for such a plea at all ignoble. All over Scotland, parish after parish clutched its purse and sought some way out of the expense which would be incurred by an election. Yet it very soon became clear that even the thought of an estimated £6000 coming out of the Glasgow rates would not prevent a contest, and by nomination day no fewer than fifty-three candidates had entered the lists.[2] Nevertheless, only five days before the election the Lord Provost was still hoping, though rather timidly, for a compromise, and at a meeting he managed to have the number reduced to thirty-nine.[3] Govan attempted to avoid an election by sharing the seats between the four constituent burghs in the parish,[4] though also without success. Before being tempted, however, to scoff at such apparently pious hopes it is well to note that later elections were not always contested. In 1876 and 1879 Maryhill managed to avoid the

[1] See p 19.
[2] *Glasgow Herald*, 19 March 1873.
[3] *Glasgow Herald*, 20 March 1873.
[4] The Parish of Govan encompassed the Burghs of Govan, Partick, Hillhead and Kinning Park. The growth of burghs had been greatly facilitated by the General Police Acts of 1850 and 1862. [See *Third Statistical Account of Scotland 1958*: The City of Glasgow, p 44.]

bother and expense; even more impressive, in view of the huge electorate involved, was the similar achievement of Govan in these years, and even of Glasgow itself in 1888.

Although Gladstone was now in the midst of his great reforms, the social climate of the day still tended to leave public affairs in the hands of a relatively small number of "gentlemen" who, for their part, expected to play the role of leaders of society. So it is not surprising that the first group to appear as prospective members of the new public body seems to have assumed that it was their natural right and duty, for they named from among themselves no less than thirteen nominees, "leaving the Roman Catholics, the Working Men, the anti-Unionists and the Women to scramble for the remaining two seats".[1] Quickly dubbed the "Eminent Citizens" by the *Herald*, this group included the leading Presbyterian clergymen and a number of notable city merchants who, as a body, eschewed any very definite platform other than a promise to do all in their power to give full effect to the spirit of the Act. But they did not long remain unchallenged and several distinct parties quickly became discernible. All were agreed that the present state of schooling in Glasgow was very bad; all were agreed that a good elementary education must now be provided for every boy and girl in the city. The only real issue at large was what, if any, religious instruction ought to be included in the curriculum. The religious question was to mar the proceedings of the school boards throughout the forty-six years of their existence, but while this may be regretted it was hardly to be wondered at. For centuries the churches had provided for, and controlled, Scottish education, and they were unlikely to feel that their usefulness had now ended, or to give up their old position of prominence without a struggle. On the other hand, a body of opinion saw in the coming of publicly financed education a chance to be rid of clerical control and overmuch emphasis on theological formulary in schools, the time thus gained to be given over to a more thorough secular training. The Act of 1872 had left much scope for argument over this point for, unlike Forster's measure which categorically forbade school boards in England to allow the teaching of any distinctive creed or catechism, the Scottish Act laid down no very

---

[1] *Glasgow Herald*, 15 March 1873.

clear ruling. During its inquiries the Argyll Commission had been much impressed by the fact that it was common practice in Scotland for children of all denominations to mix freely in schools, and many a witness had testified that the system worked well and was generally accepted by parents.

Two main parties thus emerged: the one anxious to retain the age-old catechising of the children, the other determined to abolish it. This latter, calling itself the Scottish National Education League, framed a six-point programme:[1]

1 National Education.
2 Compulsory Education.
3 Maintenance of a high standard of education.
4 Definitely no catechism in schools.
5 Reading of the Bible, however, wholeheartedly approved, though it was to be read as literature, or history, or for moral training, and not given any specific sectarian interpretation.
6 No denominational schools—all must be absorbed in the secular state system.

It would be wrong to suppose that the members of the League were necessarily atheists or even non-churchgoers; indeed, three of their candidates were ministers of religion. Most were sincere and worthy men who could not in their consciences reconcile publicly financed schooling with sectarian indoctrination. Nor did they fail to argue the futility of attempting to explain to children mysteries which must always remain mysteries. Theological doctrine was quite beyond the comprehension of the children and therefore a waste of time. The very vocabulary of the catechism—fore-ordained, summarily comprehended, inordinate notions—could have no meaning. As one experienced teacher remarked, "It was disheartening work."[2]

The Roman Catholics constituted a third party, one whose role on the school boards was bound to be somewhat anomalous. While it was true that a number of Catholic children had in the past attended Protestant schools, apparently without much difficulty on either side, yet these were very few in comparison

[1] *Glasgow Herald*, 20 March 1873.
[2] *Glasgow Herald*, 24 March 1873.

to the thousands of their faith who lived in utter ignorance of the simplest cipher, partly because there were no suitable schools for them to attend. By 1873 the Roman Catholic population in Glasgow was considerable. A proportion came from the Highlands, but the great majority were of Irish origin and largely illiterate. What Roman Catholic schools there were in the city compared handsomely with the best of the Protestant schools, but the total accommodation available was deplorably deficient. The prevailing national interest in education was, of course, fully shared by the Catholic authorities, and all the more urgently perhaps because the tendency was towards increasing control by the state, always anathema to the Roman Church. Moreover, Bismark was currently embarked on his struggle with the Papacy and within two months was to employ his May Laws in an attempt virtually to extinguish Catholic influence in schools and universities. And was it not to the Prussian system of state education that so many pamphleteers in Britain pointed in high admiration?

There was no reason why the Catholic schools should not have become part of the Board System in 1873; at least, there was nothing in the Act to prevent such an arrangement. Public opinion, however, was not ready for an accommodation whereby board schools might follow different forms of worship according to their individual convictions. The Protestant parties demanded the extreme positions of religious instruction according to the lights of the Presbyterian churches, or else no religious instruction at all. Therefore the Catholics chose to retain control of their own schools and their own children by keeping them outside the public system, even although this meant a considerable financial sacrifice. But as citizens and ratepayers they were on an equal footing with the rest of the electorate, and now determined to secure representation on the Board in order to "safeguard their rights as far as possible, to press for such local relief as was available and to keep a check in their own interests, on excessive expenditure".[1]

Thus, when the voters went to the polling stations to elect the first School Board of Glasgow they had three main parties from which to choose: ministers and laymen of the Scottish churches who advocated the continuance of "use and wont";

[1] *Glasgow Herald*, 20 March 1873.

the anti-catechist League, to whom were allied the Congregationalists, Evangelicals, Baptists and the Trades Delegates; and finally the Roman Catholics. In addition, there stood as independents a few men who, though small in number, were to exercise a considerable influence on the result of the election. They also took their stand on the religious theme, either on the extreme left or the extreme right.

THE ELECTION RESULTS

It had generally been taken for granted that the Roman Catholics would secure three seats. So it proved. A few days before the election the Central Committee of the Catholic Association published a call to all Catholics. "If you will come to the poll we can return THREE CATHOLIC candidates. In the full confidence that every catholic elector will do his duty on the day of the election, three catholic candidates have been nominated:

Rev Alex Munro (St Andrews)
Rev Valentine Chisholm (St Johns)
Hon Francis Kerr (late officer in the Pope's Zouaves)."[1]

All three nominees not only were returned but secured second, third and fourth places in the poll. In considerable measure the ease with which the Catholics carried their representatives on to the Board was due to the peculiar method of voting by which each elector had fifteen votes at his disposal (there being fifteen vacancies for the Glasgow Board) and could distribute them among the candidates as he thought fit. Anyone giving all his fifteen votes to one candidate was known as a "plumper". It had been pointed out that this method of voting was open to certain objections, especially that a well-organised party, even though small, could gain a disproportionate voice.[2] That the Catholics were well-organised there was never any doubt, a conviction amply demonstrated on election day. Committee rooms were set up where supporters were carefully instructed in where and how to mark the voting paper so that each Catholic candidate

---

[1] *Glasgow Herald*, 11 March 1873.
[2] *Glasgow Herald*, 3 March 1873. For a development of this point see Chapter 11.

received five votes, and they were then marshalled into the polling stations. Cabs were used to bring along the aged and infirm. It was a splendid piece of organisation and a very necessary one in view of the widespread illiteracy among them.[1] The number of voters whose papers had to be marked by the presiding officers because of inability to read was 4021, of which many were said at the time to belong to Catholics.[2]

The Presbyterian group formed a solid core in the middle of the list, but a notable feature was the almost complete rout of the League which had managed to squeeze in but a single representative, the Rev Dr Walter Smith. Easily at the top of the poll came Henry Alfred Long whose success reflected the strong anti-Roman element among Glasgow's citizenry. "I, for my part, could not shake hands with the Pope; I could only punch his head,"[3] said this complete Orangeman, and it seemed that many shared his opinion. At the opposite extreme stood another independent, the Rev John Page Hopps, who advertised himself as "the only candidate who is in favour of the Secular System in public and state-aided schools". If publicity was a key to success then Hopps was a certain winner, for on the day before the election the *North British Daily Mail* carried no less than ten separate manifestos, occupying twenty inches of space, extolling the virtues of John Page Hopps.[4]

Yet it is likely that many of the members were elected on personal grounds rather than party politics. The earlier election at Eastwood had returned two doctors and a local employer of labour, and a correspondent to the *Herald* suggested that the former had probably been supported by patients of all denominations while many of the latter's workmen may have plumped for him.[5] Similar influences appear to have operated in Govan where three members were well-known and much respected employers, and where voting tended to be on a regional basis between the four burghs. Whatever the reason, there can be no doubt that the first School Board of Glasgow contained a majority of quite outstanding personalities, men who had already proved themselves in other walks of life and

[1] *Glasgow Herald*, 26 March 1873.
[2] *Glasgow Herald*, 28 March 1873.
[3] *Glasgow Herald*, 24 March 1873.
[4] *North British Daily Mail*, 24 March 1873.
[5] *Glasgow Herald*, 5 March 1873.

were among the elite of their respective professions. Several were already well-versed and experienced in educational affairs, half-a-dozen were established authors, there was a sprinkling of successful businessmen whose skill was soon to be so useful, while men like the Rev Dr Robert Buchanan, Mr Michael Connal, Mr Alexander Whitelaw and Mr William Mitchell typified the best kind of Victorian educational and social philanthropists. Their worth was recognised by one of their own headmasters who, when president of the Glasgow branch of the Educational Institute of Scotland (EIS) some years later, said,

> "I believe I state a commonly recognised fact when I say that as a rule, the first School Boards were composed of men of good position, of robust intelligence and of broad views on educational matters. To the liberal and, on most points, sound views by which the members of these first School Boards were animated much, perhaps most, of the subsequent prosperity of our schools is due."[1]

MEMBERS OF THE FIRST GLASGOW BOARD

Alexander Whitelaw

A leading industrialist and commercial figure in the city, Whitelaw was a nephew of James Baird of Gartsherrie Iron Works at Coatbridge, a partner in the Eglinton and Gartsherrie Ironworks, a director of many commercial and philanthropic institutions and director of the Chamber of Commerce. He was an active philanthropist from his earliest days at Gartsherrie where he gave much attention to the welfare and education of the employees' children.[2] His firm was erecting schools and caring for poor children long before 1872, and it was said, "Gartsherrie Academy is the finest public building in Coatbridge."[3] These schools catered for 4500 children at a cost of £3000 annually.[4] As well as being one of the managers of the Ferguson Bequest, Whitelaw was also a principal trustee of the

---

[1] James Milligan, *Is Teaching a Profession?* Inaugural Address as President of the Educational Institute of Scotland, 1889.
[2] Proceedings at the presentation of Whitelaw's portrait to the Corporation of Glasgow, 29 December 1880.
[3] *The Bailie*, No 34, 11 June 1873.
[4] Andrew MacGeorge, *The Bairds of Gartsherrie*, privately published, 1875, pp 93–4.

TABLE 1

MEMBERS OF THE FIRST SCHOOL BOARD OF GLASGOW AND THEIR PLATFORMS

Name	Denomination	Number of Votes	Official EC	Official UP	Declared Catechist	RI as heretofore with conscience clause	Sabbath School Union	Temperance League	Eminent Citizens	Scottish National Education League	Trades Delegates	RC	Orangemen	Independent Secularists	Notes
H A Long	EC	108,264			×								×		
Rev A Munro	RC	50,331										×			
Rev V Chisholm	RC	49,558										×			
F Kerr	RC	46,225										×			
J A Campbell	EC	45,730	×		×	×	×								
Rev R Buchanan	FC	45,590	×		×		×	×	×						
A Whitelaw	EC	39,776				×									
Wm Kidston	FC	38,735		×	×	×		×							
Rev R Jamieson	EC	25,484	×		×	×	×	×	×						
Rev A Macewan	UP	23,216		×	×		×	×	×						
Rev J P Hopps	Unitarian	21,141												×	Extreme secularist. No Bible in school.
Rev P H Waddell	Latter Day	18,858												×	Secularist. No catechism, Bible for parents who want it.
M Connal	FC	18,308		×			×		×						
Rev W C Smith	FC	16,126							×						
Wm Mitchell	FC	16,017				×				×					

This table indicates only (a) official support from a recognised party or group. (b) personal declarations in Election Manifestos.

$£\frac{1}{2}$ million willed by his uncle for religious and educational work in the Church of Scotland. The uncle seems to have been a hard man in his lifetime for his legacy was cynically described as "the highest fire insurance premium ever paid",[1] but there is no reason for believing that a similar view was held of the nephew. At the first meeting of the School Board he was unanimously placed in the chair. Only a year later he became Conservative MP for Glasgow and, while the Board lost by his absences at Westminster, his influence there was to prove of considerable benefit on several occasions when the Board came into conflict with the Scotch Education Department and sought to modify Departmental policy.

Michael Connal

Similar to Whitelaw in several respects, Connal was a more reticent man and rather averse to public office if it involved fighting for a place. But he felt an obligation to accept such responsibilities were he pressed to take them up. Although head of a large merchant and shipping company, perhaps Connal's chief qualification for membership of the School Board was his work among lads and youths in the East End. Still to be seen, though dimly, on the railway arch which spans Graeme Street is a plaque which was put there at the time the City Improvement Trust swept away some of Glasgow's worst squalor; "Here stood Davidson's Court where the Spoutmouth Bible Institute was founded in 1848." Connal was the founder. He had begun his social work in the area ten years earlier and, besides his philanthropy and bible classes, had helped to introduce his young men to mechanics' institutes and the Penny Savings Bank. Perhaps he found his greatest pleasure in such work when he took his boys on outings to Garelochhead or Arran, country holidays which provided the example for the later Fresh Air Fortnight movement. At the first election for the Board the poorer classes tended to give their votes to men personally known to them rather than to ideas, for they did not much read newspapers. Connal was one of those men. From 1876 to 1882 Connal was chairman of the Board and thereafter

[1] quoted in W H Marwicks, *Economic Developments in Victorian Scotland*, London: Allen and Unwin, 1936, p 177.

continued to serve as a member until his death in 1893, being knighted for his services to education.[1]

Harry Alfred Long

Long was another who owed his successful election to his labours among the under-privileged and the destitute. Completely unknown outside Bridgeton until the School Board election,[2] he was already a well-kent figure on Glasgow Green and in the surrounding district where he founded and managed his Working Men's Evangelical Association. Long described himself as a missionary, and certainly his description well-fitted his low salary[3] and his bigoted zeal. His organisation did not confine itself to the words poured out in over two million tracts, leaflets and books, but undertook also the more telling deeds of bedding and feeding the unemployed and of finding many of them work. Long could frequently be seen ranting on the Green against all and sundry, but especially against Popery, and it was from the Orange element in Glasgow that his chief support was derived. He remained a member of the Board, with only one triennial break, until 1901. The violence of his opinions gave him a rather ugly look, yet *The Bailie* was able to say in later years that "he cherishes no personal rancour towards his enemies—one of the kindliest of men".[4]

The Rev Alexander Munro

Long's natural antagonist was the Rev Alexander Munro, senior priest of St Andrew's Catholic Church and a principal Roman Catholic publicist. Of Protestant parents, Munro possessed the extreme convictions which are so often to be found in converts. He had spent some years teaching at the Scotch College in Valladolid and was the author of a number of books. Notable among these was his *Calvinism and its relations to Scripture and Reason*, to which Long retorted with *Priestly*

[1] F H Georgesson, An "*In Memoriam*" *Sermon*, privately published, Glasgow, 1893; and A Gillespie, *Sir Michael Connal and his Young Men's Institute*, privately published, Glasgow, 1898.
[2] *The Bailie*, no 25, 9 April 1873: "Not one in five hundred could answer the question, 'Who the deuce is Long?'"
[3] £150 for over thirty years.
[4] *The Bailie*, no 1223, 25 March 1896.

Hypocrisy Unveiled. Thus, the two men were already at loggerheads before 1872, and it was inevitable that this mutual antagonism should be carried into the deliberations of the School Board whenever religious matters intruded. Munro served the Board for eighteen years, by which time new honours had been conferred upon him, including Doctor of Divinity and the papal title of Monsignor. By 1888 *The Bailie* felt that he was "held in high esteem by all". Munro's co-religionists were the Rev Valentine Chisholm, parish priest of St John's, and Francis Kerr. Kerr was utterly unknown in Glasgow in 1873, being resident so far away as Roxburghshire. He remained a very shadowy figure and was not nominated in 1876.

The Rev Robert Buchanan, DD

Buchanan stands out clearly as one of the most prominent churchmen in nineteenth-century Scotland. He arrived in Glasgow in 1833 on a call from the Tron Kirk, once the pulpit of Chalmers. Within a year he became closely associated with the new Glasgow Educational Association which had been formed with a view to improving the very poor and very insufficient educational provision of the city. One of the Association's major projects was the founding of a Normal School system, and on the sub-committee appointed to deal with this task David Stow had Buchanan as a colleague. When the Disruption came in 1843 Buchanan followed Chalmers, and the succeeding years were occupied in feverish building of new churches and the sessional schools which went with them. By now Buchanan was the leading Free Church figure in Glasgow. In 1849 he published *The Ten Years' Conflict*, a standard history of the Disruption. The full flood of Free Kirk missionary zeal carried Buchanan into the Wynds which surrounded his church and in which lived some of the most poverty-stricken classes in Glasgow. Here the Free Tron established two schools, one in Miller's Place and the other in Old Wynd, and it was as the result of experiences there that Buchanan produced his lecture *The Schoolmaster in the Wynds* which, as a pamphlet, ran into several editions.[1] The Free

[1] See N L Walker, *Biography of Dr Robert Buchanan*, London: Thomas Nelson and Sons, 1877; and *The Bailie*, no 29, 7 May 1873.

College Church was built specially for him, and he was so highly regarded as to be presented with 4000 guineas by the wealthier members of his Church.[1] He died in Rome only two years after election to the School Board.

James A Campbell

In 1825 a first son was born to Sir James Campbell of Stracathro.[2] A second son, Henry, later adopted the additional surname of Bannerman, as required by a relative's will, and went on to become leader of the Liberal Party and Prime Minister. But although Henry Campbell-Bannerman achieved national fame he by no means overshadowed the eminence of his elder brother in the affairs of Glasgow and of Scotland.

Like several other members of the School Board, Campbell was one of the city's leading businessmen[3] who had long given much of his time and labour to social and educational work. Long before 1872 he was "more or less connected with some of the old parochial schools",[4] and in the lengthy discussions which preceded the Education Act he had taken a prominent part, giving a series of public lectures on "The Education Question".

On election to the School Board Campbell supported the Catechist Group, as befitted a strong adherent of the Church of Scotland and one who was for many years a member of the General Assembly and of several of its committees. Politically he opposed his brother, acting as Conservative Party manager in Glasgow for some years before himself entering parliament where he sat from 1885–1906 as Member for the Universities of Glasgow and Aberdeen. Among his many activities on behalf of Glasgow University was that of convener of the committee set up in 1865 to raise funds for Gilmorehill, a position he retained until the committee's dissolution thirty years later. Beginning with the Scottish Universities Commission of 1868, Campbell was a member of all the Royal

[1] Extract minute from the Records of Session of the Free Church College, Glasgow, 28 April 1875.
[2] The boy was born in his father's home at 129 Bath Street, which later became the offices of the School Board, and the site of which is still occupied by the Glasgow Corporation Education Department.
[3] J and W Campbell, Wholesale Drapers and Warehousemen.
[4] *Glasgow Herald*, 11 May 1908. Obituary.

Commissions on education thereafter. He was Deputy Lieutenant of Lanark and Forfar, JP of both, honorary fellow of the EIS, the receiver of honorary degrees from Glasgow and St Andrews, Privy Councillor—and member of the first School Board of Glasgow.

J A Campbell died within a fortnight of the passing of his statesman brother.

The Rev Walter C Smith, DD, LLD

Smith was yet another of the long line of distinguished ministers who filled the pulpit of the Free Tron Church. A man of great personal charm, he was much beloved by his congregation.[1] In the literary field he had many works to his credit on religious themes, but was probably best known for his prolific production of poetry.

The Rev Robert Jamieson, DD

Dr Jamieson, who "may be taken as a specimen of the best type of Scottish clergyman", was[2] minister of St Paul's and Moderator of the Church of Scotland at the time of his election to the School Board.

On the Board his charitable spirit and moderation served a very useful purpose. "It is in no way out of place to say that Dr Jamieson is a better member of the School Board than he was a Moderator of the Kirk. He stands, together with Doctors Buchanan, Smith and Macewan, as a buffer between the narrowness of Messrs Kidston and Long on the one hand, and that of Father Munro and the Rev Page Hopps on the other."[3]

The Rev Alex Macewan, DD

Minister of Claremont United Presbyterian Church and Moderator of the United Free Church, Macewan was noted for his liberal views. He had the curious distinction of having a new organ lying idle in his church for fifteen years while he

[1] *The Bailie*, no 27, 23 April 1873.
[2] *The Bailie*, no 122, 17 February 1875.
[3] *ibid.*

fought outside prejudices against it.[1] He is famous for having
had a famous professorial son who, among his other achievements, was the founder of the Historical Association of Scotland.

The Rev P Hately Waddell, DD

As a Latter Day preacher Dr Waddell could not count on any
organised support, but probably was elected to the Board
because he was well known among the working classes. He was
a great and enthusiastic lecturer on Burns and had written a
Life of the poet. He engaged on a translation of the Bible into
Lowland Scots though only the Psalms were published.

William Kidston

Kidston lived on his property of Ferniegair in Helensburgh
but had his business in town. A very strong churchman fully
committed to upholding the church's role in the education of
children, he stood on the extreme right of the use and wont
issue. "He knows that it is well for the immortal souls of
children that they should learn the carritch, and his opponents
are but wicked unbelievers who ought to yield or be crushed."[2]

Kidston turned out to be one of the hardest working members
of the Board.

The Rev John Page Hopps

Hopps was a native of Cambridge who had come to Glasgow
to take over the pulpit of the City's only Unitarian Church in
Bath Street. Under his energetic leadership the Unitarians
flourished in the city as neither before nor since.[3]

An out and out secularist in education he joined the Board
determined to prevent, if he could, any form of religious
teaching in schools. The Bible might not even be read. Hopps
and Long were already old controversialists and enemies[4] and
carried their theological differences into the Board.

[1] *The Bailie*, no 38, 9 July 1873.
[2] *The Bailie*, no 23, 26 March 1873.
[3] L B Short, *Pioneers of the Scottish Unitarians*, pp 110–18. Published
privately by the author, 1963.
[4] *The Bailie*, no 24, 2 April 1873.

Hopps is remembered in the Scottish Hymnary as the author of the children's hymn, "Father, lead me day by day".

William Mitchell

In 1873 a little-known calico printer and businessman, advocate of use and wont, Mitchell in later years turned out to be the most diligent and valuable member of the Glasgow School Board. He served on it for nearly thirty years, and *The Bailie*, usually more given to scurrility than praise, commented that he was "pre-eminent among its fifteen members. . . . As a servant of the ratepayers he is better value than all his clerical colleagues, with a few other drones to boot, rolled into one."[1]

---

[1] *The Bailie*, no 737, 1 December 1886.

Chapter 2

THE ELECTION OF 1879

As the second Board's period of office drew to a close there began the usual negotiations for an uncontested election. Needless to say, these broke down, but this time for a very different reason from any that had arisen previously. It was the demand for economy. During the first year of School Board operations the rate levied for education was fourpence in the pound, for each of the following four years it remained steady at threepence, but in 1879 it had gone up once more to fourpence. Now it became known that the estimates for the next year meant a probable increase to fivepence. Immediately there were loud protests, and five "Ratepayer Candidates" were nominated with retrenchment as their platform.

They based their attack on the two most costly items of expenditure, building and salaries. Already the Board had borrowed £401,800 at an interest rate of $3\frac{1}{2}\%$ and had a considerably larger building programme planned.[1] The Ratepayer Group opposed further building on the grounds that it was unnecessary as there were still enough voluntary schools to supply the need. It went on to claim that the surviving sessional and other private schools were superior to Board Schools in the quality of education given.[2] While the latest Government returns did, in fact, show that the Board Schools were earning less grant per pupil than schools outwith the Board's control, this can be accounted for largely by the different type of child in the two groups of schools, for the new public schools had been deliberately sited in areas of greatest need whose children had often never been inside a school before while, on the other hand, the good sessional schools catered for a higher class of child and demanded substantial fees. The fact was, however, that many of the remaining independent schools had already decided to close and were merely hanging on until such time

[1] Report of Finance Committee 1879.
[2] *Glasgow Herald*, 1 March 1879, Letter to Editor.

as the Board could provide for the children. Although average attendance in all types of school had increased by some 15,000 pupils since 1873, there yet remained a very considerable leeway to make up before every child in Glasgow could find a place in an efficient school. In subsequent years it was found quite impossible to restrict the building programme. Consequently, economies had to be sought elsewhere.

Salaries of teachers was the obvious target, and particularly the very high remuneration being earned by several headmasters in the new large schools. Two of these men had earned over £700 in the last financial year—more, it was quickly pointed out, than many a university professor.[1] In their campaign speeches the Ratepayer Candidates promised to limit teachers' salaries to a maximum of £400, though excepting the High School from this limit.[2]

In their denigration of the retiring Board the Ratepayers directed their attack mainly against the clergy. Even today it is commonly asserted that the churches were over-powerful on the school boards and that their influence was not always in the best interests of education. The early years in Glasgow do not bear this out; all evidence indicates that the ministerial members were men of outstanding integrity deeply concerned to do all within their power for the children of the city. Indeed, it was this very disinterestedness upon which they were now attacked. The Ratepayers denied all allegations that they wished to depose the clergy on religious grounds, and their educational liberalism was never questioned. Ministers were unsuited to sit on the Board, not for deficiencies in their educational policies, but because they pursued these policies without due regard to the financial burden involved. They were said to lack experience in the efficient handling of large sums of money and should now therefore be replaced by businessmen who were obviously the people best fitted to look after the public's cash.[3] This was a most ironic claim to make at a moment when Glasgow was reeling from the disastrous collapse of the City of Glasgow Bank.

The members of the retiring Board who were offering

---

[1] *Glasgow Herald*, 19 March 1879. Election Campaign Meeting.
[2] *ibid.*
[3] *ibid.*

themselves for re-election formed a remarkably united body. They claimed that the Board had in no sense been divided within itself regarding the policies it had pursued. As one of them remarked, "In the Board, Priest and Presbyter, Radical and Tory were alike unknown",[1] and, except for the Catholic nominees, the old Board now shared the same campaign platforms and a common election manifesto.

Father Munro in his election speeches on the whole supported the measures which he and his old colleagues on the earlier Boards had taken, but he naturally was concerned to keep down the rates in view of the fact that although the Catholics paid this levy their children did not share in the benefits. He denied that the ordinary teachers were being overpaid, but suggested that the salaries of headmasters ought to be curtailed. In thirty-four schools now under the Board, £30,841 was the total expended on salaries, and of that total £11,677 went to headmasters alone, giving them an average per man of £364 while the average for the ordinary assistant teacher was only £81.[2]

Economy was the main issue at the third School Board election, and the results were to demonstrate the power of an appeal to the purse, for the Ratepayers carried four of their candidates into the new Board—Mr A G Collins, Mr J Colquhoun, Mr W Fife and Mr J Fleming. Henceforth a measure of division and contention was introduced into the Board which had previously been absent. The original high principles and the scholarly men gave way to something rather less. The idealism of these earlier members and their dismay at the new trends may best be illustrated by quoting from the private diary of the Board chairman, Michael Connal,[3] writing at the time of the 1879 election and of subsequent Board meetings:

"The *Herald* and *News* very fair in their criticism; the *N.B. Daily Mail* is unjust and ungenerous towards the Board—I wish to see the Education Bills of 1872 and 1876 a success. O Lord, keep me humble and true to what is right (15 March 1879).

"The Committee meeting of the School Board passed off so far well; so much so, that I was not prepared for a most unpleasant

[1] *Glasgow Herald*, 21 March 1879. Election Meeting of Logan and Aikman.
[2] *Glasgow Herald*, 11 February 1879. Election Meeting of Father Munro.
[3] *Diary of Sir Michael Connal*, 1895.

meeting on Thursday last, when the four ratepayers' candidates, leagued with the Roman Catholics and Mr Martin, outvoted us and carried their point, arresting further payments to teachers and reviewing the whole expenditure. This cannot be taken per saltum; six years work cannot be compressed into the experience and information gathered in ten days. These men seem determined to crown their successful candidature by showing the citizens good grounds for their rash assertions. Cuthbertson resigned his post as Convener of the Property Committee, but has since been induced to retain it. I felt so heavy at heart that I would willingly, but for the call of duty to the community and the great cause of education in the country, have retired from the Board. The community may come to see that the post cannot but be filled eventually by men of liberal views as to remuneration. They must take more interest in the election for the future (12 April 1879).

"I feel more and more the pressure of the School Board as to the money responsibilities of it. The present is a crisis in the education of the country, and the example of Glasgow will be followed by other communities. The narrow question of saving the rates may lead to arresting the expansion of ideas as to the remuneration of teachers and as to accommodation which has been shown in working out the Act hitherto (19 April 1879).

"I felt a repugnance in going to the School Board today. There is so much difference of opinion about things of no great moment (30 July 1879).

"Monday last, 8th inst., quite a field day at the School Board. I prayed for grace to do what was right. . . . The new men are too overbearing" (10 September 1879).

Connal's comment that the electorate must take more interest in future is not without its significance. In 1873 the percentage of the electorate which had voted was 51%. In 1876 it had declined to 39% and in 1879 had dropped as low as 30%. Glasgow did not seem much interested in education now that the novelty had worn off.

Chapter 3
TEACHERS' SALARIES

During the first two triennial periods of the Board no definite scale of salaries was evolved. It seems that salary was based, naturally enough perhaps, on past practices in the grant-aided schools, though even these were so variable, depending as they so often did on fees, either in whole or in part, that there was no simple rule to follow. An added difficulty when trying to discover the rule-of-thumb adopted by the Board is that, since there is no way of knowing the previous experience of a teacher at the time of his appointment by Glasgow, it is impossible to relate this factor to his salary on appointment. While there are no reliable figures to prove that the salary offered by the Board was at least equal to that prevailing in the past there are several good reasons for supposing this to be so:[1] the members of the Board were reasonable and liberal men who may confidently be expected to have taken such a view, there was no lack of candidates for posts, and this was the principle followed by some other Boards in the area.

Of the five categories of staff—monitors, pupil teachers, ex-pupil teachers, assistants and headmasters—the scales for the first two are known definitely. Monitors were paid at the rate of 15/- per month.[2] Because it was exceptional to quote salary monthly and because monitors were only engaged on a temporary basis, it is possible that monitors were not paid any salary during the summer holiday month of July. In March, 1874 the following scale was adopted for male pupil teachers:[3]

1st year of apprenticeship	£12
2nd ,, ,, ,,	£15

[1] On the other hand, when the New Salary Scheme was put into effect the headmasters claimed that "several of our number had higher salaries under their former management than are paid them now". Memorial from Headmaster to the School Board of Glasgow, para 7, 1879.

[2] Minutes of Board in Committee, 31 March 1874.

[3] The scale for girls is unknown but certainly was less. Govan paid girls between £2 and £5 less than boys.

3rd year of apprenticeship		£18
4th „ „ „		£21
5th „ „ „		£25

Only two thirds of this sum was paid over unconditionally. For example, a first-year boy did not receive a monthly payment of £1, but only of 13/4d. The remaining third, £4 in the first year, was "only to be made after the pupil teacher has passed the examination before Her Majesty's Inspector and produced a certificate of good conduct and attention to duties from the Headmaster".[1] Consequently, a considerable portion of the pupil teacher's salary depended both on pleasing his headmaster throughout the year and on satisfying the Inspector at the annual examination. Ex-pupil teachers received about the same as senior pupil teachers, but their tenure was very precarious and depended upon their gaining entrance to Normal School within a limited time.

In 1875 the normal male assistant's salary ranged from £52 to £90 with the great majority earning £70, £75 or £80. By 1879 only five men were earning less than £80, while at the upper end of the scale seven received £120, seven £150 and one man reached £170. A number of these better-paid individuals were graded "Second Master".

TABLE 2

DISTRIBUTION OF BASIC SALARIES

Salary £	70	75	80	85	90	95	100	105	110	11
Men	..	..	......	......	....	....	......	.	...	
			......	......	....		..			
				......	....					
				......	....					
				......	....					
				.	.					
Women			......	......	......	......	.	......		
			......	......	......	......		......		
			....	......	......					
			......		......	.				
			......		......					
			......		.....					
			......							
			......							
			.							

[1] Minutes of Board in Committee, 31 March 1874.

Table 2[1] shows the salaries being received by all teachers under the School Board in 1879, one dot representing one teacher. It should be noted that the extreme cases mentioned in the previous paragraph are not shown. Perhaps the most noticeable comparison of the scales between men and women is the debarring of the women from the higher and better paid posts. Never considered for headships, they were also limited in their promotion prospects as assistants. Not one woman earned more than £100 while nineteen men exceeded this figure, several of them by a considerable margin. But there was another source of income for many women teachers—that part of the Government grant for the training of pupil teachers which was given to the teacher responsible for them. No less than sixty-eight women were able to augment their salaries from this source. Table 3 shows the gross income when pupil teacher payments are taken into account. The men gained comparatively little, but the pattern for women is considerably modified. The number of women earning over £90 has now increased from twelve to thirty-nine, and one of these ladies reached £118. Clearly, pupil teacher grants were of great importance to the women teachers on whom the main burden fell.[2]

If the determination of assistant teachers' salaries was difficult, those for headmasters perplexed the Board even more

TABLE 3

DISTRIBUTION OF SALARIES WHEN PUPIL TEACHER INCREMENT IS INCLUDED

Salary £	70	75	80	85	90	95	100	105	110	115
n	..		.....	......	......	......	......	.	..	
			.....	......	......		......			
				......	......					
				......	......					
				..	......					
					......					
					....					
men	.....	......	......	......	......	......	......	.		......
		......	......	......	......	..	......			
		......	......	......	..		.....			
		......		......						
		......		......						
		......		......						
		..		.						

[1] From the Annual Reports on every school, 1879.
[2] There were two reasons why the task of training pupil teachers was the responsibility mainly of women:

for it was the headmasters who were to be most affected by payment by results. Assistants received a fixed amount irrespective of results, and it was only when the question of a salary increase arose that their efficiency was taken into account. Should their work merit an increase they received it, otherwise they did not. But with the headmaster the declared policy of the Board was that his salary would be determined *directly* by the amount of Government grant earned from examination passes and by income from fees paid by. the children. Here again they were simply following custom. The great problem, however, was to decide in what proportions of these money sources the headmasters should be rewarded. Bewildering variety prevailed during the early years as this random selection for 1875–76[1] indicates:

Headmaster	School	Roll	Salary
Wilson	Dobbie's Loan	740	£50 + $\frac{1}{3}$ fees + $\frac{1}{3}$ grant
McNaughton	Rockvilla	311	£25 + $\frac{1}{2}$ fees + $\frac{1}{2}$ grant
Harvey	Springbank	311	£60 + $\frac{1}{2}$ fees + $\frac{1}{3}$ grant
Gilchrist	Grove St	523	£120 only
Donald	St Rollox	400	£400 only
Milligan	London Rd	409	£250 only
Jardine	Buchan St	833	£100 + $\frac{1}{4}$ fees + $\frac{1}{4}$ grant

The only reasonable explanation for such variations is that the bargain struck between the Board and the headmaster was based on the salary he had received in his previous school. Many of the headmasters were teaching the same children or were working in the same building and had merely changed their employer. Invariably the managers of schools which were transferred or discontinued requested the Board to retain the services of the existing staff without their suffering any personal loss. Probably each man was reluctant to change from a salary

---

(a) There were many more girls than boys.

(b) Clause 70(c) of the Scotch Code laid down that pupil teachers must "be of the same sex as the certificated teacher under whom they serve, but in a mixed school may serve under a master, and may receive instruction from him out of school hours, *on condition that some respectable woman, approved by the managers, be invariably present during the whole time that such instruction is being given.*" (Italics are the author's.)

[1] From the Annual Reports on the respective schools. All other salary figures for individuals also come from school Annual Reports.

formula the effect of which he knew from experience, but it must have been a very nice decision to choose between such combinations as £25 + ½ fees + ½ grant and £60 + ½ fees + ⅓ grant. Unfortunately, the final sum earned that year by Mr McNaughton from the former system or Mr Harvey from the latter is not known. It will be seen that size of school appears to have little bearing on salary. The £150 difference between Mr Donald and Mr Milligan, whose schools had a similar roll, might be accounted for by the circumstances of their appointments, for while Mr Milligan was a new headmaster in a new temporary Board School, Mr Donald had taught for many years in an old established and successful St Rollox which had been managed by generous patrons.

The trend over the next few years is best illustrated by following the fortunes of individual headmasters. A definite Board policy as to how salaries ought to be determined becomes evident, but it must again be emphasised that no uniform system was imposed throughout the schools; the peculiarities already discussed remained, but became fewer and fewer as the headmasters were transferred to new schools and opportunity was taken of revising their salary structure.

At the end of 1876 Mr Donald of St Rollox was transferred to a new permanent school at Thomson Street which held 886 pupils. At first his salary formula did not alter, indeed it was becoming the common one among heads, but the records now show the effects of this composite salary system in detail and give the eventual net salary.

Mr Donald (Thomson St) Accom 886

1877 Minimum	£300	
1878 Salary £80 per annum, *plus* ⅓ fees (after deducting pianoforte fees £52 8s 0d) £274 11s 7d *plus* ⅓ grant £243 1s 5d and *plus* £1 5s 0d for teaching pupil teachers	£598 18s	0d
1879 Salary £80 per annum, *plus* ⅓ fees £308 7s 5d *plus* ⅓ grant £287 13s 4d	£676 0s	9d
Maximum salary allowed	£600	
1880 Salary under New Scheme contained in Report of Committee on Teachers' Emoluments	£487 14s	2d

Mr Liddell (Oatlands) Accom 1286

1877 Minimum	£300		

1878 Salary £80 per annum, *plus* ⅓ fees
£294 9s 7d *plus* ⅓ grant £397 7s 2d — £771 16s 9d

Maximum salary allowed, £600 *plus* £24
for teaching pupil teachers — £624

1879 Salary £80 per annum, *plus* ⅓ fees
£304 7s 8d *plus* ⅓ grant £417 12s 8d — £802 0s 4d

Maximum salary allowed — £600

1880 Salary under New Scheme contained in
Report of Committee on Teachers' Emoluments — £470 7s 10d

Mr Laidlaw (Crookston) Accom 1135

1877 Minimum — £300

1878 Salary £80 per annum, *plus* ⅓ fees
£352 7s 6d *plus* ⅓ grant £324 15s 3d — £730 2s 9d

1879 Salary £80 per annum, *plus* ⅓ fees
£332 0s 11d *plus* ⅓ grant £337 0s 2d — £749 1s 1d

Maximum salary allowed — £600

1880 Salary under New Scheme contained in
Report of Committee on Teachers Emoluments — £508 5s 3d

An examination of the above examples clearly shows that
four stages of development took place within as many years:

1 guaranteed minimum salary;
2 payment by results;
3 imposition of a maximum salary;
4 greatly reduced salary under the Ratepayers' Scheme.

1 Guaranteed minimum salary

The years 1874–9 saw a very rapid building programme in
progress during which twenty-seven large new schools were
opened. In the first year of a school's existence it was not
possible to relate the salary of a headmaster to the results of the
examination because no inspection had taken place. In any case,
it was unreasonable to expect the school to have got into full
working order until a settling-in period had elapsed. For the
first year, therefore, the headmaster was guaranteed a fixed

income, and £300[1] was the sum given in all schools excepting
only one or two of the smaller ones where only £250 was the
figure.

2 Payment by results

Now at last the Board felt able to implement its ideal of
basing the rewards of a headmaster on the results he could
produce in his school. He was expected to reap only where he
had sown, and the £80 + $\frac{1}{3}$ + $\frac{1}{3}$ became general. It is most
unlikely that any of the headmasters complained of this
arrangement, for they immediately began to receive incomes
far in excess of anything previously within the imagination of
an ordinary schoolmaster. As early as 1878 several Glasgow
heads were approaching £600 per year, while Mr Laidlaw
rejoiced in his £730.

3 Imposition of a maximum salary

No sooner had the Board achieved its long desired aim of
payment by results than it was considerably startled by its
unforeseen effects. Overnight a teacher could aspire to become
one of the best paid men in the community, for there were few
other professions in the 1870s that could promise such steady
and such high incomes. The fact was that there were now two
new factors which made the old form of payment by results
inappropriate. The first of these was the size of the new schools.
They had been designed for upwards of a thousand pupils, a
number far in excess of all but the most exceptional school prior
to the Act of 1872. Even with only a moderate showing at the
annual examination the Government grant was bound to be
much larger than had been normal in the past. Not only were
the schools very large but the children necessary to fill them
came along without any exertion on the part of the headmaster;
compulsory attendance provided the pupils for him. Even the
old argument that by running a superbly efficient school he
would establish a reputation for his school and so attract extra
pupils had lost its force. Now that there was so little to choose
between buildings, equipment and skilled staff, there was less

[1] Minutes of Board in Committee, 12 May 1874.

incentive for a parent to send his child to a school at a greater distance from his home than some others. Compulsory zoning of schools was never introduced by the School Board, but in practice most children attended the primary school nearest to their homes. The second traditional source of income for the master, that of fees, was also no longer appropriate, for the parents had no choice but to send their children to school and to pay the fees whether they liked it or not. The personality and skill of the master did not now affect the school's income from fees.

The legislation of 1872 rendered payment by results a wholly unsuited form of remuneration for individual teachers. To some extent it could still be maintained that it might be used as a basis for a pool of money from which to pay teachers as a body, but not an individual headmaster. The very high salary being earned by several headmasters in Glasgow caused the Board to revise and to modify its policy when, in 1879, it imposed a maximum permissible salary of £600. The Board had, in fact, virtually abandoned its own principle of payment by results, yet it continued to insist that this was the ideal by which it was guided in determining teachers' salaries.

4 The Ratepayers' Scheme

As has been described in an earlier chapter on the Election of 1879, the high salaries of some of the teachers did not escape the notice, nor evade the wrath, of that section of the community which felt it was being forced to foot the bill. The Ratepayers in their vigorous attack on the retiring Board did not suggest that the principle of payment by results and a proportion of the fees was a wrong one. Indeed, it was their complaint that the Board was not applying this principle fully or properly, and that the *total* paid in salaries ought not to exceed total school income derived from Government grants and school fees combined. This would ensure that teachers' salaries, far and away the largest single recurring item in educational expenditure, would have no effect on the education rate.

Immediately the new Board entered on its duties in 1879 it became clear that the atmosphere of the boardroom would henceforth be altogether different from the past. For six years business had been conducted with a sense of great urgency, the one thought in everyone's mind being to make good the serious lack of schooling in the city. Apart from early squabbles over the religious issue it was seldom that the Board found it necessary to divide on a motion, but now the Board was rent into two almost equal factions, each bitterly opposing the policies of the other. The surviving members from the Old Board formed what they themselves regarded as the party of educational progress, which progress could not be maintained without paying for it. Their names were Michael Connal, the Rev Dr Logan Aikman, the Rev Dr James Dodds, William Kidston, Harry A Long and William Mitchell. In all that was to follow it is worth noting that these men were the strong advocates of the Established and Free Churches and of the catechism: the Church Party was the liberal party. The opposing group of economical reformers consisted of the three Catholic representatives, Rev Dr Alex Munro, Rev Cuthbert Wood and James McCluskey, the four Ratepayers, Collins, Colquhoun, Fife and Fleming, and one town councillor, James Martin. There were thus eight economists to seven liberals—a narrow majority of one, which was to prove sufficient to alter completely the original disinterested single-minded character of the Glasgow School Board, and also severely to damage the good relations which had hitherto existed between the Board and the teaching staff.

Of the economical reformers the Catholics may be fully excused since they had excellent grounds for complaint against paying rates in the benefits of which they did not share. But all the others were directly accountable to ratepayers and committed to a policy of retrenchment on purely economy grounds. Perhaps it was a pointer to the future that the first city councillor to sit on an education board used his vote to cut expenditure—even although he was not one of the "Ratepayer Nominees" at the election and had given no indication of his intentions in the matter.

Shortly after the new Board was convened the Chairman read the financial statement and went on to move a motion that the School Rate be raised to fivepence. Collins countered this proposal with an amendment: "That the rate be continued at

B*

4d for the year 1879–80, and that therefore the word fourpence be substituted for five in the motion."[1]

The amendment was lost, partly because the economist group was not present in full strength, but this incident marked the opening of the struggle.

The real tussle took place in the Teachers and Teaching Committee, and although the Committee Minute Book for these months is missing the secondary sources make quite clear what took place behind locked doors. After a long and stormy meeting of the full Board the following motion was carried by a majority of one: "That it be laid down by this Board as a principle to be aimed at as that on which teachers should be remunerated, that the aggregate fees and grants in the Board Schools should meet the current expenses, including the salaries of the Teaching Staff; and that it be remitted to a Sub-committee to frame a scheme showing how this principle would work in the present schools—the sub-committee to take account of, and report on, any exceptional cases where they consider the principle could not be equitably applied, consistently with efficient education in the City."[2]

Thus the Ratepayers had carried their election promise that teachers' salaries would not exceed the combined income from fees and grants. The Special Sub-committee now prepared proposals as to how this might be achieved in practice. However, an interim report dealt not only with salary but with the size of staff, which suffered an immediate reduction: "The maximum school staff shall, in future, be one Assistant or two Pupil-teachers for every 300 scholars instead of every 200, in addition to the staff required by the Scotch Code."[3] Glasgow was able, therefore, to continue to boast of a staff/pupil ratio in excess of government regulations, but these were minimum requirements and can scarcely be regarded as being over-generous at the rate of one assistant, or two pupil teachers, for every eighty scholars after the first sixty.[4]

In the more serious matter of salary the individual members prepared and submitted their own schemes, but only that of the Ratepayers stood any serious chance of being adopted. It was

[1] Minutes of Board in Committee, 7 May 1879.
[2] Minutes of Board in Committee, 18 June 1879.
[3] Minutes of Board in Committee, 21 May 1879.
[4] Scotch Code, Art 32(c), 1879.

forced through against fierce opposition, and many delaying or tempering amendments were brushed aside. As each clause of the New Scheme was voted on and passed, Connal, Long, Mitchell and Kidston recorded their dissent. The two latter members had their reasons for dissenting from the measure written into the minutes, and those of Kidston are given in full in the Appendices[1] as is also a protest lodged by the Headmasters' Association.[2] The most vehement and outspoken opponent of the New Scheme was Kidston, which is not surprising as he had been Convener of the Teachers and Teaching Committee since the beginning, and it was his policies and his own achievements which he now felt to be in danger of collapse. Moreover, the primary duty of revising the salary scales had been taken out of his hands by the appointment of the Special Sub-committee in which he was not included and on which the Ratepayers had an easy majority. So bitterly did Kidston fight the salary plan that the economists forced his removal from the convenership of the Teachers and Teaching Committee. The final motion to do so was very temperate in tone, but the original motion better indicates the high feelings which were running at the time. "Mr Kidston, Convener of the Teachers' Committee, having, at the last meeting of the Board, used language with reference to certain members of the Board, implying that they had been returned to the Board for the purpose of destroying the efficiency of the Board Schools; and it being expedient to discountenance the imputation of such motives, this Board hereby censure Mr Kidston for the language so employed, and remove him from the Convenership of the Teachers' Committee."[3]

THE NEW SALARY SCHEME

The scheme recommended by the special committee and finally adopted by the Board was as follows.[4]

Headmasters

1 A fixed salary of £100, which may be raised to a sum not

[1] Appendix A, pp 229-31.
[2] Appendix B, pp 222-3.
[3] Minutes of Board in Committee, 23 September 1879.
[4] Minutes of Teachers and Teaching Committee, 4 October 1879.

exceeding £150 in cases where the fees are low and difficult of collection.

2 One fourth of the fees.

3 One fourth of the grant.

4 When the emoluments from the above reach £350 only one eighth of the fees and grant is given in excess of that sum.

5 The minimum salary is to be fixed at £200 or £250, according to the class of school.

6 The maximum salary to be £500.

7 Before the proportion of grant due to the masters was calculated there was to be deducted from the income of the school the ordinary school expenses, over which the master had greater or less control. The Committee made this proposal in the view that it was expedient that the headmaster should be interested in the school being conducted with due regard being had to economy. The expenses actually deducted are the charge for Books, Apparatus and Stationery, Repairs to Furniture, the Water Rate, Fuel and Light.

Assistants

1 Masters were to receive from a minimum of £70 to a maximum of £100, with intermediate grades of £80 and £90.

2 Mistresses rose from £60 to £90, with intermediate grades of £70 and £80.

Pupil teachers and ex-pupil teachers

New scales were also prepared for these members of staff. They are described in Chapter 10, "The Pupil Teacher".

The new salary scale for headmasters meant the reduction of grant proportion from the old one third, first to one quarter and then one eighth, the reduction of minimum salary from £300 to £200 or £250, the maximum to be £500 instead of £600, and the raising of the fixed wage by £20. The majority of headmasters suffered a considerable financial loss, as may readily be seen by referring back to the three examples already given. The figures for Mr Liddell are the most remarkable. Within two years his salary dropped by £154, but had the £600 limit not already been imposed in 1879 and had he continued to earn, therefore, on the old one third fees and grant method his loss can be reckoned at over £300. However, not all head-masters suffered so severely as those whose schools were either very large or in good grant-earning areas. For example, Mr Small at Bridgeton Public School with only 330 pupils was earning £200 until the new scheme raised this sum to £231. Out of thirty-nine schools the change in scales brought increases to six masters of £31, £25, £20, £13 and £7.

The most important question, of course, is not so much the effect of the new scale on individuals as on the education of the children, but here so many variables and imponderables intrude that a satisfactory answer is not possible. Apart from other factors, it is most doubtful if the teaching staff worked either more or less hard than they had done before. All that can be said with certainty is that the educational standards of the Glasgow schools, as measured by the times, did not decline but continued to improve over the succeeding years. Nevertheless, one of the economy measures must surely merit outright condemnation on grounds of health as well as education. To impose on the headmaster a pecuniary interest in limiting the use of books, materials and apparatus was a most retrograde step which, in the hands of some men, could seriously hamper the work of a school. And one wonders if a vigilant headmaster, intent on turning down the gas and turning off the water taps, reluctantly jeopardised the eyesight of his children and caused them to sit with dirty hands or to shiver in rooms less warm than the winter weather demanded.

In conclusion, it will be recalled that the chief aim of the economist party was to bring the cost of teachers' salaries within the total income from fees and grants. This objective was achieved and maintained for the next fourteen years.

Chapter 4

THE BOARD'S POLICY REGARDING
THE QUALIFICATIONS OF TEACHERS

The Education Act of 1872 did not demand that all teachers in public schools should have been trained, but only that the principal teacher of a board school must be certificated.[1] Certification was generally achieved as the result of a satisfactory performance during a full Normal School training course of two years.[2] Practically all entrants to the Normal Schools had already spent some years as pupil teachers.[3] At the end of their apprenticeship the pupil teachers took a government examination, and those who did well in the advanced subjects of mathematics, Latin or Greek had a special merit mark placed against that subject. Such distinction was of considerable importance to the candidate as it entitled him not only to enter the training college but to attend university classes as well. The Scotch Education Department paid 75% of all fees, and as both church training colleges in Glasgow provided the remaining 25% a promising student received the whole of his teacher training entirely without cost to himself (apart from a small sum for books) as well as two years at university.[4] Moreover those wishing to complete their university course up to graduation were encouraged to do so by financial aid from such bodies as the Church of Scotland Education Committee or, after the recommendations of the Endowments Commission, Hutcheson's Hospital.[5] The proportion of male students taking the joint course appears to have been remarkably high, being, for example, an average of 55% over the three years 1884–6 in the Free Church training college.[6]

---

[1] Education (Scotland) Act, 1872, Art 56.
[2] But note that the Code (Art 47, 1873) required a minimum of only one year.
[3] "96% at least" Evidence of Rector of Free Church Training College before the Committee of Enquiry into Education in Scotland, 1888.
[4] *ibid*, paras 142–6, 267.
[5] *ibid*, para 142.
[6] *ibid*, para 222.

From the beginning the School Board of Glasgow pursued the policy of employing only trained teachers.[1] It had, however, avoided a good deal of personal hardship by accepting untrained staff who were already in the service of schools which came under the Board's control by transfer or purchase, but by 1886 only two assistant masters and nine mistresses who had not undertaken a training course remained in Glasgow. By comparison, the city could boast of 603 certificated teachers at this time.[2] Of course, Glasgow probably was more fortunate in this respect than many other boards. Being a populous area with two training colleges gave Glasgow an advantage from the start, and to these factors were added a reasonable salary scale, a large number of responsible posts, good promotion prospects because of the large number of schools, and proximity to a university where teachers could acquire a degree through part-time attendance. In 1887 the Chairman of the Board affirmed that Glasgow was well satisfied with the present training system and that the Board got the kind of teacher it sought: "We have no difficulty in the supply. At the same time the supply is not above the demand. When the students leave the training colleges they get places almost immediately. We do not find it necessary to raise the salaries. Teachers' salaries in Glasgow are fair but nothing more . . . I have no doubt we get the choice both of men and women, and we find they suit our purpose remarkably well."[3]

In most Glasgow schools there was a category of teacher known as an ex-pupil teacher. These were time-expired pupil teachers who were awaiting admission to the Normal Schools. Provided a pupil teacher had passed "Well" in at least three out of the four annual examinations during his apprenticeship the Board retained his services until the time came round for the July entrance examination to the training colleges. "We will keep you on as an ex-pupil teacher, and if you pass we will retain you until the Normal School opens in January of next year. If you do not pass high enough to get in—having fallen,

[1] Not all boards could make a similar boast. When asked if some boards still took untrained teachers (and this as late as 1887) HM Chief Inspector replied, "I am afraid some continue to take them because they get a cheaper rate."

[2] Committee of Enquiry into Education in Scotland, para 3.

[3] *ibid*, paras 94–5.

however, not below the second class—we will keep you as an assistant teacher for another year, and give you another opportunity of taking the examination."[1] That is to say, the Board allowed its pupil teachers two chances to get into one or other of the training colleges, but if they failed to gain entrance at the second attempt they were dismissed. These ex-pupil teachers thus constituted a second class of uncertificated teacher though each remained employed for a maximum period of only two years.

There was also a special group of teachers in the schools, though a very small one indeed, which provided another exception to the normal rule of the Board to use none but trained men or women. These were university graduates wishing to take advantage of Article 59 of the Act which made provision for a graduate to receive certification on the Department's satisfying itself as to his competency in teaching. The Code of 1878 further required the graduate to have done some teaching in schools for at least three months.[2] But it is interesting to note that the Glasgow Board apparently did not continue to employ these men even after they had received Departmental recognition, so convinced was the Board that a teacher must be properly and fully trained at a college for his task. This point was made clear by the Clerk to the Board in his evidence to the Parker Commission:[3]

Q But you do not take any graduates from the University who have not been at a training college?

A No. The Board have taken graduates at their own request and allowed them to go through the training required by the Code in one of their schools; but this is done as a favour to the graduate, and one of the conditions attaching to it is that he is not to look for a permanent appointment after he is certificated.

Q You put a graduate through the required course of training, and yet you do not think him qualified for the purpose?

A Graduates apply to us as a favour to be allowed to go into one of our schools for the 12 weeks. . . . That he is granted wholly as a favour to the individual. . . . The Board never considered a

[1] Committee of Enquiry into Education in Scotland, paras 3, 4, 21.
[2] Art 47(c).
[3] Report of Committee appointed to inquire into certain questions relating to Education in Scotland (Parker Commission), paras 5–7. See also para 110 ". . . latterly we had so many offers of men in that position that now we do not give them any remuneration. We get their assistance, such as it is, and they get the practical training."

> 12 weeks training a sufficient course, especially when they are
> able to get a sufficient number of teachers trained for the full
> two years.

In other words, the Glasgow School Board drew a very definite
distinction between a "trained" (and therefore certificated)
teacher, and one who was merely "certificated". And the latter
was not favourably regarded.[1]

Yet it would be wrong to assume from this that the Board
disapproved of the university man; quite the contrary. What the
Board especially desired was the Normal School trained
teacher who had supplemented his education by university
studies. It agreed wholeheartedly with the view that "the
Normal School-trained and university-trained man . . . is the
highest type of a teacher. I find that the university training
results in the student getting a wider grasp of a subject. It has
often been said that the university makes the man, and that the
training college makes the teacher."[2] Holding this opinion
so strongly the Board early came to an arrangement with the
university by which those of the Board's teachers who were
fitted for a university course and who wished to pursue one
were allowed time off from their normal duties to attend
university classes. These classes took place for two or three
hours in the morning,[3] although it is not known how many days
in the week were involved.

Every encouragement was given the teachers to better their
own education:

> "It has been a matter of sincere gratification to the Board that so
> many of their Assistant Masters are now University Graduates. . . .
> The Board have uniformly given favourable consideration to

[1] This was also the view of HM Inspectors who ". . . while fully recognising the advantage of adding university education, were unanimous and
decided in preferring the Training College man, not only to the acting
teacher, but to the average untrained graduate" (*ibid*, p 3). It should be
noted, however, that they were thinking solely in terms of elementary
schools. In the higher schools scholarship, rather than professional tech-
nique, was the criterion of a good master. The Glasgow Board's preference
for the trained man, whether graduate or not, did not extend to the High
School. Glasgow seems to have been exceptional in the view it took of the
three-month-trained graduate. Laurie, Professor of Education at Edinburgh,
asserted that such men had a distinct advantage over the ordinary Normal
School product, and that ". . . they had all got positions soon, and good
positions too, and the best positions are reserved for them. The best places
frequently fall to them" (*ibid*, paras 768–72).
[2] *ibid*, para 37.
[3] *ibid*, para 54.

applications addressed to them by Assistants for permission to attend College. This can only be done in any case where it is certain that the school will not suffer, but subject to this, the Board are anxious to do all in their power to encourage Assistant Teachers to prosecute their studies. The Committee ventures to express the hope that this continues to be largely done, even after their university course is finished. There probably never was so good a supply as at present of teachers of average, or it may be, slightly above average qualifications; but what the country lacks at present, and in all probability will lack more, is teachers of high qualifications, not only as regards scholarship but as regards the complicated work of managing a modern school."[1]

It is unlikely, however, that mere exhortation and congratulation would by themselves have sufficed to induce staff into taking university courses had the Board not also helped in some more practical form. And this it did by continuing to pay the teacher his full salary: "Thirty-five assistants, by permission of the Board, are this year attending the University. They are at the same time acting as assistants. This has been the rule of the Board for the past six or eight years. They are relieved from a portion of their duties to do that, and are still paid at the same rate. The Board has never taken a penny of these teachers' salaries for their absence in attending college. . . . They believe they do not lose by the bargain."[2] There was a gentleman's agreement that the teacher should not forsake the classroom for some other profession as soon as he had obtained his degree. Probably few other boards were so generous and liberal-minded with their staff. This was certainly true about the great majority for only the largest and wealthiest areas could afford to grant their teachers such privileges, but even Edinburgh only gave permission for their staff to attend university ". . . in exceptional cases and on special grounds".[3]

That this policy of the Board did much to improve the quality of its staff there can be little doubt. There is nothing in the records to suggest that any of the original or early teachers were graduates. Twenty years later, out of a total male staff of 332, Glasgow had sixty-six graduates.[4] In addition, 139 men had attended university for at least one full session, some of

[1] Report of Teachers and Teaching Committee, 1882.
[2] Committee of Enquiry, 1888, paras 8–9.
[3] ibid, Report section, p 4.
[4] Report of Teachers and Teaching Committee, 1893.

whom would go on to complete their courses. This must be considered a worthy achievement by both men and School Board, for both the quantity and the social background of male pupil teachers were poor and a repeated topic of comment and cause for some concern.[1] Few of the women teachers concerned themselves with higher education, no doubt because the universities still did not admit them on an equality with men. Yet in 1887 three Glasgow mistresses held the LLA certificate,[2] and their number was to grow.

---

[1] Committee of Enquiry, 1888, paras 114, 241.
[2] *ibid*, para 42.

Chapter 5
PROVIDING THE PLACES

There was no doubt in the minds of those on the new Board what was the most immediate and urgent task before them—to build the schools which were needed for the thousands of illiterate children of the city. But how many thousands? Already the statistics gathered by the Argyll Commission were out of date. So the Board, as required by the Department, undertook a swift but thorough census of all existing schools. The classification adopted was one which the Board continued to use throughout the years to come and is therefore worth noting. Schools were divided into six main classes: those inspected by the Scotch Education Department, those inspected by the Home Office, "Higher Class" schools (being defined as those which charged fees of over ninepence a week), Free and Charitable schools, Private Adventure, and Unsatisfactory.

To qualify for the last of these categories a school had to be very bad indeed, for the Board well knew that it would have its work cut out to eliminate even the grossest caricatures of schools. In later years the Board would be able to condemn many more schools as "Unsatisfactory", but for the moment some of those which qualified were like the Dame's School which was held in a but-and-ben. The teacher lived in the kitchen, while the room served as classroom, gymnasium and playground rolled into one. "The dame who taught the school was a bit of a philosopher and did not believe in her pupils being idle. She therefore had the wooden bottom of the bed taken out, and to the recess thus cleared she relegated the little ones in rotation when not being taught. And thus it was that while she had a class in hand the remaining young spirits were playing 'jing-a-ring' in the happy hunting ground of the bed recess."[1] Other proprietors of adventure schools found rather different ways of solving their problems. One of the census takers visited such a school in an old weaver's shop. "On asking for the

[1] John McMath, *Progress of School Building in Glasgow*, 1873–92, p 10.

52

'master' a small boy, who appeared to be in charge for the moment, came forward and in a stage whisper said, 'Please, sir, this is the day we pay our fees, and he's in the shop next door'." He was, remarked the investigator, ". . . combining porter with penmanship and geography with Glenlivet".[1]

Of the other classes, Private Adventure schools were generally very small, often very bad, and were soon largely to disappear; Free and Charitable schools gradually diminished in number, though one or two even outlasted the School Board itself; Higher Class schools, many of them "for young ladies", also tended to disappear quite rapidly; the Home Office was concerned with reformatories. None of these groups of schools (with the exception of the High School) was the concern of the School Board. Schools inspected by the Scotch Education Department included many Roman Catholic schools as well as all those under the direction of the Board.

The Board's census showed that there were in Glasgow 87,294 children of compulsory school age.[2] To provide for them there existed 228 schools of all kinds having accommodation for 57,290. Thus, in terms of desks alone there was a deficiency of 30,000 places. However, the total school roll for the city was only 52,644, showing that fully 35,000 Glasgow children received no schooling whatsoever. If average attendance is taken into account the picture was worse still as this added another 10,000 absentees. In other words, putting the most generous interpretation on these figures only about 60% of children ever went to school at all. In some districts the situation was far worse. For example, south of the river a mere 8143 places, many very bad, served a potential school population of over 18,000.[3]

Even after allowing for Roman Catholics, who would go to their own schools, the task before the Board was a huge one. It decided, as its initial aim, to provide for an additional 22,000 scholars in thirty or so new schools.[4]

Individual members of the Board now spread out through the town seeking suitable building sites, the while trying to make

[1] John McMath, *Progress of School Building in Glasgow*, 1873–92, p 10.
[2] ie, between 5 and 13 years.
[3] First Report of Progress in preparations for providing new Public Schools, 1874.
[4] Summary of Work, 1873–82, pp 3–4.

their inquiries as casual as possible and hoping to remain unrecognised, for it was certain that such a spree of public spending would encourage owners of land to raise their prices. By the end of the year the Board had acquired twenty-nine sites, and had submitted them to the Education Department for approval and payment of grant. At this point progress was brought to a sudden halt for the Department refused to sanction the plans, and for four months not a stone was laid while the Board, joined by others including Govan and Dundee, argued with the Department.[1] Letters flew back and forth, a deputation went to London, and MPs lobbied the government (fortuitously Alex Whitelaw had been elected to Parliament only a few months after becoming the first Chairman of the Glasgow School Board).

The quarrel centred round the Department's demands that the new schools should be single storey buildings with long rooms no wider than 22 feet. Such buildings would have required much more spacious sites than those proposed. The various boards were dismayed at these requirements. While single storey constructions might be very well in the country, in towns where land was at a premium nothing less than two storeys, and more likely three, would be economic. Moreover, the Department had based its grants on average cost of building schools throughout the country in 1865! Building costs had jumped in the intervening eight years, especially in rapidly growing towns like Glasgow and Govan. Glasgow reckoned that if forced to comply with the Department's wishes the increase in costs thereby entailed would itself absorb the whole of the building grant.

Eventually the Department capitulated. Classrooms could be up to 32 feet in width and school boards might arrange the furniture as they saw fit.[2] This early skirmish led to one or two architectural features of board schools which became well known to generations of children, for the Department still insisted that ". . . the boys and girls should enter by separate stairs, and should not mingle until they were under the eye of the teacher in the classroom."[3] Thus the separate playgrounds,

---

[1] Letter Book No 1, 11 February 1874 and 5 March 1874.
[2] Minutes 6 April 1874.
[3] J McMath, *op cit*, p 11.

the doors marked "Boys" and "Girls" and, inside, strange and wonderful double sets of stairs which testified to the ingenuity of architects in reconciling official requirements with thrifty space saving.

The construction of half-a-dozen schools began immediately. But it would be over a year before they would be ready for occupation, and something had to be done at once to give the untutored thousands the education to which they were now by law entitled. The School Board members were impelled by a great sense of urgency. Lacking proper schools for the time being, they leased and pressed into service an odd assortment of buildings and rooms: ". . . halls, old factories, derelict churches and similar buildings, some of them awfully pictur-esque in their decay",[1] became schoolrooms. Far from ideal, dirty and draughty, these makeshift quarters introduced Glasgow's poorer boys and girls to the benefits of schooling. Most, of course, were able to be abandoned after a few years when the permanent schools were ready, but meantime visitors were not astonished to come upon a class of shivering youngsters struggling (perhaps!) to concentrate on the words of their teacher, who herself laboured under the handicap of holding up an umbrella to keep off the snow coming down through the holes in the ceiling.[2]

The first permanent school, called Rose Street,[3] opened in October 1874. It was a three storey rectangular building about 30 yards by 12 yards, and had been adapted for school purposes from what was formerly part of a workshop. This building was to accommodate 741 pupils. Rose Street continued to function as a school in one form or another until 1966, by which time it was an annexe of Adelphi Terrace School. In June of that year, Adelphi Terrace itself moved into adjacent modern buildings, the need for an annexe was eliminated, and so the first school to have inscribed on its facade "School Board of Glasgow" was pulled down to make way for a girls' hockey pitch.

Rose Street was merely an existing structure altered and improved. It was another year before the first group of brand new schools were opened. Of these seven schools all but one

---

[1] J McMath, *op cit*, p 8.
[2] *ibid*, p 9.
[3] This street was later renamed and is now Florence Street, Gorbals.

were still in use ninety years later. The other, Sister Street, had been the very first site acquired by the Board, which as early as August 1873 was urging the Education Department to allow an immediate start on construction so great was the need in Bridgeton.[1] Ironically, of all the schools built by the Board, this one had the shortest life. It soon had to be sold to the North British Railway Company, and was demolished in 1889 to make way for what is now Bridgeton Central Station.[2]

The first school to come under the authority of the Board, however, was neither a new building nor was it a new institution. It was, in fact, the oldest school in the city and one of the oldest in Scotland—the High School of Glasgow. The High School was one of eleven burgh schools which were specially named in the Act as Higher Class Public Schools, and these were to be taken over by the school boards of the respective areas. Accordingly, the Town Council of Glasgow, the former managers of the High School, handed it over to the new authority. Among several serious problems of the High School which were thereby inherited by the Board was the alarming one that ". . . the premises were considered far from suitable for the Grammar School of so great a city".[3] The town council had long been acutely aware of the need for new premises but nothing had been done and, clearly, the present was no time for the Board to contemplate building just when all efforts in that direction must necessarily go towards providing schools for those who had none. So the old quarters in John Street were patched up and enlarged a bit, and likely enough the High School would have had to make do and mend for some time to come but for a fortuitous event. At this time, Glasgow Academy had a comparatively splendid building in Elmbank Street, and the School Board was able to negotiate its purchase for £32,000. The High School moved into its second-hand home in 1878. Out of their own pockets three members of the Board did what they could to make the premises even more fitting for the "Grammar School of so great a city", for it happened that the original design of the building had called for four statues of famous thinkers to grace the front of the building.

---

[1] Letter to SED, 12 August 1873.
[2] Sister Street School was replaced by Calton School.
[3] Report on the Work of the High School Committee, 1873–81.

This had never been carried out, but the inspiration which had thus been denied the scholars of the Academy was now provided for the High School boys who entered their new quarters under the gaze of Homer, Cicero, Galileo and James Watt.[1] Let into the wall of the Elmbank Street building at this time also was the lintel stone of the ancient Grammar School of Glasgow. It had originally been rescued from the remains of this very old school by Mr Michael Connal who had then presented it to the High School when it was still in John Street. Connal, soon to be Sir Michael, was by now the Chairman of the School Board.

THE DEMISE OF NON-BOARD SCHOOLS

As soon as the first School Board was constituted and long before it had been able to provide a single additional school place it was inundated with letters from the managers of existing schools notifying the Board of their intention to discontinue the work. It soon became clear that the efforts of the Board to provide new schools were likely to be nullified by old ones closing down. The danger had been foreseen: "I would say to managers of good schools, 'Don't be in a hurry to transfer your schools, for the School Board will have quite enough to do in the meantime with the new schools which are needed'."[2] Few heeded the request. Rather despairing appeals by the Board in similar vein fared no better.

There were two main groups of existing schools; those which received grants in aid, and those which did not and consequently were entirely dependent on their own means. The great majority of the latter swiftly disappeared after 1873. Some had been operated by charitable and philanthropic societies for whom the raising of funds had always been difficult. Now that the state had taken on their mantle their sponsors were glad to withdraw. The other self-supporting schools were Private Adventure, and these simply collapsed under the impact of the new system. The Argyll Commission had shown that most Private Adventure schools were little short of hovels run by

[1] The cost of these statues was borne by several of the School Board members.
[2] J A Campbell, speech quoted in *Glasgow Herald*, 22 March 1873.

men and women who were themselves as bereft of any learning as the children they professed to teach. Parents had no need of such places when, at no greater cost, their children could be sent to buildings palatial by comparison, rich in equipment, in the charge of properly trained teachers, and efficiently organised and conducted by a school board. Five years after the Board began its work schools of this type had declined in number from sixty-five to twenty,[1] and the trend was to continue. Yet while, for the most part, the change was educationally desirable, it also had the very embarrassing effect of unloading 7000[2] children for whom new schools had to be built all too soon.

The grant-aided schools were mostly run by the churches. A number of these sessional schools had high reputations while all were controlled by well-intentioned men. In such circumstances the School Board had good cause to hope that the church sessions would continue to accept the responsibility of educating their children for a few more years until such time as the Board had managed to cater for the many thousands without any form of schooling. It proved a pious hope on the whole. Some congregations had long been unable to afford to rebuild schools which were far gone along the road to decay and were inefficient. The Government had continued their grants only because the continuation of such schools was preferable to putting the children into the street. Now, however, the grant was refused, and the schools inevitably closed. The responsibility was now the Board's. When, for example, Camlachie Subscription School lost its grant the School Board was forced to provide a substitute and the best it could manage straight away was the lease of a disused bottle works at Vinegar Hill. Perhaps in a case like this the cure was no better than the disease.[3]

Even the efficient schools were soon given up by the churches, for congregations were unwilling to make voluntary contributions for schools in addition to paying through the rates. Not one Protestant Church proved ready to pay the price of assuring a truly Christian education by keeping its school under its own

[1] General Summary of Work, 1878.
[2] *ibid.*
[3] *Glasgow Herald*, 1 May 1876.

control. Within a few months of the passing of the Act, and even before the school boards were actually convened, there was a marked drop in contributions to the education funds of the churches. The Free Church was compelled to reduce the grant it paid to pre-Disruption teachers and ". . . all other classes of teachers are suffering a proportionate reduction".[1] Once the school boards began to function this trend in the church became even more pronounced. "An impression seems to prevail that no need now exists for the continuance of this scheme ie The Education Fund and contributions to it."[2] Much to the discomfiture of the School Board its first eighteen months of operation saw twenty-six schools discontinued. When five years had passed, sixty-five schools had been given up by the churches, and Glasgow lost the last of her sessional schools in the early '80s.

The initial aim of the Board, it will be recalled, had been to build about thirty new schools in order to provide 22,000 additional places. By the end of the second triennial period the building programme had progressed well, twenty-seven schools having been completed with a total accommodation of 25,494. Yet the Board had sadly to admit that it had been unable to accomplish what it had set out to do, largely because ". . . the number of schools discontinued has been so great".[3] In fact, the additional 25,494 places made available by new schools had to be set against 25,687 places lost by the abandonment of 143 pre-Act schools. The situation was not quite as bad as these figures suggest for, apart from its new schools, the Board operated several schools which had been transferred to it by churches or other bodies, as well as thirty or so temporary schools. Even so, it seems quite certain that during the first ten years the Board did little more than absorb the children transferred from other schools, plus finding room for another 10,000 in temporary accommodation of a most unsatisfactory kind. In January of 1884 Mr A J Mundella, Vice President of the Privy Council, during his visit to Glasgow gave a speech before a large audience, in which he referred to an article which had appeared in the *North British Daily Mail* that morning,

[1] *Free Church Monthly Record*, Feb 1873.
[2] *Free Church Monthly Record*, Oct 1873.
[3] Eighth Report of Progress in preparations for providing new Public Schools, 1881.

claiming that out of 90,000 Glasgow children of school age, 33,000 were absent every day. Mundella, while offering mitigating factors, agreed that this was ". . . a statement which is perfectly correct in fact".[1] Perhaps even more powerful evidence of the still lamentable lack of school places were some comments made during a Board meeting in 1879 by Mr Wm Fife. Fife had been one of the severest critics of the first two Boards. During the election campaign for the third Board he charged them with gross extravagance, caused partly by an excessive building programme.[2] Fife was elected on an economy ticket. After three years' personal experience of the problems facing the Board, this same man publicly announced that many more schools would be needed. It is interesting to note that one effect of Fife and his fellow "Economists" was virtually to bring building to a complete halt for three years in spite of the great need; between 1879 and 1882 only one school was built.

No blame for these disappointing results can be laid at the door of the earlier Boards. They had set themselves the target of "about thirty" new schools to provide 22,000 places. They built twenty-seven schools which, together with a dozen schools which had been transferred and which were regarded as permanent, gave accommodation to 33,000 pupils. All this in six years. It was an achievement never again matched. Yet an event outwith their control, the abandonment of sessional and private schools, left almost as many children without access to school as before. And into this situation had come the "Economists".

Thereafter the further provision of schools continued steadily, and even when there was space for all children the need to build was never quite satisfied. On the whole, the population of Glasgow increased little during the fifty years of the school boards, but more and ever more schools were required as one district died and another grew up elsewhere, as educational changes called for secondary schools or as the leaving age was raised. The last school planned by the Board was Bernard Street. Work on its construction was held up for

[1] *North British Daily Mail*, 19 January 1884.
[2] For a very full exposition of the critics' views in this controversy see James Caldwell, *Educational Endowments of the City of Glasgow; a Review of School Board Education in Glasgow*, 1884.

a time by the Great War, and within a few months of its opening the School Board of Glasgow passed into history.

THE TRANSFER OF SCHOOLS

The Act of 1872 made it permissible for school boards to accept into their charge existing schools whose managers were willing to transfer them. Apart from one or two conditions such as that existing teachers were to be retained and that the original owners might have the use of the schoolroom so long as it did not infringe other details of the Act, the transfer had to be an outright gift. While very many managers were willing, and even anxious, to have the Board take the burden of education off their shoulders, naturally enough few were prepared to hand over their property without any return. Serious difficulties arose as to the exact interpretation of the transfer clauses, which delayed matters for a while.

In many cases of offers to transfer, the Board declined to accept because the premises were so small or so dilapidated that they would have been a liability. Instead, the Board promised to make new provision for the locality as expeditiously as possible, and urged the managers to maintain their school in the meantime.[1]

Where managers of reasonably decent schools were unwilling to transfer the building and were determined to discontinue the school, the Board was usually able to obtain temporary use by leasing it for a few years. "The rule which we have acted upon in cases where the managers refuse to transfer, but desired us to carry on the school, is that we carry it on, paying simply the expense of tuition, the managers being at liberty to resume possession on giving reasonable notice. I am doubtful whether the Act allows us to go to this length, but necessity has forced us thus far."[2] Examples of this type of arrangement were Keppochhill Free Church School which was run by the Board from 1874 under the name of Keppochhill Public School until the permanent school of the same name was completed, and Free St George's whose temporary name was North Woodside Public School, becoming Oakbank on the opening of the permanent building.

[1] Minutes of Board in Committee, 5 November 1873.
[2] School Board Letter to SED, 7 April 1874.

Two existing schools, St Rollox and Cowcaddens Episcopal, were purchased outright. Later the Highland Society School and Albany Academy were also bought by the Board.

It is worth tracing the history of several of the schools transferred or purchased at this time, partly because they have an inherent interest of their own, and partly because many are still being used by the Glasgow Corporation Education Department in one capacity or another. What is perhaps more remarkable is the fact that a number of them are still serving their original function as schools. In many parts of Glasgow today the seeing and knowing eye may mark century-old buildings which pre-date the establishment of public schooling.[1]

St Rollox

The original school opened in Castle Street in 1827 and was built by Charles Tennant mainly for the children of employees in his chemical works. By 1858 a larger building was needed and it was put up in Garngad Road. This was the school which the Board bought from Tennants, and by utilising the master's house for classrooms was able to increase the accommodation from 470 to 800 pupils.[2] It was replaced by a new building in 1906, which today is called Royston Secondary.

Dobbie's Loan

Dobbie's Loan was the name given by the Board to the school bought from Cowcaddens Episcopal Church. It ended its career as a primary school in 1949, but is still in educational use as an annexe of the Stow College of Engineering.

Highland Society School

The Society was founded in 1727 with the object of ". . . educating and putting out to trade boys born in the highlands or

[1] eg (a) In Braid St (off N Woodside Rd) is "St Mary's Episcopal School"
   (b) At 234 London Rd, near Bridgeton Cross, adjacent to the old parish church, stands "St James' Sessional School". It is now leased by a saw doctor.
   Both these schools, like many others, have their names inscribed on the stone facade. The history of Glasgow is to be discovered by looking upwards.
[2] H A Dow, *History of St Rollox School*, 1876, p 48.

descended from Highlanders, and branches of Highlanders . . . and for other charitable and laudable ends".[1] By 1831 it supported four day schools and two night schools, all of which were now brought together into one building in Montrose Street. There were just over 800 pupils, girls as well as boys. In 1886 the directors decided to sell their school as it did not seem worthwhile incurring the heavy cost of repairs which were then needed at a time when the working classes were moving away to distant parts of the town, and when, moreover, board schools provided ". . . not only elementary education but secondary and technical education"[2] as well. After a few years as a public school, then as the pupil teacher institute, the building was sold to the West of Scotland Technical College which demolished it in 1902 to make way for the new College, now Strathclyde University.

Albany Academy

Albany Academy was a superior private school in a rather superior district. In 1895 it sold out to the School Board, almost certainly because two years previously Woodside Public School (only a few hundred yards away) had instituted a secondary department. Albany Public School replaced the Highland School as the pupil teacher institute. It now serves as an annexe of Woodside Secondary.

The City Schools

These were the old High School properties, enlarged by the Board and divided into separate schools for boys and girls. Eventually they shared the fate of the Highland School when the Technical College was built.

Freeland

Freeland was a transferred sessional school in Taylor Street. Thirty-five years later the inspector's report clearly showed that public schooling took a very long time indeed to improve

[1] Summary of Progress of Glasgow Highland Society, 1861.
[2] Glasgow Highland Society: Amended Constitution and Rules, 1886.

educational conditions in some parts of the town. "Both the premises and the equipment are unsatisfactory. The situation of the offices is altogether objectionable; there is no cloakroom accommodation; the desks have no back supports; and the lighting in some rooms is very defective. In three of the rooms there are two classes and two teachers, and in some cases free floor space is entirely limited. It is to be hoped that the school will very soon be entirely discontinued."[1] It remained in use until 1966 as an annexe for girls and infants of St Mungo's Primary School.

Kay Public School

Kay Public School was the name given to the sessional school of St Stephen's parish church, transferred in 1882. It continued as a primary school until 1909, after which it was a special school for physically defective children. Soon Kennyhill took over this function, and Kay became the Decorative Trades Institute. But the war soon took away the students, and from 1917 it was used by the old Allan Glen's as an annexe. Today it is an annexe of the College of Printing, and can be seen at the corner of Renfrew and Renfield Streets.

Bridgeton Public School

Bridgeton Public School had been an undenominational school. After its transfer the original name was retained. Its later vicissitudes included a spell as a school for half-timers under the factory acts. This building was demolished only recently to make way for the new John Street Secondary.

Hozier Street

Hozier Street is a good example of an extant sessional school, probably the oldest one still in use today. It was opened in 1851 by Bridgeton Free Church, and has continued an uninterrupted life as a primary school for 120 years. Its present name is John Street Primary.

[1] Inspector's Report, 1907. The school had 390 pupils, eight teachers and four or five rooms.

Alexander's

Alexander's was a charity school. It was rather severely criticised by the Endowments Commission, and was taken over by the School Board shortly afterwards. The parents, however, were far from pleased, for they would now have to pay fees. From the point of view of the Chairman of the Board, the official opening was marred by these angry people: "Went to the opening of Alexander's School under the School Board. A very unpleasant meeting. The people in the district not prepared for free education being done away with, and apparently taken by surprise. It shows the effect of training a community in dependence . . . the whole thing has been a school of unthrift . . . a charity school in the worst sense."[1] Today Alexander's is an annexe of St Mungo's Academy, called St Kentigern's.

ARCHITECTURE AND FURNITURE

From the beginning the School Board decided that its schools would be large, certainly no smaller than to accommodate 800, and in practice virtually all the new schools took 1000 and upwards. While the Board claimed that large numbers made for educational efficiency, undoubtedly the main motive was one of economy. "Small schools are necessary evils when the population is sparse, but in populous districts the larger the better."[2] Such huge schools were an innovation for the times, and may have done much to give board schools that soullessness which seems to have pervaded most of them.

Departmental regulations required a floor space per pupil of 8 square feet,[3] a figure generous enough to permit of a goodly crowd in a moderately sized building. Most schools were given three storeys and not over-large playgrounds. There were separate playgrounds for boys and girls. Unlike London and some other boards in England, Glasgow spread the work among the city architects, and thus benefited from a greater range of design, although the limits imposed on the architects by Code requirements and confined building sites inevitably cramped

[1] *Diary of Sir Michael Connal*, 2 August 1886.
[2] Letter of Glasgow School Board to Rutherglen School Board, 26 June 1874.
[3] 10 sq ft from 1880.

C

their style and restricted variety. Architects, of course, like other craftsmen, work to the fashion of the day, which further tended to make all the schools similar in their essentials.

To a remarkable degree design was conditioned by the need to have separate stairways for boys and girls. The earliest schools solved the problem by having a central well, either wholly or partially enclosed. Within this well the two sets of stairs inter-twined, one on top of another, and wound their way up to the different landings whence the classrooms were set off to left and right. Once having set course on one of the stairs, one had no choice but to follow it to its conclusion and might well discover only then that the desired destination was impossible to reach by that route. Then the only remedy was to retrace one's steps to the ground floor and try the other stair. Some-times a person on the second storey, wanting to visit another room on the same floor, and which he could perhaps even see only a few yards off, was compelled to descend to ground level by one stair and then come back by the other. They were, indeed, very confusing to all but the most experienced navi-gators. One old body was discovered wandering round one of these schools, and rather breathlessly explained her dilemma: "Hech, sirs, this is a braw schule, but it's unco apt to ravel ye: I've been wandering here for twenty meenits, an I canna get oot."[1] The design may still be seen (and experienced) in, for example, Dobbie's Loan, Kennedy Street, Tureen Street, or Henderson Street.

Later schools, such as Strathclyde or Cuthbertson, adopted the plan of moving the stairs quite apart from each other and setting them round a central hall, a development now possible because the hall had become an essential educational require-ment for drill and communal meetings of the school. The final stage of this form, perhaps, is the design of Bernard Street School. Here the large central hall is actually an open-air playground, the classrooms surrounding it on all four sides.

For heating purposes, and before the introduction of radiators, 4 inch pipes were run through the building. There was no means of regulating the heat from one room to another, so that some classes stewed while others froze. Which was the more fortunate is hard to say as ventilation too was uncertain

[1] I McMath, *op cit*, p 12.

in its performance. And the very best efforts of engineers sometimes came to naught in the face of the human factor: one teacher was found to have stuffed the ventilation shaft with newspaper because she simply could not stand the draught, preferring the familiar smell of ninety young overheated bodies.[1]

In the older schools pegs were sometimes provided within the classrooms for the children's coats. A little later the well of the staircase was fitted as a proper cloakroom. However, it was quite common for cloakrooms deliberately to be omitted altogether, for example at Finnieston, for it was known that here and in similar districts the children were too poor to possess coats.[2] To provide for them would therefore have been an extravagance.

The offices[3] were invariably outside of, and at a distance from, the main building, requiring the children to run out through the rain. Even when they got there the boys, at least, found no roof over their heads. Automatic flushing of urinals was unknown, and cleanliness depended upon the janitor sluicing a bucket of water along the channel. The common type of closet was in the form of a long trough with nine to twelve partitioned divisions over it. Some had to be flushed manually by the janitor after the interval (the ideal at any rate!); an advanced form incorporated automatic flushing every six hours![4] This system of sanitation obtained during practically the whole of the School Board period. As late as 1909 thirty-nine schools were being modernised by replacing the old trough system with individual WCs.[5]

Glasgow was proud of its wash basins, the invention of a headmaster and the master of works.[6] Water was run into a long lead trough from which it passed through perforations into little shallow basins. As the children dipped their hands into the bowls, so the water overflowed and the scum ran off down the drain. A perfect system! Wonderfully hygienic—and haply cheap, for only the janitor could turn on the water.

---

[1] J McMath, *op cit*, p 25.
[2] D McKail, *Extrinsic and Intrinsic Conditions Affecting School Children*; *a study of some schools and school children in Glasgow*, 1909, p 29.
[3] The euphemism of the time for lavatory.   [4] D McKail, *op cit*, p 30.
[5] Annual Report of Property Committee, 1909.
[6] J McMath, *op cit*, p 18

Lighting was by gas. One cluster of open flame jets hung from the centre of the room, though in time this gave way to a better arrangement whereby the flame was enclosed in a glass and several pendants were distributed around the room.

The old form of schoolroom was, of course, a largish rectangular space, often indeed the whole length and breadth of the building. In this one room were two (or more) classes conducted by two teachers and several pupil teachers. Small imagination is required to suppose that little could be taught and little learned in such conditions. The inspector's report on Springbank, an early temporary school, is only one example of many such. "The school continues to be greatly overcrowded, and this makes good organisation impossible. The discipline is as good as can be expected. . . . A curtain to shut off part of the Large Room and additional desks are absolutely necessary . . . the noise arising in the Large Room from so many being taught together causes inaccurate and careless work. . . . The work of the school is very elementary. Upwards of 400 children were present, but only eight were as high as the Fourth Standard."[1] These 400 children were being taught by one man, one woman and five pupil teachers.

The new schools did away with comprehensive classrooms. Now the teacher, with her pupil teacher, had a room to herself in which to teach her 105 scholars.[2] It certainly was a great improvement, especially when in time numbers came down to more manageable proportions. Yet it was still far from ideal. Most rooms were divided by nothing more soundproof than thin wood and glass partitions. It was not easy to snap out the correct answer to nine times six when the class next door was chanting their eight times table. And there was always the thrilling, and inevitably distracting, sound of some unlucky miscreant suffering punishment. Then, too, many a room interconnected with the one next door but had itself no direct access to the outside corridor. Anyone entering or leaving had to pass through one class, and frequently two others, with consequent disturbance.

Until about 1890 all pupils' desks were of the so-called "Glasgow" type. They were very heavy desks from six to nine

---

[1] Inspector's Report, 1875.
[2] An average figure for 1881.

feet in length and having a sloping table top. A fixed bench seat was placed about four inches behind the desk, and the bench had no back support.[1] The lack of a backrest was deliberate. Since several children sat on the one form the only way most of them could get out was by stepping backwards over the seat, a manoeuvre only possible in the absence of a back. Even when a new style of desk was eventually introduced the old ones remained in use for a very long time to come. Twenty years later the undesirability of children having to sit all day long without any support for their backs was at last being recognised. "The Board continues to supply back supports to the seats of the 'Glasgow' type of desk where the desks are in good condition", and always, of course, the usual justification for not completely replacing these relics of the bad old days, ". . . thus a considerable saving is effected".[2]

The new desk was the invention of the headmaster of Washington Street. It took only two pupils, and was a marvel of ingenuity incorporating several cunning ideas. It consisted of a cast iron frame with on one side a wooden table, and on the other a wooden seat. As the seat was designed to hinge upwards when not in use, there was no longer any need for the foot of floorspace behind, which had been so wasteful. Desks could be placed in file one directly behind the other, the front of each desk providing both seat and a backrest for the child in front. The table was hinged along the middle of its length, and thus could be made to serve a dual purpose; folded down it formed a level surface for writing on; folded up it was a sloping book rest, a little ledge being provided to take the book. Additional assets were slots for slates and a shelf for books.

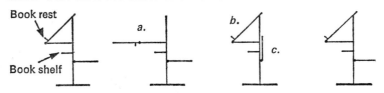

a. Desk position for writing.
b. Desk position for reading.
c. Seat and desk raised for egress of pupil and for floor sweeping.

[1] J McMath, *op cit*, p 21.
[2] Annual Report of Property Committee, 1909–10.

It might seem obvious that the new dual desk would have been an unqualified improvement for the physical comfort and well being of the children. A medical investigator was not so sure, however. He claimed that classrooms were just as crowded as before, and indeed that overcrowding was sometimes demonstrably greater after the introduction of the dual desk, since it did not require, nor even permit, a passage space behind each seat, and consequently the air-space available to each pupil in the class was less.[1] No doubt the desks were occasionally used in this way, but other evidence shows that in reality class numbers had decreased somewhat by the time that the doctor was writing.

The schools built by the Glasgow School Board are not, with one exception,[2] much prized for their architectural beauty. That would surely be too much to expect. The times demanded utility, the demand was urgent, school architecture as such was born only with the school board system itself, and the school rate was vigilantly watched by a public still suspicious and resentful of lavish public spending—and still having an effective voice to curb it. In the present age of built-in obsolescence the most damaging charge heard against board schools is that they were built too well! But in their day they were objects of great civic pride and symbols of social progress.[3]

---

[1] D McKail, *op cit*, p 18.

[2] Scotland Street School, the creation of the Glasgow architect of distinction, Charles Rennie Mackintosh.

In the small architectural handbook "Glasgow at a Glance" (ed Young and Doak, 1965) St Rollox School (now Royston Secondary) is also given an honourable mention.

[3] A list of the schools built by the School Board of Glasgow is given in Appendix C, pp 234-6.

Chapter 6
THE HALF-TIME SYSTEM

The first legislation for the compulsory education of children was enacted in the Factory Act of 1833, and the essential provisions of this forty-year-old law still applied when the School Boards began operations in 1873.

The relevant clauses, which referred to children under thirteen years of age and whose hours of labour were limited to eight per day, were:

20 "... every child ... shall attend some school to be chosen by the parents or guardians of such child, or such as may be appointed by any Inspector . . .; and it shall be lawful for any inspector to order the employer of such child to make a deduction from the weekly wage of such child—not exceeding the rate of one penny in every shilling, to pay for the schooling of such child; and such employer is hereby required to pay the sum so deducted according to the order and direction of such inspector.

21 "... such child shall, on Monday of every week ... give to the factory master or proprietor, or to his agent, a schoolmaster's ticket or voucher, certifying that such child has for Two Hours at least for Six out of Seven days of the week next preceding attended his school.

22 ". . . whenever it shall appear to any inspector that a new or additional school is necessary or desirable to enable the children employed in any factory to obtain the education required by this Act, such inspector is hereby authorised to establish or procure the establishment of such school.

23 "Inspector may disallow master's salary if incompetent.

This Act applied only to Textile Factories as did the amending Factory Act of 1844 whose educational provisions were slightly different from the earlier Act and are given here, in brief, as they introduce an alternative form of half-time schooling:

29 Children may be employed at eight years (previously nine).
30 Maximum daily hours of employment to be $6\frac{1}{2}$, except:
    (a) if Dinner Time begins at 1 pm then the morning shift of children may work 7 hours per day;

(b) if employed before noon the child may not be employed after 1 pm (except if working alternate days).

31 In a factory where children are restricted to 10 hours per day they may work ten hours on three alternate days of every week, and provided that the child attends school at least 5 hours between 8 am and 6 pm "of the same day of each week day preceding each day of employment in the factory". But no school was required on a Saturday.

38 If not working the system permitted under Section 31 but working every day then:
(a) child must attend school for 3 hours daily;
(b) but if attending school after 1 pm only 2½ hours daily were required between 1st Nov and 28th Feb.

39 Every factory occupier shall "pay to the schoolmaster of such child towards the expenses of educating such child such sum as the inspector may require, not exceeding Two Pence per week, and shall be entitled to deduct from the wages of such child any such sum as he shall have been required to pay for such expenses not exceeding the rate of One Twelfth part of the weekly wages of such child".

In 1867 the Workshops Act further extended the compulsory education of working children into new spheres, and offered yet another way in which this schooling time could be accumulated (the Factory Acts Extension Act, 1867, included children in any manufacturing process in an establishment of fifty or more employees and the Workshops Act was intended to do the same in smaller places):

14 (i) Every child who is employed in a Workshop shall attend school for at least ten hours in every week.
(ii) In computing the time for the purpose of this section during which the child has attended such school there shall not be included any time during which such child has attended either:
(a) In excess of 3 hours at any one time, or in excess of 5 hours in any one day . . .
etc.

Even yet the possibilities had not been exhausted, and the Coal Mines Act of 1873 managed to find a formula of its own: twenty school hours must be put in in any one fortnight.

Thus, when the half-time children began to come into the Board Schools there were four distinct methods by which they might make up their time in school.

1 Morning and afternoon sets (3 hours each day Mon–Fri);
2 Alternate days each week of 5 hours each day);
3 Any two days (5 hours each day);
4 20 hours per fortnight, either by:
    (a) not more than 3 hours in any one day; *or*
    (b) 5 hours in any one day; *or*
    (c) 12 hours in any one week.

Even if the half-time system had not been disliked by schools for other reasons it is easy to see the chaos that must have existed if some children attended for half of each day, others

Act	*Trade or industry*	*Method of half-time education*
Factory Acts 1833, 1844, 1850, 1853, 1874 Factory Acts Extension Act 1876 Lace Factory Act 1861 Ropeworks Act 1846 Factory and Workshops Acts 1870 (Bleachworks), 1871 (Jews), 1871 (General)	Cotton, wool, hair, flax, hemp, jute, lace; rope-works; earthenware, tiles; lucifer matches, cartridges; paper-staining, fustian-cutting; blast furnaces, copper and iron mills, foundries, machinery, metals; india rubber, gutta percha; paper, glass, tobacco; letter-press printing, book-binding; printworks, bleaching and dying works; plus all premises of 50 or more employees manufacturing an "article" for sale	1 or 2
Workshops Act 1867 Factory and Workshops Acts 1870, 1871	"any room or place whatever—in which any handicraft is carried on" (under 50 employees)	1 or 2 or 3
Coal Mines Act 1873	Mines of coal, iron-stone, shale, fireclay	4 which included 1 or 2 or 3

came only on Tuesday and Thursday, while some put in an appearance on any two days in the week and then perhaps not always on the same two days every week. It was possible, for example, for a school to be full to overflowing on Monday and Tuesday and then to be half empty for the rest of the week. "This is, of course, in many ways most disastrous. In providing, as we feel bound to do, for the due instruction of all scholars at the beginning of the week, the school staff for the last three

c*

days is considerably in excess of what is required, and thus is incurred a waste of expenditure which has to be met by liberal private contributions."[1]

This question of the times at which working children could make up their school attendance is but one instance of the extreme complexity and confusion which had been reached by 1874 due to the large number of Acts and Amendments which piled one on top of another. The previous page gives a list of the pertinent Acts which covered half-time education, the trades and industries under these Acts by 1874, and the ways in which the education could be taken.

That the half-time system was highly unpopular with both employer and child alike there can be no doubt. When there was talk of its being extended to roperies, a Manchester firm protested strongly on behalf of themselves and apparently of the children also.

". . . The Trade may be fairly stated as the most healthy in the kingdom, not even excepting that of agriculture, for the children are in most cases employed where the atmosphere cannot be otherwise than pure, for frequently in sheds 100 yards by 10 yards, not more than 16 to 20 people, young and old, are employed. It would be very unfair to class such places with manufactures such as cutlery, lucifer match making, and others similarly injurious. Indeed, to say that rope and twine making is injurious at all is absurd, for it is a positive benefit to a child. What employment indeed can there be that so much resembles play, what workshop that so much reminds the boy of the playground? They turn a wheel that is so easy to work that for very pastime's sake they will try how many revolutions they can make the wheel take at one effort, and their attention is centred on the result as if their reputation depended on it; their work is exceedingly light, they are constantly changing position, either sitting, walking or running; they lift no heavy weights, they have no straining pulls, they have plenty of good fresh air, are protected moderately well from the inclemency of the weather, are not exposed to a particle of dust arising from any fibre, and their employment is clean, cheerful and light, and that it is exceedingly renovating to the constitution can be readily proved by the sickly appearance they exhibit after being taken out of the rope walk to work in the close mills and weaving sheds, and the noisy injurious machine shops, such children being always taken out of the rope walk to work in such places for the sake of a few pence more per week than they can earn when they get to about 11 or 12 years. That the children who are employed in

[1] Factory and Workshops Commission, 1876, vol I, p 161.

this trade of rope and twine manufacturing present a far more healthy and robust appearance than the children who work in confined workshops no one can deny, and to close this part of the argument, their time is spent in singing and play."[1]

Yet in spite of the obvious difficulties the half-time system created for an employer, young children continued to be used in large numbers, though to what extent varied greatly from district to district. Many witnesses were of the opinion that relatively fewer half-timers were employed in Scotland than in England. Writing a few years after the passing of the original Factory Act, an inspector noted a considerable decrease in the use of children in Scotland.

"Few of them are now employed in the factories at Glasgow, Belfast, Carlisle, Dundee and in all places where it is not difficult, from the state of the population, to procure young persons from the age of 13 years upwards. The proprietors of the factories uniformly attribute this change to the provision of the Act which occasions inconvenience to them employing one set of workers for a shorter time than the rest, and in procuring certificates of attendance."[2]

The Commissioners of 1875 also found themselves perplexed by the countless objections to half-timers in Scotland. Addressing the clerk of the Glasgow School Board they said,

"From some cause or other the half-time system has been much more fully carried out in England than it has in Scotland, and we have a great deal of evidence that in some places it is working very satisfactorily, and we have been assured by boards and schoolmasters that wherever the children have been well grounded in the first place the half-timers can keep up fairly with the other classes, but that would not I presume, be your experience?"[3]

A later question produced a quite revealing answer,

"Admitting that the half-time system has completely broken down in Scotland, to what causes do you attribute that; do you think there is anything in the half-time system inconsistent with the habits of the people in Scotland; are the usual dinner hours of the Glasgow workers inconsistent with the children attending half-time?" "As far as I am aware they are not. You could scarcely say that the system has failed in Glasgow, for so far as one can ascertain, it has never been adequately tried."[4]

[1] Factory and Workshops Commission, 1876, vol I, p 157.
[2] Factory Inspector's Report, 1846.
[3] Factory and Workshops Commission, 1876, paras 15, 637.
[4] *ibid*, paras 15, 666.

At one point of the inquiry the Chairman of the Commission was driven to exasperation, "It is an extraordinary thing that in England it is worked with such complete efficiency, and yet is so much resisted in Scotland."[1] This same theme of the discrepancy in practice between England and Scotland arose once again during the inquiry of the Departmental Committee on Partial Exemption from School Attendance in 1909. By this time, although London, Manchester and Liverpool had virtually no half-timers, they still existed in large numbers in other parts of England. In Scotland, on the other hand, they had become almost extinct according to the evidence of a factory inspector: "A great deal of my work has been in Scotland, where half-timers have been abolished except in Dundee. That is the only place now that has any half-time employment. Comparing the Cheshire and Lancashire child with the Glasgow child who is kept at school until he is 14, I think the advantage is not on the side of the Lancashire child. There was one half-timer in Paisley the year before last; last year there was not one."

Q Why has the half-time system been abolished in Scotland? Is it a matter of public opinion?
A I think so. I think it was recognised that the education in the schools was of more advantage to the child than working in the factory.
Q Has there been much half-time in Scotland in recent years?
A There has been no half-time in Glasgow or Edinburgh during the fifteen years that I have been inspecting (ie since 1893)— absolutely none.
Q Are you speaking of textile factories, or of all?
A Of all factories.
Q How was it abolished?
A By the School Boards who have absolute discretion in the matter of refusing to exempt children.
Q They all refuse to exempt?
A Glasgow does not exempt at all; Dundee does.
Q How many half-timers are there?
A Under 200. Exemption in Scotland can only be got on the grounds of necessitous circumstances. It has no necessary relation either to efficiency or to attendance.
Q They have never held that the Factory Acts overruled the bye-laws in Scotland? The bye-law is supreme; that is admitted in Scotland?
A It is not the bye-law. It is the Scotch Education Act of 1901.

[1] Factory and Workshops Commission, 1876, paras 15, 409.

Section 71 of the Factory and Workshop Act of 1901 does not apply to Scotland.[1]

How far this inspector was correct in her opinions will be discussed later when considering the reasons for the decline of the half-time system in Glasgow, but her evidence and that of earlier witnesses show that there was a widespread feeling that the system was far more successful in England and that it flourished there for some time after it had become moribund in Scotland.

Nevertheless, what statistics are available suggest that in some years the proportion of half-timers in Scotland was, in fact, not much lower than that of England, and it may be that observers were led to an inaccurate view by the much larger total numbers in the south as well as by the apparent thrawnness of the Scots to work so complicated and unsatisfactory a system. Figures relating to half-timers are very suspect in regard to accuracy, but official returns indicate the relative numbers in Scotland, England and Ireland. In Table 4 the figures concern textile factories only and take no account of other industries.

TABLE 4

HALF-TIMERS IN TEXTILE INDUSTRIES[2]

		1867	1874	1878	1885	1889
gland	Boys	40,000	56,150	46,300	36,900	35,200
	Girls	41,200	57,450	51,850	39,200	38,650
tland	Boys	950	3,600	3,250	4,300	2,900
	Girls	1,550	5,000	5,150	5,800	3,900
land	Boys	600	1,500	1,600	2,100	2,500
	Girls	1,250	2,250	2,400	3,350	3,450

(Numbers taken to nearest 50)

The reasons why half-timers should be so thoroughly disliked within the schools are nowhere more vividly given than by one of the school inspectors.

[1] Report of Departmental Committee on Partial Exemption, 1909. Evidence of Miss Mary Paterson. See also Second Report of Board of Education, p xxviii, where some of the difficulties are set out.
[2] House of Commons Returns.

ANSWER OF D ROSS, INSPECTOR OF SCHOOLS
(RENFREWSHIRE ETC) TO FACTORY AND WORKSHOPS
COMMISSION OF 1875

"My district, especially Renfrewshire, contains a large manu-facturing population; I have met altogether about 1000 half-timers in, I think, 40 schools. The great majority of these attend on the alternate day system. I cannot say how far the bias of my position may distort my views unconsciously; but tested educationally I see little difference, in so far as the children themselves are concerned, between the alternate day and the half-day systems. My experience is that both are bad, and the question has again and again come before me. Do not these half-time sets as they are at present worked out defeat the object of the Education Act of 1872? I have watched the half-timers narrowly; only on one occasion was I able to say that they passed with any credit.

"Their chief characteristic is rudeness. The boys have about them a sort of impudent and independent air, and the girls are marked by a coarseness that I do not find even in schools that are filled with children drafted from the gutter or the street. Too frequently there is a sort of precocity along with this coarseness. They look worn out and seem to be underfed, when they are not jaded or haggard. Their influence upon the other children is almost always bad, their habits are filthier and their language more obscene than one finds amongst ordinary Scotch children. The reason is that they are generally not the children of the respectable and hard-pressed poor, but those of the careless and selfish classes, who look upon children as inconvenient evils when they are not bread winners. These half-timers thus neglected and early cast upon their own resources, are precisely the class that in this district is bringing pauperism and rates up, and themselves down. At 13 they are young men and young women, they marry early, treat their numerous offspring as they were treated, they lose sight of their parents who retire upon the paupers role, and they in their turn are lost sight of by those who should support them. By this process in Renfrewshire, the Irishmen and a section of the Scotch are suffering, and not those only but those who have to support them. Half-timers bring their coarseness into school. They are more restless and more difficult to control than other children; whenever they can they move about from school to school; they are not, it is true, welcomed very much by teachers who are anxious to pass their scholars well; for if they pass at all on the day of inspection their pass is bare, and their want of intelligence may affect the grants under the Scotch Code, just as their restlessness and tendency to disobedience may endanger the discipline grant for the whole school. That they stand in the way of good discipline, that they swell the failures as indicated on the schedule, that they do not manifest ordinary intelligence, and that they generally give an unpleasant odour to the report upon the school, are facts well enough understood.

"The two systems looked at from the point of view of the mixed public school, are two evils. But of the two, the alternate day system is the less. The reason lies in the matter of organisation. I have not yet met a teacher—and many of the teachers in my district are very competent men—I have not yet met a teacher who professed himself to be able to organise a school attended by *half-dayers*, upon any plan that would give justice both to the regular pupils and to the irregular half-timers. I can put the difference between the two systems thus: As regards the schools, both are bad; as regards the half-timers themselves, both are very bad, but by the 'alternate day' system, the half-timers only are sacrificed; by the other both the half-timers and the school are sacrificed. In any case the half-timers are thrust to the wall, and the reason is very obvious. Teachers and school boards will not organise special classes in the common school for their instruction, because this would be a waste of teaching power. They must, therefore, try to keep up with the classes of the school. But this they cannot do; for either they must lose some subjects altogether, or they must attempt all, and do their work imperfectly. They are required to go over the same work as the other children in something like half the time. And in this struggle every thing is against them. The circumstances of their homes, the fact that they are jaded and worn out, and their want of habits of application, render them incapable of getting up their tasks half so well as their more fortunate schoolfellows. Hence, they fall hopelessly behind. This perpetual hopelessness, operating upon bad subjects, results in general carelessness and disgust for school life. . . . If I were allowed to express my opinion that experience in Renfrewshire has deposited in my mind, the expression would take the form of a protest in the interests of education, of the poor children themselves, and of society against the crushing operation of Acts, which enrich a small section of the community at the ulterior expense of all the rest."

From the educational point of view the half-time system undoubtedly gave some degree of education to some children, but often it was so defective as to be almost nugatory. Here again the picture varies greatly from place to place, but there is no doubt of its miserable inadequacy in Glasgow before the Education Act came into force. The Argyll Commission clearly showed how the Factory Acts were evaded by means of a large trade in attendance certificates from bogus, or at least ineffective, schoolmasters. Respectable schools could pick and choose their pupils and so would have nothing to do with half-timers. "The result has consequently been that mere adventurers have in all our dense mill-working centres opened Half-time schools.

These men, as is frequently and correctly said, earn a livelihood not by teaching but by signing certificates. I remember inspecting a half-time school of an attendance of about 300, whose whole staff consisted of a certificated teacher and a non-certificated assistant. A few good passes were made by the pupils in reading, several in writing, but hardly any in arithmetic; nothing was professed to be taught but the three Rs. The real facts of the case were that the children had been taught in good schools before they entered the mills, but as soon as they

TABLE 5

HALF-TIMERS IN SCOTLAND BY TRADES (1871)[2]

	Total	Textiles	Metals	Leather	Chemical Works	Food	Building	Paper	M
Boys	3566	2222	193	21	21	144	94	30	8.
Girls	3418	3108	2	1	6	60	8	10	2

TABLE 6

DETAILS OF MISCELLANEOUS TRADES[2]

	Tobacco	Rope-making	Bricks and Tiles	Letter-Press Printing	Litho-graphy	Match-making	India-Rubber	Engrav-ing	Ot
Boys	302	253	47	35	27	20	25	16	1
Girls	41	1	12	21	15	56			

became half-timers they were compelled to leave these schools and resort to the institution to which I allude: There they were put into the lowest standards and, as they could not but remember some of their previously received instruction, they made of course a few passes."[1] And this was a school which received a government grant (though subsequently removed from the list). There were many worse adventure schools in the factory districts; indeed, the half-timers seem to have been one of their major sources of revenue and their sole reason for existence.

In 1875 a Royal Commission was appointed to inquire into the working of the Factory and Workshop Acts, and its report provides the best and fullest information available about the half-time system. It gives figures of the number of half-timers in the various trades for the whole of Scotland (Tables 5 and 6).[2]

[1] Factory and Workshops Commission, 1876, vol I, p 207.
[2] ibid, vol I, appx B(d).

The most striking features of these statistics is the over-whelming proportion of the half-timers who were employed in the various textile trades. Out of a total of 3418 girls employed in all industries no less than 3108 (ie 91%) worked in textiles. Only three other single trades engaged more than twenty-five girls; preserved meat and fruit (33), matchmaking (56) and tobacco (41). The work of boys was a good deal more diversified, though here also textiles occupied the majority (62%), and again numbers were very small in individual trades except for bakehouses, biscuits and confectionery (122), ropemaking (253), bricks and tiles (47), printing and engraving (78), and tobacco (302). The high concentration of half-timers in only a few forms of occupation was to be a most important factor in the decay of the half-time system, since any decline in these particular trades would tend to eliminate demand for the services of young children.

THE EDUCATION ACT AND THE HALF-TIME SYSTEM

The Education Act of 1872 had as its most important principle that children must attend school full-time until thirteen years old. At once this raised the question of whether the Education Act superseded the Factory and Workshops Acts. If so, the half-time system was automatically ended. Of course, the same doubts had arisen two years earlier in England, but Scotland apparently was not content to accept the experience of the South. Some zealous school boards attempted to compel all children under 13 to attend school full-time. Selkirk went so far as to take a test case to law where it was decided that the Education Act did not over-rule any previous legislation other than that specifically mentioned in the Act. This was also the view taken by the SED which issued a circular[1] for the guidance of inspectors which, while laying down no definite ruling on the matter and leaving the final decision to the discretion of school boards, cautiously gave its opinion that the Act did not over-ride the Factory Acts. "You will bear in mind that the 73rd Section fixes one, but does not profess to fix the only, claim to exemption from the compulsory powers of the Act." Consequently, it was within the discretion of the school boards

[1] Committee of Council on Education in Scotland, 1873–74, p lxxviii.

to accept half-time, and the Department believed that half-time was a fair substitute. It was further pointed out that the Scotch Code made provision for half-timers by giving a grant for making only 150 attendances instead of the normal 250, and that under Section 17(a) no grant was payable to a school if a child was refused admission on other than reasonable grounds. As the Department held half-time to be "reasonable" it followed that a school which refused to accept half-timers would receive no grant.

Thus the half-time system continued alongside the new. Not only did this lead to many practical difficulties in integrating the two methods in common schools, but it also illuminated the educational deficiencies of the half-timers as never before. Whereas factory children previously had been assured of some degree of schooling, however poor, while thousands of others received none at all, now the advantage was completely reversed and it was the half-timers who could never hope to reach the educational attainments of children blessed with full-time schooling.

HALF-TIMERS IN GLASGOW

One of the most striking features in regard to the position of factory children in Glasgow at this time is the very large discrepancy between the numbers of those given in official returns as at work under the age of thirteen and the figures of the School Board showing children who were receiving education under the Half-time system. This is true even allowing for the fact that government statistics are for Scotland as a whole or, sometimes, for the West of Scotland, for a considerable proportion of the textile factories and the myriad workshops were within the city boundaries. It is difficult to know what to make of the available figures. It seems clear that the factory inspectors were themselves unable to keep a check on this facet of their work. Factory owners had little difficulty in evading the law; even when a sudden call by an inspector took the manager by surprise, children were easily got out of the way for a while if their presence might prove embarrassing. Schoolmasters' certificates were of little real use, being seldom supplied on the Monday (as required by law) and, in any case, the employer had far too many more pressing matters to which to attend, to bother about trifling records of this kind. Too few in number the inspectors were already over-worked. Sometimes they were even unsure of their own jurisdiction as the chief inspector himself admitted at the inquiry of 1874.

Q Are you acquainted with most of the bakehouses?
A No, I have never inspected one, because I have always understood that they were not under our jurisdiction, and I never went into them at all.[1]

Moreover, there was no compulsory registration of Factories and Workshops, so that many places were unknown to the inspectors unless they came upon them by mere chance. The inspectors did not even have an office in Glasgow and so were difficult to contact, and were even more difficult to get to act in cases of complaint as the School Board, for one, discovered: "We find great difficulty at present in there being no official place of business in connection with the inspectors. We do not know where to apply to them at the moment. If we wanted to communicate with the inspectors, there is no public office that we are aware of in the city."

Q Have you found that a practical difficulty?
A I have. I have written twice to London on two different occasions to know the names of the inspectors and their addresses in Glasgow.[2]
Q When you come across cases of children who are at work and not attending school, is it your habit to make application to the Inspector of Factories?
A I have complained to the inspectors, and I have given the names of certain masters who have children upon the school roll who have never attended. I gave the inspector a list of four schools on one occasion, and I never heard anything more about it. He complained that he had too much to do, and I think he has too much to do.[3]

Thus the evidence of the Board's Principal Attendance Officer. Yet another pitfall of half-time statistics lies in their having been taken on one particular day in the year, for a considerable number of the trades using half-timers were seasonal: eg calico printers only required them for three

[1] Factory and Workshops Commission, 1876, paras 15, 640.
[2] ibid, paras 15, 611–15.
[3] ibid, paras 15, 642.

months in the year, ropemaking similarly depended on the weather, as also did brickworks.

One thing is certain; prior to the Education Act the education clauses of the various factory acts had never been punctiliously carried out in Glasgow, and very many children were at work without having to attend school as the law demanded. This was borne out by the evidence of William Mitchell, Convener of the Attendance Committee of the Glasgow School Board.

"The working of the Factory and Workshop Acts is unsatisfactory in the following respects: The total number of children at Half-time Schools bears a small proportion to the number of children from 9 to 13 in this city who are at work. There are about 40,000 children in the city from 9 to 13. The Board cannot form an accurate estimated number of these at work, but even the lowest conceivable estimate is far above the total number found in half-time schools which only reaches the total number of 840. There are five half-time schools in connection with works in the city. There are ten adventure schools in which there are half-timers, and four Board schools in which there are half-timers. . . . I may state also that in one of the half-time schools in connection with a factory, one of the largest, the number fluctuates so much that some weeks whilst they have 150 half-timers, the next week, perhaps, they may have only 60 or 70. There is no uniformity to the time during which half-time education is given. In some schools it is given on a portion of every day, in others on alternate days, and in others on two or three consecutive days of each week, three days one week and two days the following week. There is thus no possibility of providing separate schools for each class of half-timer, and no sufficient number of one class for special schools. Mixing them with regular scholars is unsatisfactory to both. The attendance of half-timers is irregular and capricious. If a work has occasion to put away certain hands, and this without any notice to the School Board, to a considerable extent the provisions of the Act are evaded. . . . Employers seem to be very lax in carrying out the provisions of the Factory Acts. The school rolls especially kept for employers in the schools are not inspected by them in all cases and checked, and children are constantly found in potteries, ropeworks, tobacco works and bleachfields, who are not at half-time schools, although they are under 13. Children are there without their names being on the master's books at all."[1]

Just how reliable were the statistics of this time was underlined by the Report of the Departmental Commission on Factory Statistics in 1895. "It is out of the question to procure

[1] Factory and Workshops Commission, 1876, paras 15, 597.

such returns [annual return of persons employed] from work-shops. Their number is too great to cope with. . . . Hitherto, the efforts in this direction so far as the Factory Dept. is concerned, have been spasmodic, and undertaken at uncertain intervals . . . eg 1871, 1885, 1889, and no doubt they represent to a certain extent the position of British manufactures at the dates named, but they are otherwise of no value whatever as representing the continuous growth or decay of any given industry or group of industries, and can in no sense be said to be of more than approximate accuracy." The figures pertaining to textiles were more reliable than others, but: "With respect to this class, it appears that, on the last occasion on which a return was called for, none was received in at least 4500 instances. It is, moreover, extremely doubtful whether those which were sent from this class could be considered as correct."[1]

It is in the light of the above remarks that the tables given on page 80 must be considered. Thus we have no real means of knowing the number of Glasgow children at work during the first few years of the School Board. Undoubtedly, it was far in excess of the 840 known to be attending schools under the Factory Acts; perhaps three times that number would not be unlikely. By the 1880s, however, this period of grace had passed, for by now the school attendance officers had gained a long experience of their work, there were more of them so that the city was adequately and regularly covered, annual censuses of the child population had provided a more certain indication of how many should be at school, and the work of the officers could no longer be thwarted by the plea that school buildings did not exist.

In 1873 only five works in Glasgow operated schools for their young employees. They had 433 pupils, though this number fluctuated wildly and weekly. Little is known about these schools, and the last of them disappeared in 1884.[2]

As may be expected, the School Board's attitude to half-timers was not particularly sympathetic in the early days. It already had a hard enough task in providing for the ordinary child without the added burden and complications which accompanied half-timers. Indeed, it was not even clear that

[1] Report of Departmental Committee on Factory Statistics, 1895.
[2] General Summary of Work: Triennial Reports 1882–1906.

school boards were duty bound to bother with factory children, while their unsettling influence in ordinary schools was only too well known. The Glasgow Board attempted to avoid the unsatisfactory mixing of full-time pupils by expressing their opinion "that Section 72 of the Act gave the School Board power to refuse to accept half-time attendance in any case where they were not satisfied that the child is sufficiently advanced in elementary education previously".[1] However, one or two employers soon began to press the Board to provide school accommodation for their workers, notably Watson Bros of Dennistoun Rope Works, and John Jex Long, "Manufacturer of congreve matches, Vesuvians, fusees, and blacking, timber merchant and saw miller". Long's matchworks at 727 Duke Street was by far the largest in Scotland. After consulting the SED about the advisability of establishing purely half-time schools, and whether they were duty bound to do so, the Board began to consider buying "the top flat of a weaving shop consisting of one room 70' long, 21' broad, 10'-4" high sufficient for 180 children",[2] in East John Street. Even so, the Board's attitude remained cool, and is well illustrated by its reply to the employers: "The building in East John Street would be used chiefly for half-timers, but the Board would agree to open such a school only when they have reasonable assurance that a fair proportion of the cost will be covered by the school fees. It may be well to remind you that, while it is the duty of the Board to provide accommodation for the elementary education of children from 5 to 13, they are under no special obligation to provide schools for half-timers. At the same time, they consider it quite competent for them to establish such schools and carry them on. In doing so they will, of course, expect the hearty co-operation of the employers."[3] Eventually two schools were opened in the latter half of 1874, principally for the use of half-timers, and they speedily gained the reputation of being "the most difficult to manage within the district of the Board". Both of these schools were temporary buildings leased for a number of years; one was known as London Road (No 83) and the other as Glenpark[4] (34 Wilkie Street). In one respect

[1] Minutes of Board in Committee, 2 October 1873.
[2] Minutes of Board in Committee, 3 July 1874.
[3] Letter to Watson Bros, 1 July 1874. See also Appendix D, p 237.
[4] Now demolished.

Glasgow was fairly fortunate in that virtually all half-timers were confined to the eastern part of the town, in and around Bridgeton. This allowed the half-timers to be concentrated in only a few schools, thus leaving the others undisturbed. Other Boards also followed this practice of isolating factory children whenever possible so that they might not contaminate others with their coarse habits and tendency to indiscipline. In Govan, for example, the half-timers were crammed into a little school at the Cross.

For some years the majority of half-timers were housed at Glenpark and London Road, the inspectors' reports of which amply bear out the reasons why "some teachers of ordinary schools are glad to get rid of them".

> "A large number of the scholars are half-timers from the neighbouring factories and, though from 10 to 14 years of age, are so backward in their education that they are only able to pass in the First Standard."
> "This school is attended by a very poor class of children."
> ". . . drawn from the very lowest of the population."

Yet it is remarkable how successful were the staffs in coping with such unpromising material. Although any degree of academic attainment could scarcely be hoped for, the reports of the annual inspections never failed to comment on the splendid work being done by the teachers in the face of conditions so discouraging.

> "This school is conducted with very satisfactory vigour, and in view of the proportion of half-timers, is in a state of very creditable efficiency."
> "The school is conducted with vigour, ability and success, and its condition in respect of both discipline and instruction reflects great credit on the Headmaster and his staff."
> "Good order is maintained and the pupils sing well."
> "From the energy of the present Master much better results may be expected next year."

(The inspector's confidence in the ability of this headmaster of London Road was not misplaced, for he went on to become *Doctor* Milligan of Garnethill.)

The buildings of both these schools were, however, very poor. In 1878 the inspector called London Road "the most wretched premises that are now used for school purposes in Glasgow". Accordingly, the leases were allowed to lapse,

London Road in 1879 and Glenpark in 1881. To replace them the Board took a three-year lease on a building at 19 Campbellfield Street which was used exclusively for half-timers, both boys and girls at first. Known as Campbellfield Hall this half-time school is not to be confused with the large permanent Campbellfield School a few yards along the street. Fortunately, the log-book of this half-time school survives, and provides a picture of the trials and tribulations of the work there. Perhaps more important, however, is the evidence it provides of one powerful reason for the early disappearance of half-timers in Glasgow.

Campbellfield Hall was opened in May 1880, and during the next two years the number of children on the roll averaged about 470. Comparison with the table on page 92 shows that this was rather more than half the total number of half-timers in the city and it follows, therefore, that almost as many again were scattered throughout other schools. In 1882 and 1883 there was an increase in the number of half-timers which brought the roll of Campbellfield to over 600; a quite intolerable figure for the accommodation available, even when allowing for the fact that only half of that number were present on any one day. A warning note from HMI that "the average attendance must no longer exceed the number for whom accommodation is provided otherwise next year's grant may be seriously endangered"[1] compelled the Board to open a second Half-time School. Their choice fell on Bridgeton Public School whose ordinary pupils were transferred elsewhere, and all the girls from Campbellfield moved into Bridgeton in August 1883. But only three years later the number of half-timers in Glasgow had declined to such an extent that Bridgeton was able to revert to its original role and Campbellfield took practically all the half-timers in the city, both boys and girls. Yet another three years, when the school roll had fallen to under 150, and the lease was not renewed. After 1889 no school in Glasgow was set apart specifically for half-timers. At first practically all these children attended Sister Street, but within a few months this school was demolished to make way for the new Bridgeton Railway Station. The half-timers were forced to migrate once again and were distributed among other schools in the East End.

[1] Inspector's Report, 1883.

The log of Campbellfield Hall reflects some of the problems besetting a school of this kind. Chiefly, these were either troublesome boys (girls are never mentioned as giving any bother) or recalcitrant employers. Boys found it fairly easy to "plunk" school and to go to work instead, while employers often winked at the practice or even connived in it. The consequent irregularity of attendance had its inevitable effect on the children's schooling which, in turn, affected the grant which could be won at the annual inspection. The grant for attendance also suffered. Headmasters attempted to counter the temptation of the children to work when they ought to have been at school by compelling them to "make up time" the following week, but little success attended their efforts. The school income further suffered by the refusal of the children to leave their work on the day of the inspection in order to take the examination. A simple solution would have been for the inspection to be held on two consecutive days yet this was never done.

No better picture of life in a half-time school could be given than to quote typical extracts from the log book; they speak for themselves.

"On account of the hard frost, the children felt extremely cold and uncomfortable, and were much more troublesome to manage—not easy at the best."

"I am attempting to make the attendance more regular by insisting upon the children making up their time at school."

"The number of scholars who have never been absent [during the past six months] is 32."

"I wrote a letter to the Match Works asking the directors to insist upon the better attendance of their half-timers. A few of the children were sent here to make up time, but not all I reported."

"Some of the Leith Coy. lads have not made up time this week."

"The Leith Coy. boys have not made up time yet. An employer of labour named Livingstone in the London Road has positively refused to pay 7½d being arrears of a lad in his works. I have written to him again calling his attention to the Act which holds him responsible for all fees."

"Mr Livingstone has paid the arrears under protest."

"Reported several cases of boys not attending school who were working. In one case, John McGraw, the Master, pleaded ignorance, and [I] sent him about his business."

"Two lads under age are employed by Peter Brown, London Road."

"Smith & Coy. kept Wm John Murphy working on his school day and asked the boy to say he was ill."

"The boys from Rutherglen Ropery came one day this week."

"All the boys from the above work are playing truant."

"All the lads from Eastfield are absent. A few of the Rope Work employers have been persuaded to conform to the regulations regarding payment of fees."

"The lads from Eastfield Ropery still play truant."

"John McGillvary has been complaining of a sore chest to the Officer for three weeks, and all the time has been working full-time."

"The Match-work boys are very difficult."

Yet however tough these working lads may have been, we are reminded sometimes that they were still very young children at heart for "Alexander Robertson ran off home today. He had been swearing in the playground." And even the headmaster could prove himself human and kindly: "The school was closed yesterday in honour of the Queen's Birthday. As the lads here today were working I have granted them a half holiday."

The impossibility of enforcing good attendance under the half-time system proved to be one of its most serious defects. Table 7 shows just how very seldom many half-timers actually went to school.

TABLE 7

ATTENDANCE AT CAMPBELLFIELD HALL HALF-TIME SCHOOL

Year	1881	1882	1883	1884	1885	1886	1
Roll	591	610	344	344	152	209	
Number qualified to take examination	234	369	138	257	114	121	
% not making 150 minimum attendances	60%	40%	60%	26%	27%	43%	4

In order to qualify for grant-earning purposes half-timers were required to make 150 attendances annually (as opposed to 250 in the case of full-time children), but in five out of the seven years cited over 40% of all half-timers failed to attend school for as much as seventy-five days in the year. Add irregularity to infrequency and it is little wonder if the factory children remained largely illiterate. Of those who scraped together sufficient attendances to take the examination a goodly number reached Standards IV or V and acquired a fairly reasonable ability in reading (see Table 8) and writing, although attainment in arithmetic was always rather lower.

TABLE 8

PASSES IN READING AT CAMPBELLFIELD HALL

andard	I	II	III	IV	V	VI	Total	Total Roll	Grant for Organisation and Discipline
1	15	38	54	45	38	3	193	591	Lower
2	20	70	95	61	55	1	302	610	,,
3	3	17	44	40	20		124	344	,,
4	12	41	67	73	44	3	240	344	Higher
5	5	12	24	32	24		97	152	,,
6			5	53	46	1	105	209	,,
7	1	8	27	60	30	5	131	267	,,

A curious, though significant, sidelight on half-time schools is the way in which, on occasion, they could be used for the punishment of wayward staff. Mr Lamont, headmaster of Dobbie's Loan, became ill in 1883, and the Board ". . . while gratified to hear of the improvement in Mr Lamont's health, hoped he would not return to duty for a week or two".[1] But two years later the Board became less friendly to Lamont for he had become involved in debt and his creditors had lodged an arrestment with the Board against Lamont whose "liabilities amounted to £449 odds which includes the sum of £21 8s 2d of fees not paid over to the Board".[2] After considering the matter and taking Lamont's professional skill into account, the Board decided to give him another chance on condition that he satisfied his creditors within a specified period, though ". . . it is not considered expedient that Mr Lamont be continued as Head Master of Dobbie's Loan School, but that his name be continued on the list of headmasters".[3] Accordingly, Lamont was banished to Campbellfield Hall where he laboured (and with success) until its closing three years later. He was no longer trusted with the school monies, the fees having to be collected by one of the assistant teachers. The man whom Lamont replaced went to Dobbie's Loan, and one can almost hear the relief in his voice when told of the new arrangement,

[1] Board in Committee, 21 October 1883.
[2] Board in Committee, 21 April 1885.
[3] ibid.

"The Convener reported that he had seen Mr Wilson who had very cordially agreed to the Board's proposal."[1]

THE DECAY OF THE HALF-TIME SYSTEM

The half-time system of education petered out in Scotland long before full-time attendance became compulsory for all children; in Glasgow, no half-timers are recorded after 1896. It has already been shown that, at first, many children were at work without ever attending a school of any kind, but it has also been suggested that there is probably a reasonable correlation between those at work and the figures of those in half-time schools by about 1880. School Board records give the following numbers at school (Table 9).

TABLE 9

NUMBERS OF HALF-TIMERS AT SCHOOL IN GLASGOW, 1880-96

Date	Boys		Girls		Total	Notes
	In Public Schools	In Sessional Schools	In Public Schools	In Sessional Schools		
1880					938	
1881	228	21	414	90	753	
1882	308	33	512	53	906	
1883	363	5	490	19	877	
1884	323	4	375	2	704	Last Works School closed
1885	188		255		443	
1886	106		176		282	
1887	62		131		193	
1888	48		113		161	Sister St (124 Kelvinhaugh St Rollox (4)
1889	42		90		132	
1890	43		91		134	
1891	42		54		96	
1892	28		45		73	
1893	13		37		50	Calton (43) Dalmarnock (
1894	2		16		18	Barrowfield (3 Calton (10) Dalmarnock (
1895			6		6	Calton (6)
1896			8		8	Calton (6) Parkhead (2)

Whatever the reason for the disappearance of half-timers it certainly was not due to any direct process of law. Neither parliament nor School Board did anything to alter the Factory

[1] Board in Committee, 21 April 1885.

or Education Acts as they applied to the education of working children.

The most important single cause for the decline undoubtedly lies in the economic vicissitudes of the time, especially from 1884 onwards. In this year began a severe trade depression which was to prove a very prolonged one extending over many succeeding years. It will be seen from Table 9 that the number of half-timers during the four years 1880–83, while fluctuating somewhat, remained around the 900 mark. But 1884 shows a most decided drop of nearly 200, a still greater decrease took place the following year, and henceforth the figures show an ever-downward trend. Furthermore, no factory maintained a school for its half-timers after 1884, probably because the number of children was insufficient to justify one. The year 1884 was a quite decisive turning point in the half-time system. The inference of the figures in Table 9 is amply borne out by the Log Book of Campbellfield Hall.

1884 June 13: The attendance is considerably down this week owing to dull trade. Preston's Roperies and the Match Works have suspended 20 lads.

Nov. 14: John Clark Junr. & Coy. (Cotton Manufacturers) have dismissed 10 lads as they have no work for them, and I am afraid there are more to follow.

1885 Jan. 9: The attendance is very much down owing to dull trade. Clark's Mill alone have suspended 60 half-timers.

Feb. 12: The attendance is very much down as the Un-employed were asked for their fees this week.

At this time the school contained only boys, but girls were affected just as badly, and both groups had become so small by October 1886 that the girls returned to Campbellfield which was now the only purely Half-time School in Glasgow. Less than three years later even a single school was not worth keeping open, and on 1 March 1889 the headmaster recorded his final entry, "School was closed today." Half-timers lingered on for some years more, but they were a dying race.

We have already seen what a very high proportion of all half-timers were employed by the textile industry; in Glasgow this meant cotton. "The experience [American Civil War] proved how dangerous to the community a specialised unilateral expansion can be. Cotton in its era of great growth had ousted from the West of Scotland the other traditional industries of flax and silk spinning and throwing to such an extent that when the crisis came there was nothing else on which to fall back. Glasgow, except for one large flax spinning mill and one or two silk throwsters, was a cotton town."[1] The rapid decline of the cotton industry in Glasgow during the latter half of the nineteenth century is well known. Competition from Lancashire captured the trade in all but the finest of woven goods from Glasgow. Writing in 1896 (the last year, be it noted, of any recorded half-timers) a factory inspector said that there were then 25,000 fewer power looms employed in the textile trade in Glasgow than there were twenty years previously, and that there remained "only two cotton spinning mills in Glasgow . . . this used to be an important industry, but ten or twelve mills were burnt down in Glasgow during late years and have not been rebuilt."[2]

The fate of the cotton industry largely decided the fate of the half-time system also, for Glasgow was turning more and more to heavy industries which were quite unsuited to the employment of such young children. It is interesting to note in passing what might have happened had Glasgow retained its earlier connection with flax, for in Ireland, where the number of employees in the flax trade increased from 21,000 in 1850 to 68,000 in 1895 as many as 9% of these were children under thirteen years of age.[3]

Besides textiles, only a few other trades are mentioned by the half-time schools, and it may therefore be assumed that these engaged the bulk of the remaining children. Most prominent among them were ropemaking and matchmaking, both of which also suffered from the depression in trade.

Once the decline had begun there were many other influences at work tending to hasten the process and, in the end, to prevent the half-time system from re-establishing itself. Employers had never liked it. Over and over again they had vowed they would have nothing to do with half-timers if only they were not essential to the trade. Here, as has so often happened,

---

[1] *Third Statistical Account of Scotland*, 1958, vol V, p 241.
[2] Mary H Irwin, "Women's Industries in Scotland", Proceedings of Royal Philosophical Society, 18 March 1896.
[3] D L Armstrong, "Social & Economic Conditions in the Belfast Linen Industry, 1850–1900", *Irish Historical Studies*, 1950–51.

necessity proved the mother of invention, new methods were evolved to replace the disappearing children, and the satisfactory results frequently confounded the pessimists. If half-timers were a nuisance prior to the Education Act, they become even more so under the strict control and energy of the School Board, which pestered the employers with demands for the better attendance of their children and compelled the factories to provide school books and to pay for them. Several trades preferred the children to work by the half day, but the Board's half-time schools only operated the alternate day method, and the employers necessarily had to comply.

Frequently the wages of children in factories and workshops were so low for a full week's work that, even for the almost destitute, the rewards of half-time labour simply were not worth the candle. For example, before the introduction of the half-time system into the calico printing trade, children's wages were 2/3d a week. Or, again, in the tobacco spinning shops where "the tables at which the men work are surrounded by a number of small boxes or hutches about 3 ft square, which each contain, buried in tobacco leaves, a dirty little half-clothed boy, who is engaged from morning till night in separating the leaves, pulling out the stalks, etc."[1] For this "the dirty little half-clothed boy" received the weekly sum of from 1/3d to 2/6d. Even school might well have been thought preferable to such a wage minus a penny taken off at source for school fees. Furthermore, these tobacco boys were not paid by the manufacturer but by the journeyman they assisted, a practice to be found in a few other trades also. In bad times, with his own wage diminished, a man simply could not afford to pay a boy. There is also occasional evidence that the adult worker was beginning to regard the low pay of children as a threat to his own wage packet, and the growth of the trade union movement during the late nineteenth century was bound to be unfavourable to child labour.

Another most important contribution to the death of the half-time system was the strenuous efforts of the Roman Catholic authorities to provide their own children with an education comparable to that given in the Board schools. In 1873 there were only ten grant-aided Catholic schools in

[1] Children's Employment Commission, 1862, Vol IV, p 80.

Glasgow. By 1889 the Catholics had twenty-seven schools and the total roll had increased by 7000. As only the very poorest parents sent their children into the factories, and since the Catholic section of the community formed a considerable portion of this unfortunate class, it followed that large numbers of half-timers were Catholics. "The persons employed in the cotton factories have little to distinguish them socially from the great body of the working population except, perhaps, that there is a large number of Irishwomen among them, whose manners are somewhat coarse."[1] School attendance officers were sometimes baulked in their work by parents refusing to send their children to school on the grounds that no Catholic school was available. Stephen Mitchell, the tobacco manu-facturer, commented on the same problem when discussing the limitations of the evening school which had been set up by his trade for its boys in 1864: "One of the great obstacles is the unwillingness of R.C. parents to let their children come to a general school."[2] By 1890 this excuse was no longer valid for there was ample accommodation in Catholic schools, and the forces tending towards full-time education applied equally to Catholics as to Protestants.

Twelve years after the Education Act no less than sixty-six private adventure schools had closed down. Ejected half-timers perforce had to go elsewhere which meant, in effect, to Board schools, where they were unwelcome and discouraged except in those schools specially set apart for them. For the first time a real and effective check was kept on these children and their movements by a strong and efficient authority. No longer was it possible to evade the legal requirements of school attendance —or at any rate, it became far more difficult. The policy of the Board's attendance officers further strengthened the trend towards wholetime schooling. "When I find a child in what is supposed to be a workshop and not a factory, I invariably put him as a defaulter under the Education Act, and I would require full-time attendance till I have proper explanation from the parent."[3] And once he had been got to school the child usually stayed. Sheer inertia alone ensured this.

[1] D Bremner, *Industries of Scotland.* Edinburgh: A and C Black, 1869, p 294.
[2] Children's Employment Commission, 1862, vol IV, p 85.
[3] Factory and Workshops Commission, 1876, paras 15, 625.

Two other possible reasons for the ending of the half-time system remain for consideration; the abolition of school fees and the effect of adverse public opinion. The first move towards free education came in 1889, and within two years all children between five and fourteen were entitled to free schooling. As the half-time system was already on its way out the ending of fees cannot be regarded as a primary cause of its decline, but it may well have had the effect of sealing its fate. There undoubtedly were a considerable number of parents who scarcely had the means to pay even the smallest contribution to the education of their children and who were yet too proud to seek the remedy in recourse to public assistance. There is, and was at the time, a widespread belief that education was held in higher esteem by Scotland than by some other countries, and this is probably true. Some weight must therefore be given to this factor also when determining why the half-time system ended so soon. In 1862 a hand loom weaver exemplified both aspects of this final paragraph, the almost touching Scottish faith in the power of learning and the desperate need in some quarters for relief from school fees.

"I have eight children living . . . Only two of them have ever been at school, and neither of these for a year. All that any know beyond this I have taught myself, but I shall be content if the younger can only read. I might have got them free education, but only at the parish school, by humbling myself as a pauper. That will never do. Though I never applied, I believe that I must plead poverty and get a line signed by a minister and an elder. It is a poor thing for a man to demean himself and plead for that which is a natural right. Education is a natural right. If the mind is not fed how can it grow? The State should educate and see that a child gets its due. I would let people say what they like about interfering with our independence."[1]

[1] Children's Employment Commission, 1862, vol II, p 227.

Chapter 7
THE DEVELOPMENT OF SECONDARY EDUCATION

The history of the development of secondary education in Scotland between 1872 and 1918 is not merely complex but also obscure. Very little has been written on it, and standard textbooks tend to list one piece of legislation following so hard upon another as to leave the reader suffering from mental indigestion. Moreover, all writers make the point that education in Scotland after the 1872 Act was administered by a Committee of the Privy Council, and it operated from Dover House in Whitehall. As a consequence, the argument runs, Scottish education was too much influenced by English thinking and practice, and was retarded in its progress by an alien power ignorant of, and unsympathetic to, the Scottish tradition. It is a view that, while pandering to the ego of the Scot and to his anglophobia, is too simple by far.

The policy of the School Board of Glasgow towards secondary education cannot be properly understood without some consideration of the national picture. In particular, it is first necessary to attempt an answer to two questions: What *was* the Scottish tradition in education—and especially in secondary education? What precisely was meant by *secondary* education?

THE SCOTTISH TRADITION

Every Scot knows of John Knox. He was the Great Reformer. Every Scot knows that among Knox's Great Reforms was that dealing with education. Every Scot knows, though nearly every Scot chooses to forget, that, "From a variety of causes, partly from the rapacity of those who, more powerful even than John Knox, obtained possession of the resources which he had hoped to secure for this purpose, and partly from the carelessness and apathy of the people in later times, this ideal was never carried out."[1] As the rapacious, the powerful, the careless and the apathetic were every whit as Scottish as Knox himself, the question remains: What was the Scottish tradition? But whether fact or fiction, the ideal proclaimed by Knox was accepted in later years by those few whose special concern was for education. The Knoxian "tradition" became a most potent force in Scotland. Unfortunately, its influence can be harmful as well as beneficial. It is harmful when it is accepted as the only true tradition, blinding its devotees to other traditions in Scottish education and to other practices in Scottish education. In particular, the "school in every parish" was not applicable in towns, and therefore of small importance in Glasgow, other than for the strong belief that all children should be schooled.

The second of the best-known Scottish traditions is the ideal of the "lad o' pairts". This tradition holds that every clever boy was spotted early as a potential scholar, that the master tutored him sedulously in Latin and other higher subjects, and in due course the boy moved on to the university. Here again, however, the facts are less encouraging. The area of the Dick and Milne Bequests in the north-east of the country was justifiably famed for its success of this system. In other places throughout the land, if a boy was lucky he found himself in a school with an able and keen master. Plenty did not. As far as Glasgow was concerned there is abundant evidence to suggest that the "lad o' pairts" seldom got beyond the 3 Rs. What might be possible in a small country school was quite impossible in a large town. No schoolmaster could put to one side seventy or eighty or ninety children, while he concentrated on the two or three bright ones, no matter how brilliant.

Probably the fondest belief of the Scot is that his educational tradition is a classless one; that the high and the low, the rich and the poor went to school together. In large degree this is a self-congratulatory delusion. Said the Duke of Argyll in 1869, "It is the universal custom all over Scotland that men in very different classes of society should be educated together in the parochial schools. You will have the children of the poorest labourer sitting beside the farmer who employs him, the children of the clergyman of the parish, and even in some cases

---

[1] Lord Balfour of Burleigh in an address at the opening of an extension to Glasgow High School, 1887.

of the landed gentry, sitting on the same bench and learning from the same master, the same branches of instruction."[1] But it should be noted that the Duke limited his observations to "the parochial schools". With country villages, their very remoteness, combined with very poor and sometimes non-existent transport, no doubt often compelled such mixing. In big towns it was not necessary, and it did not happen. In passing, the Duke's phrase, "and even in some cases" clearly indicates that the attendance of the Master of Ballantrae, or wherever, at the local school was exceptional. The Glasgow practice was not at all egalitarian; one of the most marked features of the Glasgow educational scene noted by the Argyll Commission was the social distinctions that existed between the schools. The best sessional schools charged high fees, and thus effectively excluded the lower classes. The scholastic progression of James Bridie (no mean Scot!) in the Glasgow of the 1890s is as typical of his class and of his nation as the more generally accepted rural version. As a very little boy in Dennistoun, he and his brother ". . . set out daily to Miss Carter's School, where the weekly fee was 1/6d". Soon, "The first real school I went to was the High School of Glasgow. . . ," but then, ". . . in the following year the family fortunes must have improved, for I was transferred to the Glasgow Academy for the Sons of Gentlemen".[2]

Thus the three traditions, Knoxism, the "Lad o' Pairts", and the Egalitarian, were of small practical importance in Glasgow in the later nineteenth century. In so far as they were effective at all, they belonged to the countryside. They were a part of the Scottish heritage, but only a part. For there were also other traditions though not all as well publicised or as frankly acknowledged today.

THE MEANING OF SECONDARY EDUCATION

Forster's Education Act was quite specific in its purpose and precisely limited in its aim: to provide public elementary schooling up to the age of thirteen for all who wished to have it.

---

[1] Quoted by S J Curtis, *Education in Britain Since 1900*, London: Andrew Dakers, 1952, p 239.
[2] James Bridie, *One Way of Living*, London: Constable, 1938, p 40.

Beyond the Board School was the Grammar School which remained outside government control. That is, government supplied *primary* education, independent agencies *secondary*. The division between the two stages was clear and unequivocal.

In Scotland, however, the intentions of the 1872 Act in its relation to secondary education was a matter of debate and dispute. As the wording of the Act did not limit the new schools to elementary education in so many words, Scottish opinion claimed that this implied that secondary education also was within the province of the School Boards and that public money should be made available for secondary work. In practice, the Scotch Education Department refused to accept this interpretation of the Act, and accordingly paid grants only to the elementary schools and for the Specific Subjects taught within them. The argument between the Department and Scottish educational opinion continued for the next twenty years before secondary education was at last recognised for grant-earning purposes. Perhaps victory would not have been so long delayed had Scots been agreed as to what exactly secondary education was. Unfortunately they were not. And this largely because the concept of secondary education was a blurred one in the minds of many—even the well-informed—by the variety of Scottish traditions and by the firm belief of many that their particular view of the matter was in keeping with a practice hallowed by the ages and therefore immutable.

The situation is best looked at by considering separately:

(a) higher class schools;
(b) parochial-type schools;
(c) specific subjects;
(d) the influence of the university.

Higher Class Schools

Everyone accepted that here, indeed, was to be found secondary schooling in its proper sense. These were the Scottish schools that carried a boy beyond the 3 Rs into the upper reaches of knowledge; French and German, mathematics, literature and, above all, Latin. It was here perhaps that culture was to be obtained. It was here certainly that the necessary training was given for entry to university, the professions and the commercial world. The old academies and high schools had a proud past and enjoyed great prestige.

Unfortunately, they were so few. Originally only eleven Higher Class Public Schools were designated for transference to the School Boards, although others were created later by the Boards themselves until by 1889 there were twenty-one throughout the country. Glasgow had only one, the High School. For many years this was the sole secondary school proper under public management. It was available only to boys, about 600 of them, many of whom came from outside the city. Only those able to pay the high fees could contemplate going, and consequently the High School's pupils were drawn entirely from the professional and commercial classes.

Private Higher Class Schools were an important element in the city. For girls there flourished a number of schools and colleges for "Young Ladies". For boys, the Glasgow Academy especially competed keenly with the High School.

The attitude of the School Board towards independent schools was very important as it strongly influenced the Board's thinking on secondary education. In brief, public education was not something which was inherently meritorious in itself. It had come into being merely because the old system had proved inadequate for the times; private charity could not keep pace with the ever increasing number of children too poor to buy a decent education. So the state had stepped in, but only to make good a deficiency, not to supersede existing schools. Thus it was not part of the duty of a School Board to erect and maintain a school at public expense if adequate provision was already made by private enterprise.

Most members of the Glasgow Board thoroughly approved. They believed that it was a parent's duty to provide for his own children so far as he was able; that it was a parent's right to send his child to the school of his choice; and, moreover, they believed that a private school also had a *right* to exist so long as it was efficient. Said a Chairman of the Board in 1887, "The School Boards have no desire to obtain a monopoly of education, either primary or secondary. We do not consider the Acts which we administer entitle us to any monopoly. We welcome all existing agencies. School Boards have held back, perhaps wrongly, from doing all they might have done for Secondary

Education, largely from fear of injuring private schools; and unless there be a clear demand from the community for the establishment of secondary schools it will always be difficult to get over this."[1]

Parochial-type Schools

As is well known, the Scottish tradition was to have "all age" or "all through" schools. Even the Higher Class schools were not solely secondary; they merely had a more clearly defined secondary department. The ordinary schools were, however, basically primary schools which, in the absence of a proper Higher School nearby, had perforce to retain and cater for pupils who wished to stay on beyond the usual leaving age of twelve or thirteen. These advanced pupils were very few in number, too few to be able to warrant the provision for them of the highly qualified specialist teachers, expensive equipment, and all that is implied in education at this level. In spite of the difficulties, schools and schoolmasters did what they could for these high flyers. Now and again the exceptional boy in an occasional school even got as far as the university. Just how infrequent such success was may be judged from the evidence of the Professor of Humanity at Glasgow who said in a report for the University Court, "Out of 255 first-year students in the session 1889–90 . . . only 55 proved themselves able to pass the preliminary examination in Latin. Almost the whole of these 55 were educated at secondary schools; and the experience of the past 10 years shows that it is but rarely that a student coming direct from an elementary or ordinary public school is able to pass the examination."[2] He went on to give the figures over a period of five years of those who passed in the different subjects at the Annual Bursary Competition; 232 were from secondary schools, twenty-two from public or elementary. "Thus the elementary schools carry off a very small proportion of all the places in this list; and those places are practically all gained by three schools which happen to have a higher side. The fact is, therefore, that the ordinary public schools are not able to send

---

[1] Sir John Neilson Cuthbertson, *Secondary Education from the School Board Point of View*, 1887.
[2] Evidence of G G Ramsay before the Elgin Commission, 1892, para 1443.

up students who can pass the preliminary examination."[1] So
much for the much-admired parochial system. So much for the
system so dear to the heart of the Scot, both then and now.

There were, of course, sound practical reasons for its
continuance, the chief one being the unwillingness or financial
inability of most parents in country areas to send their children
away from home to a central higher school. But this argument
could have no validity in a city. Yet so deeply ingrained was
the notion that provision for more advanced learning within
the ordinary school was the great glory of the Scottish tradition
and the mainspring of its peculiar genius, that even in Glasgow
they could not free their minds of its mesmeric charm. The
School Board consistently maintained its determination not to
do away with the traditional practice, but to encourage and
develop it. This was, it asserted, secondary education.

"It has been the ambition of Scottish teachers to carry on
their pupils as far as their parents wish them to go. Our schools
[ie Glasgow School Board] are not merely elementary schools,
but come in the place and with the traditions of the old parish
schools . . . and whatever our critics shall say to the contrary,
the Board shall certainly see that a substantial proportion of
their 66 schools shall give instruction in the Higher branches
and be suitably staffed for the purpose."[2] Another School
Board representative, when giving evidence before the Mon-
creiff Commission, strongly contended that education in
Glasgow's elementary schools was not confined to primary
work, and accordingly put forward the Board's preference
". . . that the expressions 'Elementary Education' and 'Primary
Education' should be dropped from the Order, and that there
should be used instead, education in public or other inspected
schools.

Q Therefore the School Board desire that the word 'education'
   should be used exclusively?
A Education in public or other inspected schools.
Q You wish the word 'primary' or 'elementary' omitted?
A We think it is misleading—that it is generally supposed to limit
   education to its simplest elements, whereas it is not so.[3]

[1] Ramsay, *loc cit.*
[2] J N Cuthbertson, *op cit.*
[3] Evidence of William Mitchell before the Moncrieff Commission, 1881.

Was the work done in the extended courses of the primary schools "secondary" education? No one seemed very sure. The same man sometimes claimed it to be so, only apparently to contradict himself a little later. Opinion was blurred and rather confused. Perhaps, Cuthbertson best illustrated this perplexity when he actually referred to schools of this type as "semi-secondary". Perhaps, too, he revealed the real justification for so much of the enthusiasm for these glorified elementary schools when he said, "The advantage offered by these semi-secondary schools of a good sound education at a moderate fee is one to which the ratepayers are well entitled. The much higher fee in the purely secondary school is a complete barrier to the vast majority of the people."[1]

Specific Subjects

Until 1899 a number of teaching topics were designated Specific Subjects. They were taught in the ordinary elementary schools and took the pupils beyond the minimum requirements of the 3 Rs. They carried an additional grant and so were popular with the school boards. On the other hand, Specific Subjects were much criticised[2] on various educational grounds which need not be reviewed here. Our interest lies in the fact that this extension of primary schooling contributed to the already confused attitudes towards secondary education. How far could a course in Specific Subjects be regarded as a substitute for an academic schooling at the High School?

Much depended on the subject. The sciences, such as mechanics or animal physiology, were simple in content and far from demanding. They were derided by the academic. Other subjects like Latin were very difficult. "The Third Stage of a Specific Subject is in some cases higher than the entrance examination to Glasgow University," said the Chief Inspector. In practice, the number of pupils going on to the third stage of even one specific subject was tiny indeed; few stayed even for the second stage.

Few schools could spare a teacher for the full-time training of

---

[1] J N Cuthbertson, *op cit.*

[2] For example: "Thus began the era of Specific Subjects, and what had been an educational burlesque became a screaming farce." S S Laurie, *The Scottish Code of 1899 and Other Matters*, 1889.

D*

a small elite at the top of the school. Nor were specialist teachers often available in the different subjects. Consequently, Specific Subject classes tended to get far less assistance from a teacher than was desirable. A good deal of what would euphemistically be called "private study" went on.

The advocates of true secondary schooling further maintained that there was far more to a proper secondary education than the mere business of passing an examination in one or two advanced subjects. A full secondary course created an attitude of mind, a culture, which never could be acquired in an appendage of an elementary school.

Specific Subjects were, in effect, the official stamp of approval for the all-through parochial-type of school. They allowed the traditionalist to feel that the good old Scottish practice still flourished. Now even the cities could believe that they too shared the great heritage, and that the ordinary lad, denied the High School by his relative poverty, could make his way to fame and fortune by a near equivalent route.

The Influence of the University

We are accustomed today to think of a full education as passing through three distinct stages; the primary school, the secondary school, and the university. It seems a natural progression. Yet until as late as 1890 the second of these stages was virtually non-existent in Scotland.

University educational standards were low, and many critics opined that a Scottish degree was of little merit and scarcely higher in standard than that reached in a good school. "Centuries ago a Degree in Arts was a proof of learning. Now it represents the educational status of a grammar-school boy."[1] "For the last century the University of Glasgow has been plunging with accelerating speed down a headlong course, and is now in many respects, if not in all, inferior to many of the secondary schools throughout the country. . . . The MA degree is no proof of education. It indicates the same level of education as that possessed by a boy leaving a good Grammar School, and is a miserable result from a university course."[2]

---

[1] ed James Kelly, *University Pamphlets.* c 1885, p 15.
[2] *ibid*, p 37.

A practising teacher claimed in 1889 that the newly instituted Leaving Certificate examination was intrinsically far higher than those set for the MA degree in the universities, that no graduate of a Scottish University had any hope of a classical or mathematics chair unless he had first improved himself by going to Oxford or Cambridge, that "even the best posts in our secondary schools have recently been given only to those who have had the benefit of an education at an English University", and that, while the Scottish medical classes were crowded with students from England and elsewhere, Scottish students could only get good classics or mathematics in the South.[1]

That the reader may judge for himself what truth there was in such allegations, here are a few random questions taken from Ordinary MA Degree Examination of Glasgow University in 1876.

English Literature

4. Distinguish and illustrate the following terms:
   Synecdoche, Antonomasia, Anticlimax, Antithesis, Tautology, Pleonasm, Verbosity.
7. Give some account of the most famous allegories that have appeared in our language.
9. Refer the following to their authors, with approximate dates:
   The Hesperides, Ode to Althea, Hudibras, Holy War, Absalom and Achitophel, Arcadia, Windsor Forest, Hymn on the Nativity, The Dunciad, Vision of Mirza.
10. Give a brief outline of Milton's Life, and a list of his chief works.

Mathematics

3. Prove that a quadrilateral, which has two opposite sides and two opposite angles equal, is a parallelogram.
6. Reduce $\dfrac{x^4 - 4x^3 + 8x^2 - 8x - 21}{x^4 - x^3 + 12x^2 - 7x + 49}$ to its lowest terms.

If the final examination at university was not very demanding, entrance requirements were nil. Anyone who wished to do so was able to attend university classes provided he paid his fees to the professor. As the demand for university places was small there was no necessity to impose restrictions on entry. In these

[1] James Moir, "Secondary Education". An address as President of the Association of Teachers in the Secondary Schools of Scotland, 1889.

spacious days a professor could proclaim himself to be strongly against any form of entrance test on the grounds that no one was harmed if a student attended a class and yet understood none of it.[1]

There was, in fact, a very good reason for the refusal of the universities to institute some kind of entrance test: few could have passed it. As far as teaching beyond the 3 Rs was concerned the parish school system had proved a total failure. Hardly a boy from schools outside the city was fit for university. In 1875 Professor G G Ramsay tested 261 of his students in Latin. On the basis of the standard expected of a fifteen-year-old boy at Harrow or Rugby 203 were failures. Out of the top twenty-four candidates nineteen came from secondary schools (including five from the Glasgow High School and six from Glasgow Academy), leaving only five from all the sessional schools in the city and all the parish schools in the country areas. Ramsay reckoned that if an entrance test were adopted it would exclude four fifths of all the present entrants.[2] The much lauded custom by which a relatively large proportion of Scottish boys passed on to university was due not to the splendid quality of the schooling they had received but to the wide open gates of an indulgent college which recognised the glaring deficiencies and severe limitations of the schools.

Attempts were made to require an entrance qualification, but supporters of the old system successfully resisted innovation for many years. An excluding test would have prevented many men going up to university long after they had left school, a custom very common. The Royal Commission into the Universities of Scotland in 1878 found that there was a large majority opinion against an entrance examination, for "the necessity of having to pass an ordeal before admission would prevent many from applying for admission, and would check that laudable ambition which has been a characteristic feature among Scottish students".

The effect of such low university standards was seriously to retard the development of secondary education. As long as universities accepted young boys of fourteen with no better

[1] Evidence of J P Nichol, Professor of Astronomy at Glasgow, before the Royal Commission into Scottish Universities, 1859.
[2] G G Ramsay, *A Summary of Entrance Standards and Practicality of Introducing an Entrance Examination*, 1876.

scholastic background than an extended elementary course what need was there for secondary schools? The university itself provided a bridge for these children by placing them in a "Junior Class" for a year of preparation before they began the university course proper. This was a class which did not normally have to be taken by a boy from, say, the High School or the Academy. In other words, the university supplied the means to by-pass secondary schooling altogether; the Junior Class was a kind of crash secondary course in itself.

The secondary school was being squeezed out of existence between the elementary school with its Specific Subjects and the university with its Junior Class. Critics of the system were not wanting.

"Though it is scandalous that the University should be in competition with the secondary schools, which should be its feeders and not its competitors, the University Authorities sometimes make a boast of the cheapness of the education it gives. It is both cheap and nasty. Any secondary school would be ashamed to give such an education; but in order to give a better, it has to charge higher fees. . . . How much cheaper does it seem? It gives a complete course of highly honoured education for about £35, while the High School of Glasgow cannot give a complete course of even lightly esteemed education under £70. University *honours* are cheap; High School *education* is double the price.

"In the race of teaching, then, the secondary schools have not only the fight against the University monopoly, but against the University cheapness. The University poaches upon them both with the M.A. gun and the three guinea snare [ie the fee for one university course]. How can it be expected that they can have anything but a flickering existence? That they live at all in spite of the University opposition is due to the fact that there are men who prefer education to a Degree—who love the reality as distinguished from the show of learning, and to this other fact that there is here and there a teacher who loves his work, and is willing to spend his life in comparatively unremunerated labour. . . . By teaching merely elementary subjects the University enters a scandalous competition with the secondary schools and lowers the standard of education throughout the country."[1]

The famous S S Laurie was equally critical. He proposed a compromise solution to the problem whereby the university would accept boys of sixteen and over without examination, while boys under sixteen would be told to go back to school.

[1] ed James Kelly, *op cit*, pp 44–6.

"The University is essentially a school for manly, not boyish, intellect."[1]

THE PROBLEM FACING THE SCHOOL BOARD

In the nineteenth century secondary education was ailing. As is well known, the Act of 1872 administered the death blow to a number of established secondary schools. Since no grants were payable for the running of such Higher Class schools, several Boards simply turned them into elementary schools. This was the fate of the burgh grammar schools at Banff, Musselburgh, Montrose, Peebles and Selkirk among others. But not in Glasgow. Proud of its High School, the Board was keen to develop and expand secondary schooling though money was obviously a limiting factor. Financial considerations made it essential to look around for some acceptable alternative to the clear-cut secondary education of the Higher Class schools, and the alternative must carry with it government blessing in the concrete form of government money.

The easy solution lay at hand: the ordinary parochial school had traditionally served the needs of those who wanted a higher schooling. There seemed no reason why the new Board Schools, given the necessary encouragement, should not follow in the same tradition. The tradition was, of course, largely a delusion, and most thinking men knew it to be so. Yet it was a beguiling delusion. All the more so since the system of Specific Subjects heightened the impression of giving an advanced education, as did the University practice of recruiting pupils direct from the ordinary schools.

From the start the School Board of Glasgow was determined to provide secondary education facilities for all who could and would take advantage of them. The way ahead was not, however, at all clear to the members. Nor is this surprising. No guidance came from the Department of Education, for government policy on secondary education was negative. The other factors already discussed served but to confuse and blur the whole concept of secondary education.

Glasgow's approach to the problem was to advance on a

[1] Evidence of Professor S S Laurie before the Universities (Scotland) Commission, 1878.

broad front, steadily if somewhat delicately, until by the late 1880s a definite and recognisable system of secondary schooling served the whole city. It had been reached by a groping, pragmatic approach, the outstanding features of which were a refusal to pay too much attention to tags—"elementary", "secondary"—and a certain facility for not being overawed by what seemed to be official Departmental policy, and for interpreting the Acts and Codes in such a generous manner as to allow the early development of secondary education in fact if not in name.

THE EARLY YEARS

In one respect the secondary education of the City was improved immediately the School Board came into being, for it took vigorous action to re-organise the internal administration of the High School to its great benefit. Apart from this and the continuing work of the High School Committee, the early Boards were much too busy tackling the enormous deficiencies in elementary schooling to pay very much attention to secondary work. There were the intricate financial and administrative problems of the new Act to be solved; thousands of children to be brought into the schools—and kept there; a constant shifting of pupils and staff as makeshift quarters gave way to permanent classrooms. Elementary schooling was the really urgent work of the time. Secondary education was bound to take a back seat.

It was not altogether ignored. The Board looked on all its schools as standing in the place of the traditional parish school which could, if it would, carry its pupils beyond the mere elements of reading and writing into the higher branches of knowledge. There was a strong belief that a teacher of merit and ambition would wish to introduce his pupils to mathematics and languages, and that since this was to be his chief source of satisfaction and reward and his compensation for the everyday drudgery of dunning the 3 Rs into the younger children, it would be unjust to limit him to the elementary subjects. Furthermore, it would be unwise, for the master might lose all enthusiasm for his work and be a lesser teacher as a result.[1]

[1] J N Cuthbertson, *op cit*.

Consequently the schools were encouraged to teach the Specific Subjects, though without much in the way of guidance or direction. "To begin with, the Committee left to the headmasters and other teachers very much to exercise their own discretion as to whether Specific Subjects should be taught and what these should be. In the course of time they were able to discover in what schools such subjects were likely to flourish and where they should be encouraged."[1]

By their fourth year twenty-two out of all the thirty-nine schools were professing Specific Subjects in their curriculum, but most schools were attempting only one or two topics and almost all of these were the easier choices like physiology, geography, literature and domestic economy. The more testing and truly academic subjects were scarcely represented at all. Six schools offering mathematics presented for examination a mere thirty-two pupils, five schools offered a total of twenty-one Latin scholars, while only three schools taught French. Two years later, by 1879, the picture was little better even although many of the new large permanent schools had now been erected and occupied. Thirty-nine pupils passed French, eighty-one Latin, and twenty-seven mathematics. A wise and discerning parent of the day would have sent his boy to Crookston Street, Henderson Street, Oatlands, or Springburn. Yet even the best of these good schools had little really to offer: Henderson Street obtained nine successes in French, eight in Latin, and five in mathematics. It will be readily realised how wasteful such a system was in teaching strength, and the Board was soon discouraging headmasters from allocating one of their staff to teach a mere handful of advanced pupils, for however willing the Board was to develop secondary work it could not afford to ignore the economics of the situation.[2]

The following decade brought in a goodly financial return in grants from Specific Subjects as more and more schools came into operation, but for the most part the improvement was still

[1] Teachers and Teaching Committee, Annual Report, 1881.
[2] Teachers and Teaching Committee, Annual Report, 1885. "In some schools the numbers studying particular branches are very small, while in other schools the range of subjects is apparently too wide. It is known to the Board that, in not a few cases, such small classes are taught by the master and assistants at extra hours . . . but where such teaching is carried on at the usual hours it involves a dissipation of teaching power which is much to be lamented and ought to be checked."

in those subjects which were little regarded as having much educational worth. For example, English literature was far and away the most popular Specific Subject. However, in spite of its erudite title, it consisted of little more than an extended course in reading and a few questions on interpretation. Indeed it was so simple that it was dropped from the list of Specific Subjects in 1888, becoming just an ordinary class subject.

TABLE 10

NUMBER OF PASSES IN THE EASIER SPECIFIC SUBJECTS

Year Ending	English Literature	Physical Geography	Domestic Economy	Physiology	Chemistry*	Magnetism & Electricity
1881	2962	913	1867	452	37	160
1882	3662	647	2028	500	29	173
1883	3719	1216	2248	628	59	147
1884	4398	1624	2707	923	180	137
1885	4981	2122	2794	821	205	106
1886	4688	1942	2634	1064	249	170
1887	4504	2431	2604	1199	201	300
1888		2862	1999	1941	198	510
1889		1980	1360	1735	243	537

* Only one or two schools taught this subject; eg in 1887 Dennistoun contributed 170 candidates, the other 31 were at Mathieson Street.

Table 10 shows the total passes over a period of years in the lightweight subjects. Mechanics was never attempted in any of the schools. Light and heat, and botany were hardly ever offered; occasionally one school or other put forward a few pupils only to abandon the work within a year or two. Table 11 gives the numbers passing in those subjects which were regarded as truly secondary standard.

TABLE 11

NUMBER OF PASSES IN THE ACADEMIC SPECIFIC SUBJECTS

Year Ending	Mathematics	Latin	Greek	French	German
1881	67	270	2	111	1
1882	115	338	12	153	0
1883	158	452	15	368	30
1884	218	482	14	484	32
1885	246	459	22	504	58
1886	245	459	16	567	97
1887	279	345	22	554	113
1888	396	306	26	920	176
1889	569	301	42	1120	167

NB These figures do not include the High School.

Perhaps one of the more surprising facts is the relative decline of Latin at a time when the classics were still regarded as the true mark of an educated man. The explanation would seem to lie in its unattractiveness compared with other studies, for after 1886 the Board began to discourage to the point of compulsion children under Standard VI attempting more than one Specific Subject.[1] Many appear to have preferred the modern languages and mathematics. The growing popularity of French is apparent, although scarcely any specialist teachers existed as yet.

There is a very marked improvement in all subjects except Latin from 1888 onwards, the cause of which is in no doubt: the reorganisation of Glasgow's educational endowments had at last come into effect, and a large number of bursaries were available for needy children who wished to continue their schooling beyond the elementary stage.[2]

On the whole, however, progress was very slow throughout the eighties, and the opportunities for some degree of advanced learning were even slighter than raw totals indicate since very few schools indeed provided a varied offering of courses. Several subjects were confined to a mere handful of schools. For example, in 1887 the 113 German students were either at Garnethill, Dennistoun or Woodside. No other school taught German. Greek could be had only at Garnethill or Woodside. Three quarters of the Latin pupils came from only three schools.

Another way of measuring the progress of secondary education is to consider the number of children who had passed the wholly elementary work of Standard VI. If, in addition, age is taken into account it will be seen how many stayed on at school beyond the permitted leaving age (Table 12).

Considering the size of Glasgow these figures do not suggest that secondary schooling was advancing at all rapidly. In particular, one might have expected a fairly steady improvement over the years, yet no such development occurred. The slow rate of growth was in no way due to a failure of the School Board to provide for secondary work. On the contrary, the

---

[1] In the previous year, 1885, the Scotch Code had prohibited any Specific Subject to pupils below Standard V.
[2] See Chapter 8, "Fees, Bursaries and Scholarships".

Board had always sought to encourage the higher subjects in every way open to it: by providing money where possible, by representations to Government, both privately and as witnesses before several commissions of enquiry, by giving their teachers freedom to teach to as high a level as they wished, and by carefully considered organisation of the schools. The main reason for the rather slow growth of secondary schools was a lack of effective demand for them.

TABLE 12

NUMBER AND AGES OF PUPILS BEYOND STANDARD VI

Age	11	12	13	14	15	16	17	18	Totals all ages
91–92	6	92	509	277	74	13	4		975
92–93	2	103	534	348	93	15	6		1101
93–94	8	102	446	339	113	20	1		1029
94–95	2	66	432	326	133	32	9	1	1001
95–96	1	47	415	422	151	43	14	2	1095
96–97	1	64	405	383	151	34	11	1	1050
97–98		86	395	320	160	15	6	1	983
98–99	3	56	352	374	145	40	11	2	983

We have already seen that the university was partly to blame for the early leaving of many boys. Certainly, the School Board held the university responsible for not setting a suitable standard at entrance. Said Cuthbertson, the Chairman, in reply to Professor Ramsay's criticism of the bad material reaching the university (out of 104 students who had sat the examination of the Junior Class in Latin 81 failed). "Now, in the name of common sense, as the Professor himself admits, what business had these 81 students or for that part of it, the 104, in a university at all? And how can secondary schools be expected to exist, far less to thrive, if the Professor of Humanity takes in a herd of men like that?"[1] If, then, boys destined for university, presumably the academic cream of the schools, left so young what likelihood was there of the others remaining longer at school?

There is ample evidence that there existed a general apathy towards education among the better-off classes, not only in Glasgow but throughout Scotland. As late as 1903 the Education Department reported, "It is a matter for regret to find that where liberal educational provision has been made, the

[1] J N Cuthbertson, *op cit.*

Inspectors have so often to lament that the pupils are withdrawn at an age too early to benefit fully by it . . . and is, indeed, one of the most serious difficulties against which secondary education has to contend. The only remedy for it is the growth of a more enlightened public opinion."[1] Leading members of the Glasgow Board frequently criticised the attitude of the City's merchant and industrial classes. Many sent their children to boarding school, and especially to the great English Public Schools. Moreover, it was the habit of commercial firms to recruit boys for their offices as soon as they became fourteen. They liked to get the lads in young, and seemed to want little more from them than attractive penmanship and a certain skill at totting up figures. When the Chamber of Commerce asked the School Board to introduce more language and commercial courses into the schools the Board retorted that they were anxious to do so, but that so few pupils stayed on that nothing could be done. The remedy, however, lay largely in the hands of the businessmen themselves. It was pointless to ask for special commercial training when a mere 1300 boys remained in all the schools of the city after reaching fourteen.[2]

The School Board was progressive in thought, generous with facilities, willing and keen to advance the cause of secondary education as far as possible. But its efforts were frustrated by the apathy of that section of the public which might have been most expected to lend it support and even to put ever greater demands on the Board for this form of schooling. Repeatedly the Board claimed that only a lack of demand prevented it from developing secondary work further. Show us that you want it, said the Board, and we will supply it. Cuthbertson never tired of bringing the matter to public notice. "It is little short of scandalous that a place like Glasgow can support only two or three secondary schools of the first class."[3] "The attendance, even at the High School and other Secondary Schools, dwindles to a small number in the higher forms."[4] "It is melancholy that so few Glasgow citizens give their sons the benefit of a really

[1] Committee of Council on Education in Scotland, Annual Report, 1903.
[2] Discussion between School Board of Glasgow and the Chamber of Commerce, 1885.
[3] ibid.
[4] J N Cuthbertson, *Secondary Education from the School Board Point of View.*

liberal education, and that this great community can barely support two or three purely secondary schools."[1]

The same difficulties and discouragements faced the Govan Board. Their Chairman considered the standards in Scottish secondary schools much inferior to those of England. He even sent a strong letter to the Rector of Kelvinside Academy, which his own boys attended, complaining about the low standards there, and he duly removed his sons to an English boarding school. As in Glasgow, Govan found it impossible to achieve satisfactory secondary work as the schools remained unfilled. In 1886, out of 10,000 pupils attending the parish's public schools, only 315 were presented for examination beyond Standard VI. When asked by the Parker Commission if he regarded this as a satisfactory result of the teaching of higher education in Govan he replied, "I do not." "Can you point to any reason for that state of matters, why the proportion is so small?" "I think it is the indifference of the population to the higher branches. I think the great bane of secondary education in Scotland is the little interest the people generally take in secondary education; it is quite different from the same class of people in England." In Govan also it was the professional and merchant classes that showed least interest: "While the working classes in Scotland, to their lasting honour, have been till quite recently more alive to the advantages of education than are the corresponding classes in England, the reverse proposition holds true when you reach the middle classes. It is my opinion . . . that as a rule in the middle and upper classes, English parents are more concerned about their children's education and willing to spend more money on that education than are Scotch parents."[2]

Undoubtedly, the School Boards of both Glasgow and Govan felt that the main reason for the frustration of their hopes for the greater development of secondary education was the lack of interest and support of the middle classes, the very group which might have been expected to provide a lead and that group which was certainly able to afford it. For few men at the time thought it reasonable to expect the working classes to be

[1] J N Cuthbertson, *op cit.*
[2] George Crichton, *An Educational Address delivered at the opening of the enlargement to Kinning Park School*, 1887.

interested in secondary schooling. Money was too hard to come by. In themselves fees were no great deterrent. The household economy simply demanded that the child leave school as soon as possible so that he could contribute to the family income.

The School Board never felt that government policy was any great hindrance to the furtherance of secondary education. It was true that the 1872 Act did not allot monies to secondary work, but neither, with one exception, did it seem to forbid the use of public funds for this purpose,[1] for the Act did not specifically designate grant-aided schools as "Elementary" and at no time did Glasgow ever refer to "Elementary" Schools, but always to "Public" Schools. Similarly the expression "Secondary" was avoided in official Board nomenclature. The preferred expression was "Higher Department (or Higher Subjects) in Public Schools". By this device of not using terms which might possibly lead to contentious legal definition and to Treasury objections, the Board was able to exploit Glasgow's potential for secondary schooling, fully aided by Government grants. Probably this was the great merit of Specific Subjects. Those of little scholastic worth brought in a good deal of money for inexpensive teaching. The more difficult and more expensive subjects could be financed, with the help of moderate rates and fees, to any degree to which the school was able to advance them. Cuthbertson contended that the Acts of 1872 and 1878 *took* nothing from Higher Schools and added something, and ". . . contains principles which, if carried out, will provide all the secondary education that can be wanted. Given a public opinion favourable to the movement, and the School Board in any district has ample powers."[2]

If the Scotch Education Department did not actually connive at the practice it certainly put no obstacle in the way. On one financial matter of some importance, however, Glasgow had to fight a lengthy battle. Grants alone could not sustain secondary work. Income from fees was also necessary. A school which developed a really strong higher side, found that it had to charge a fee rather above that which was normal in public

[1] The exception was in the case of Higher Class Schools. The restriction did not worry the Board, however, as the High School was self-supporting and always had been so.
[2] J N Cuthbertson, *op cit*.

schools. When, therefore, the Code of 1875 announced that no grant would be given in the case of a school charging more than ninepence[1] a week it placed the work of a few Glasgow schools in jeopardy. At the time it was scarcely noticed, for the Board was then engrossed in providing the new schools. Only later did it become an issue of importance. The regulation had been copied from the Elementary Education (England) Act, 1870. Glasgow and several other Scottish Boards contended that it ought never to have been applied to Scotland, for while it was reasonable to have a limit of ninepence for Elementary schools, the Scottish Public Schools, unlike those of England, were not and never had been purely elementary schools. If the limitation was insisted upon ". . . the schools must go on drawing from the rates to provide the higher branches as far as the ratepayers will allow them to do so. The standard of education will go down if the ratepayers object. It seems, on the other hand, extraordinary that the ratepayers should have to pay for the parents what the parents are willing to do for themselves, and that the Department, without any pecuniary advantage to the Exchequer, should insist upon a condition which tends to increase the local rate. It is difficult to see what interest the Department have in keeping down the fees."[2]

There is evidence to suggest that the Department was not responsible for the legal interpretation of the Article which denied the claim of the School Board. It emanated from the inaccessible recesses of the Treasury.[3]

It is worth noting that the Board, if necessary, was prepared to raise the local rate as far as it could be driven rather than diminish the quality of education in its schools. The school most affected was Garnethill, but so strong was demand for the exceptionally high quality of schooling which it offered that it was able to continue its progress by raising fees even after the grant-in-aid was withdrawn.

A curious sidelight on the Limitation Clause was that Govan experienced little difficulty with it. When A J Mundella, Vice-President of the Privy Council and at that time responsible for educational matters in Scotland, visited Glasgow, he was wined

[1] Scotch Code, 1875, Article VI(d).
[2] Notes by the School Board of Glasgow to the Commissioners on Endowed Institutions in Scotland, 1888.
[3] See comment by Craik, Parker Commission, paras 1625–30.

and dined. But the hospitality of Govan perhaps outdid that of her neighbouring burgh. At any rate, Govan was able to get Mundella's assurance that the ninepenny restriction would not be applied, and so Govan came to enjoy a grant for Hillhead, whose fees ranged from £5 to £6, while Garnethill was denied it, even though its fees were lower at about £4.[1]

A PATTERN EMERGES

The 1880s was a gestation period for secondary education, a time when the School Boards felt their way through the misty screen of specific subjects. Experience enabled the Boards and the Department to crystallise their ideas, which were then ready for putting before the central government when, by the end of the decade, it had become prepared to take up public secondary education as a national necessity.

In Glasgow the major developments of the period were two: the realisation that higher subjects, in order to be efficiently taught, must be concentrated in a limited number of schools; and the extremely important results of the Endowed Schools Commission. In time, the latter had the effect of intensifying the former trend.

It has already been seen that only a small number of children undertook the advanced study of specific subjects, and that because these were scattered throughout the schools of the city the number of pupils of any one higher subject in any one school was tiny. In 1886 the numbers of scholars above Standard VI related to the Schools was as follows:

0 scholars in 16 schools
less than 20 scholars in 34 schools
20 to 50 scholars in 7 schools
over 50 scholars in 10 schools

As these small numbers would be sub-divided in each school into three main streams—those taking French and German with a view to a commercial career, those studying mathematics and science for a technical future, and others needing Latin,

[1] Evidence of George Crichton, Chairman of Govan School Board, before Parker Commission.

Greek and mathematics for the university—the classes would be so small as to be extremely wasteful. An inspector commented that they were too few to do any good at all.[1] The Board had long been aware of the situation, but although convinced of the desirability of centralising advanced work was slow to force the issue because of its scruples in regard to depriving any teacher of his "right" to retain his brightest and best. In fact the Board was being over-tender, for when the headmasters were circularised on the matter most of them were found to be in full agreement with the principle of concentration. As reasonable men they well knew that it would be in the best interests of their pupils.

The first deliberate step towards centralisation followed the report of the Endowed Schools Commission. The Commission had been set up to investigate the educational endowments of Scotland and to make recommendations for their better use—a needed reform as the establishment of public schooling had made many of the old endowments out of date. By Clause 7 of the Educational Endowments (Scotland) Act, 1882, the Commissioners were directed to have special regard to making provision ". . . for secondary or higher or technical education, in public schools, or otherwise".

This instruction was fully in keeping with the wishes of the Glasgow Board, although it cavilled at the implications of the words "or otherwise" which reflected the views of some people that near-secondary schools should be established and run by a body other than the School Board. The Board claimed that it was already responsible for higher education by the wording of the original Education Act, that it had already made provision for it in several schools, and that, indeed, additional higher grade schools in the city would be superfluous as all demand for secondary education was already fully met, ". . . and in proof of that I give the illustration of what the School Board endeavoured to do in the case of the City Schools. When the High School was removed to Elmbank Street, the Board endeavoured to establish a secondary school of a lower grade in the old premises, and they gave it every advantage of a first class staff of teachers, but they found it very uphill work indeed

[1] Committee of Council on Education in Scotland, Annual Report, 1886, p 192.

and in order to make the school a success they had to introduce a primary department."[1]

In this way the School Board laid its claim to being the proper agency to control aided secondary schools in the future. But schools in themselves were not enough; provision must be made to enable the pupils to come to them. The Board therefore urged the Commissioners to set aside a considerable part of the funds at their disposal for the provision of competitive bursaries to enable pupils to remain at school for two or three years beyond the Standards.

The views of the Board in regard to secondary education were now absolutely clear, and were brought together in an important letter to the Scotch Education Department.[2] Glasgow wanted:

1 *One or more additional High Schools* similar to the existing High School. They would be solely secondary in nature or, if there must be a primary section, it would shape its curriculum with an eye to the needs of the secondary department rather than follow the standards of the ordinary public school. Special grants or endowments would be required.

2 *A uniform examination for all Higher Class Schools.* Nothing would be more conducive to the well-being of secondary schooling than a national standard of work to be reached, preferably one which was a university entrance requirement.

3 *A large number of Bursaries* in order to enable students both to remain at school and to go on to technical college or university.

4 *A High School for Girls* which would offer girls something which had always been available to their brothers.

5 *The graduation of schools*, some having higher departments and some not. "The practical question for this district seems to be, whether to grade the Public Schools after this manner or to equip special schools for the Higher Branches [ie High Schools as in 1]. Judging from their past experience, the Board are decidedly of opinion that a *combination of both plans will turn out to be the most satisfactory.*"

[1] J N Cuthbertson, Evidence before Educational Endowments Commission, First Report, 1884, para 2125.
[2] Reply of School Board of Glasgow to Circular 55 on Higher Education, 1883.

6 *Removal of the restriction on fees*, thereby allowing more money to become available for secondary development.

7 *Financial assistance for technical education.* On the whole the School Board was not keen to adopt a strongly biased technical training in its schools, for ". . . the practice of handling tools in itself would be taking up time learning what will be better learned in the workshop when the lad begins his apprenticeship". In any case, Glasgow had adequate provision for technical training outwith public schools in such establishments as the Old Mechanics' Institute or Allan Glen's. On the other hand, some laboratory work in chemistry, mechanics and technical drawing might help to keep the early leavers at school for another couple of years, so competitive bursaries should be established for them which would provide not only free schooling but maintenance allowance also.

8 *Implementation of the Educational Endowments Acts directive to encourage Secondary Education in Public Schools.*

The solution finally adopted by the Endowments Commission came into effect in 1885. Two schemes were concerned with the public schools: the Glasgow City Educational Endowments Board and the Glasgow General Educational Endowments Board. They were always known as the "City" and the "General". Broadly speaking, those endowments which were grouped under the "City" scheme had been in the control of the Town Council, and the Town Council still had a preponderating influence in their management. Similarly, the "General" comprised endowments which had been in the hands of the clergy, and now largely remained so. However, the provisions for the disbursement of their funds were virtually identical, and the two schemes can be considered as one for our purposes. Indeed, the two trusts used a common office and the same secretary.

Bursaries were available to children ". . . whose parents or guardians are in such circumstances as to require aid for giving their children a higher education". The value of the bursaries was between £5 and £10, they were tenable for two years, and 150 were offered for competition. Soon another of the Commission's schemes, the Marshall Trust, added a further seventy-five secondary bursaries.

An important aspect of these bursaries was the condition that they be tenable at schools in Glasgow ". . . in which efficient instruction is given in the higher branches", for this immediately raised the question of which schools qualified as having secondary departments. A good deal of sparring ensued between the School Board and the Trusts, many of whose governors had a higher conception of what was meant by the phrase "higher branches". They were reluctant to allow their bursars to take up their awards in what seemed little more than elementary schools. The Trusts wanted a much greater concentration of secondary work in fewer schools than the Board was willing to concede. The Board feared that masters in danger of losing their pupils to these schools would discourage them from applying for bursaries, and also that a policy of greater concentration might result in the extinction of Standard VI in many a school. That this fear was well founded is illustrated by the case of Thomson Street School which at the first competition won no fewer than twenty-six bursaries. "The withdrawal of so many scholars at once would seriously weaken the school, and cause a heavy loss in the Government grant."[1] The Trusts, which did not regard Thomson Street as a fit school for their bursars, referred the dispute to the senior inspector who concurred with their view, and added, "The Governors have, I presume, the power, and it is certainly their duty to determine, whether, from an educational point of view, it is desirable to have driblets of Languages, Mathematics and Science taught to small classes in a dozen schools, or in a smaller but sufficient number in judiciously chosen localities, with the twofold advantage of a great saving in educational power and increase of educational effect from a spirit of emulation, which can with difficulty be kept up, except in reasonably large classes."[2]

Within a year, however, the inspector reversed his decision and declared Thomson Street to be a suitable school for bursars. Why had he changed his mind? In part because the time-table had been modified. But it is likely that he was influenced, as were the School Board and eventually the Trusts, by the hard fact that so very few children stayed on to a real secondary course that they could have been accommodated easily in a

[1] Letter from School Board to the Joint Trusts. 6 August 1886.
[2] Letter from Dr John Kerr, HM Chief Inspector, to the Secretary of the Joint Trusts 4 September 1886.

single school, but this would have been centralisation carried beyond the practical travelling limitations of the day. Even several years later the Secretary of the Joint Trusts gave as his opinion, ". . . about three-quarters of the secondary education at present demanded in Glasgow does not really cover more than two years above the standards, or at all events Standard VI with Specific Subjects in Stage 1; the education in demand is practically an education which would terminate at the close of a class where the Specific Subjects were taught up to Stage 3."[1]

So the availability of a generous supply of bursaries for secondary education, which could have been expected to bring about a high degree of centralisation of this type of work, did not in fact do so. Nevertheless, it did cause the first step to be taken in this direction. Thirteen of the Board's schools were selected for "the efficient instruction of the School Bursars in the Higher Branches".[2] It was a nudge in the right direction. The forceful shove towards greater concentration and really effective secondary schools only came when the Government applied it some years later.

GOVERNMENT TAKES A HAND 1886–92

So far the Government had taken little directly to do with secondary education. Its view seems to have been that the original Higher Class Schools had got along very nicely by themselves, and as they still received little by way of public monies there was neither reason nor justification for government interference. True, the Scotch Education Department had always proved willing to permit the public schools to grow a higher department, but only provided that such growth took place within the Specific Subjects structure. How advanced the work of a school became depended entirely on the encouragement given it, both financially and in spirit, by a school board. Improvement was initiated locally, not from Dover House.

[1] Evidence of Dr F L Robertson before the Elgin Commission, para 1580.
[2] The schools, carefully chosen to cover the various districts of the City were: Abbotsford, Crookston Street, John Street, Dennistoun, Thomson Street, Springburn, Kennedy Street, St George's Road, Garnethill, Woodside, Kent Road, Overnewton, City Boys' and Girls'.
Notes on behalf of the School Board of Glasgow in regard to Schools at which the School Bursaries of the Endowments Boards may properly be held, 1886.

A concession to Higher Class Schools had been made in the 1878 Act under which a school board could use public money to pay for the upkeep of the building and some other minor expenses. There was also a permissive clause in the Act giving the Scotch Education Department power to appoint examiners of these schools, which examiners would replace those hired by the school boards or other managers of Higher Class Schools, to inspect the year's work in terms of the Act of 1872. The Glasgow Board was very keen to adopt the proposed new method of inspection which it felt would bring several desirable consequences in its train. One of these was that government inspection would be likely to bring about a uniform standard in the schools both public and private. Uniform standards would, in turn, lead perhaps to the institution of a leaving Certificate, and "such a Certificate, if it afforded satisfactory evidence of scholarship, might be accepted in lieu of an examination in general knowledge by various professional societies, and be a passport into the Senior Classes of the Universities".[1] In other words, the Glasgow School Board saw government inspection of secondary work as the first essential step towards the eventual cure of the present curse of secondary schooling—the lack of any definite purpose and value.

In spite of continual urging by Glasgow the Department did not accept its new responsibilities for eight years, when in 1886 it at last began to inspect the high schools. This seems to mark the beginning of much closer interest by central government in secondary education. All the benefits foreseen and eagerly looked forward to by the Glasgow Board speedily followed. And much more besides. Henceforth the powerful and positive influence of Whitehall was to have a very marked and beneficial effect on secondary education. Within two years the Leaving Certificate began in Higher Class Schools, and by 1892 ordinary public schools were eligible to enter candidates. A standard had been set; it had been set by the Government, and by making public schools sensitive to that standard the Government had tactily assumed some responsibility for raising the schools to it. In 1892 the first Treasury grant specifically for secondary education was given.

[1] School Board of Glasgow, High School Committee Annual Report, 1888.

To gather opinions on how the money ought to be spent an Enquiry Commission sat in London.[1] Of the five commissioners, one was the Chairman of the Glasgow School Board, another was an ex-Chairman. The representations of Glasgow were likely to be well received.

Generally speaking, what Glasgow wanted was implementation of the recommendations made by an earlier Commission which had considered secondary education in 1887 under Lord Parker.[2]

The main relevant recommendations were:

1 That secondary education should be given in schools specially designed for that work, and not in glorified primary schools.
2 That in Edinburgh, Glasgow and Aberdeen the high schools should remain under the control of the School Boards. Elsewhere a special Board should be set up to control a secondary school which would be fed by all the School Boards in the district.
3 Parliamentary grants should be given for secondary education in public secondary schools.
4 Fees should be allowed to rise as high as the parents could reasonably be expected to afford, but special arrangements were to be made for educating promising children of poor parents at reduced fees, or free.
5 Grant-aided primary schools with higher departments should be encouraged as hitherto, but should not be allowed to compete unduly with secondary schools.
6 Leaving examinations should be established at once.

Until 1892 only the last of these objectives had been gained. Now, however, a money grant was to be given to secondary schools.

Following the Elgin Commission the distribution of the grant to secondary education was put under the control of a new authority, the Secondary Education Committee, on which were represented the School Board, the Town Council and the

[1] Minutes of Evidence taken by the Committee appointed to enquire into the Best Means of Distributing the Grant in Aid of Secondary Education in Scotland. Elgin Commission, 1892.
[2] Third Report of the Committee appointed to enquire into certain questions relating to Education in Scotland. Parker Commission, 1887.

Educational Trusts. It was an arrangement not particularly to the liking of the School Board which felt that it was well able to handle another few thousand pounds of government money and to use it wisely for the benefit of its own schools. However, time brought an inevitable recognition of the Board's contentions, for in 1909 the Board's representation on the Secondary Education Committee was increased to a degree which gave it a dominant voice.[1]

The Glasgow schools share of the national £60,000 grant was £8011 16s 9d.[2] It was not a great deal. Common sense dictated that it could best be used if shared among as few schools as possible. In this way was supplied the final impetus towards concentration of secondary work in a few selected schools. Such a solution had seemed the obvious one from the beginning, but it had taken twenty years of pragmatic development to kill the old hankering for the traditional parish type of all-through school. Separate secondary schools[3] had now arrived. They were to reign supreme for sixty years until challenged by the egalitarian ideal of comprehensive schools.

GLASGOW'S SECONDARY SCHOOLS 1893–1919

In 1893 the School Board classified its schools in three groups:

1 Schools having Secondary Departments, of which there were five.
2 Schools, sixteen in number, giving instruction for one year beyond the Standards.
3 All other schools would teach no further than Standard VI.

The five schools to have Secondary Departments were the City Schools, John Street, Kent Road, Whitehill and Woodside. They were carefully chosen so as to cover the whole city, each school serving the needs of a district. They were at first referred

---

[1] Minutes of Committee of Council on Education in Scotland, 10 August 1909.
[2] Of this sum schools under the management of the School Board received £5800 annually. The rest went to the Hutchesons' Schools and the Catholic Schools.
[3] ie, *academic* secondary schools.

to as Central Schools, but soon came to be called Higher Grade Schools.[1]

Besides the five Higher Grade Schools there were two other secondary schools. These were, however, rather special cases, and received separate treatment and consideration by the Board. The first was, of course, the High School, which had always been set apart by virtue of its being a Higher Class School. The other was Garnethill, a school which had won for itself a quite unique reputation in Scotland. The story of Garnethill will be told later.

No test was required for entrance to a Higher Grade School. It was necessary for the pupil merely to indicate that he wished to continue his schooling beyond the primary stage and he would then be transferred to the appropriate school. In view of the small numbers who remained at school after thirteen it seems unlikely that there could have been many hopefuls applying for secondary schooling whose ambitions were in excess of their ability. Many ex-VI pupils would want to spend only one more year at school, and they would go to one of the sixteen intermediate schools. It was not intended that the extra year should correspond with the first year of the secondary departments in the five schools. The more ordinary higher subjects such as composition, higher arithmetic, shorthand and mathematics would be emphasised, "and above all a considerable portion of the time-table should be given to revision, with the object of building up and strengthening the scholars in the education previously acquired. The work in this group of schools should include a more thorough treatment of the subjects of primary education with very few extra branches."[2]

The value of these extra branches was later described by an inspector.

"As regards the teaching of Languages and Mathematics in the Elementary Schools of Glasgow, Latin and French are generally feeble and show no knowledge that has been worth acquiring. Mathematics is occasionally satisfactory, seldom of much account."[3]

Because children destined for the secondary schools would

[1] Not to be confused with Higher Class schools.
[2] School Board of Glasgow, Report of Committee on Secondary Education, 1893.
[3] Committee of Council on Education in Scotland, Annual Report, 1897.

often be in primary classes where the great majority of the pupils had no such ambition or ability, it was probable that they would move along in primary schools at a relatively slow pace and so would arrive at secondary level ill-prepared. To prevent this the Board urged parent and teacher to see that the pupil was transferred to the elementary side of his future secondary school no later than the end of Standard V and preferably after Standard IV. His new primary school was specially geared to the needs of the Upper Department. It was recognised that elementary teachers might be reluctant to hand over promising pupils so early, but the Board hoped to persuade them to co-operate by promising that the work done by their scholars in the Higher Grade would be taken into account when considering promotions. Their pride was appealed to by the device of naming the elementary schools in the Prize and Honours Lists of the secondary school. Just as Eton might publish

Head of School: Jeremy Smythe (Cheam),

so would John Street say,

Dux: Archie Campbell (Tureen Street).

The selection of the five schools was but the fulfilment of the destiny intended for them from the beginning. The City School, as we have seen, had inherited the old building of the Boys' High, and originally was planned as a secondary school. As early as 1877 the Board began to build new schools definitely designed for secondary work. The earliest was Garnethill. John Street, Kent Road, Woodside and Whitehill soon followed. Each was carefully placed in an area likely to provide a goodly supply of higher pupils. John Street, situated at Bridgeton Cross, was in the centre of a populous part of the city which, in spite of its general poverty, could reasonably anticipate enough pupils. Woodside was in a rather good quarter of town, as was Kent Road. Whitehill was the newest of the five schools and had been opened on the same day as Dennistoun. They were in a superior class of district, and the expression which the Board used to describe them was "Superior Schools". The intention was to develop Whitehill along the same lines as those already pioneered so successfully by Garnethill. It was to become an Upper Class School for Girls serving the east end of Glasgow. Accordingly it opened in 1882 as the Whitehill School for

Girls[1] and continued in this capacity until a large new building was ready in 1891. By now it had become disappointingly apparent that the early hopes of a large expansion of secondary work had been too optimistic. Too few pupils offered themselves. Therefore the new Whitehill Academy combined the School for Girls and the boys from the higher department of Dennistoun which then became an ordinary primary school. The Academy flourished so well that it might still have reached equality of status with the two high schools, for an inspector later wrote, "I have to suggest for the consideration of the Board whether this School, in view of its range and advancement of curriculum, its equipment, its situation, and the present condition of its attendance, would not find its most fitting status and function as a specially organised Higher Class Public School for the Eastern portion of the City of Glasgow."[2] It was not to be—at least in name.

In framing curricula for the schools there was little talk of education for education's sake, no theorising about vague cultural or social benefits of education, no seeking after the "well-rounded" boy. If the men of the day had known the modern shibboleth that schooling is "a preparation for life", they would have agreed. But for them the obvious and most insistent aspect of life was that it had to be earned. One must work. It followed that school should be a preparation for the work which lay ahead, that it should be vocational in so far as it gave the boy the basic knowledge and training he would need for the job which probably lay before him, be it profession, business or trade.

The curricula reflected the industrial and commercial needs of Glasgow's labour market. It also took note of probable employment which, in the Board's view, would be taken up by the pupils of the respective districts.[3]

[1] A month prior to the opening a Miss Hogg was appointed Headmistress. It would have been a unique appointment in Glasgow for no other school was ruled by a woman (except in the special case of the Day Industrial Schools). Yet, for some reason unknown, Miss Hogg did not take up her post, and a Headmaster had charge of this girls' school throughout its existence.

[2] Committee of Council on Education in Scotland, Annual Report, 1900.

[3] School Board of Glasgow, Teachers and Teaching Committee; Secondary Schools Sub-committee Reports on Curricula, 1893. "The Education in the Secondary Departments should be directed to such subjects as are ctly useful in commerce and in industrial occupations, along with a

Whitehill, as a sort of poor man's High School, enjoyed both a scientific and a classical course. None of the other schools offered a full Latin course, although they did a little Latin in the first two years. The City School, being in the heart of the town's business centre, concentrated on "those subjects which are directly useful in commerce". In John Street, Kent Road and Woodside science was to have a dominant place, "so as to meet the requirements of scholars likely to be engaged in different departments of industry, and also, to prepare for the scientific side of the University, or for the Technical College". Woodside would have merited a classical course also if it had not been for the existence nearby of Hillhead School and Glasgow Academy. Although neither school belonged to the Glasgow Board it was felt unnecessary to duplicate the facilities they both offered for "very complete classical and literary training".

In all five schools boys were to be given a certain amount of manual training, while girls got cookery, sewing, laundry and domestic economy. Present-day modern language teachers delighting in language laboratories will be gratified to know that languages were to be taught "orally from the very beginning". However, this was an ideal difficult to achieve at first in view of the scarcity of specialist teachers. For some years French and German were taught by visiting teachers who made their rounds of the schools.

A FAMOUS SCHOOL AND ITS HEADMASTER

Mr James Milligan was one of the many masters who lost their jobs when church schools closed down consequent upon the appearance of public schools. He naturally applied for a teaching post with the Glasgow School Board. The details of his earlier career as meticulously set out in his application were unremarkable. A native of Denny, he had served his pupil teachership at the Parish School of Falkirk before going on to the Established Church Training College in Glasgow, out of which he passed with distinction. His first post was at St

---

sound general training, including Latin, French, German, Mathematics, Drawing, Shorthand, and Elementary Science. The requirements of commerce are needed to a very large extent in all the schools, and are of the utmost consequence, even to the lads who follow trades or professions."

Andrew's Parish School, but in 1866 he obtained the head-mastership of the "Mitchell School" in Anderston.[1] There he had remained for nine years. Satisfied with Mr Milligan's references, the Board gave him the headship of London Road, one of their temporary schools. It was no sinecure. Before its recent transfer to the School Board, London Road had been the well-established sessional school of St James'. But in 1875 all the staff and nearly all the scholars were transferred to the first of the new Board schools to be built—Sister Street and Barrow-field. The results for the school were very bad, for now it was filled with reluctant and often obnoxious half-timers from the mills and ropeworks of Bridgeton and Calton. It was Milligan's job to bring order out of chaos, and the inspector, at least, had confidence in him, "From the energy of the present Master better results may be expected next year."[2]

Meanwhile the Board was planning the building of a new school at the opposite side of the city, in an area very different from Bridgeton. The district of Milton lay to the north of Sauchiehall Street. In its western parts it included the University and the splendid mansions of Park Circus. Moving east-ward the social tone certainly went down, but still remained good. Here lived those respectable and responsible citizens of the lower-middle or upper-working classes: shopkeepers, tradesmen, foremen, clerks and suchlike. Just the folk who would be ambitious for their children, willing to sacrifice to provide them with a good schooling, anxious to co-operate with the demands of school in pushing the children along the path of academic success. Here was fertile ground for a promising school, and it was recognised as such by the School Board. Garnethill Public School was planned from the start as a school likely to carry many of its pupils beyond elementary level. Everything was in its favour. Now a good man must be found to lead and direct the venture.

Mr Milligan was the Board's choice. At London Road he had thoroughly demonstrated his abilities as a teacher and as an administrator. What was more, he had proved that he was also a scholar by attending college part-time and graduating Master

[1] In Piccadilly Street. It was connected with Wellington Street United Presbyterian Church.
[2] Inspector's Report, 1875.

of Arts. In the years ahead Milligan was to make Garnethill the most outstanding public school in Scotland.

This admirable new school building had the immediate effect of killing off the little private schools which had, till now, flourished in the district. Not unnaturally Milligan found his first pupils were a very mixed bunch scholastically, but within eighteen months he had licked them into shape. Already the annual inspection was couched in superlatives: "The Standard pass is very high; general intelligence bright. Reading exceptionally good. . . . Grammar ahead of the requirements. . . . Discipline is excellent. . . . The pupil-teachers are skilfully trained and have worked very good papers." And when the inspector comments that ". . . 90 pupils are too many for one man to teach in all subjects", one can only marvel. Already, too, the school had begun that side of its work which was to bring it fame: advanced post-primary instruction. English, geography, mathematics, literature, domestic economy, French and Latin were all "highly satisfactory".[1]

Nothing could better describe the tone of the school, its thrusting energy, its quite apparent sense of purpose and its obvious success than the reports of inspectors over the next two or three years.

> 1881 This large school is in a most prosperous and efficient condition. The accomplished Head Master, Mr Milligan, evidently exercises a very real and effective control over every detail of its working, and the results of his energy, tact and firmness are manifest at every turn. Excellent discipline is maintained in all departments, and throughout the whole course of my protracted examination the demeanour of the pupils gave me unqualified satisfaction. With the exception of a slight weakness in the fifth, the standard work was done with an accuracy which, in view of the large numbers presented for individual examination, may be characterised as faultless. Reading is throughout fluent, and generally intelligently expressive. In the higher classes I could have wished, perhaps, for greater distinctness of enunciation both in Reading and answering in the case of some of the older girls. Writing, both on slates and paper, was neat and careful. The children exhibited bright and ready comprehension of the lessons read in the second and third standards, and have made wonderful progress in Grammar. The answering in Geography and History was full, ready and accurate. A large

[1] Inspector's Report, 1880.

amount of really good work has been overtaken in a very judiciously selected list of Specific Subjects. I was particularly pleased with the natural style of Repetition and the admirable answering upon the subject matter in the class in English Literature, taught by Miss Hamilton. Industrial work is carefully attended to, and many excellent specimens of plain white seam, knitting and darning were shown. The pupils sing with great taste and spirit. The features which appear to have evoked the very high terms of praise in which the Infant School is spoken of in the Report upon it for the previous year are still prominent in that department. The little pupils show admirable proficiency in their studies; they sit and stand, wheel to the right and left, and walk across the floor on the tips of their toes at the word of command, with a precision of movement which I have never seen equalled. During the hour and a half which I spent in the room, but for the little sound occasioned by the process of examination, one might have heard a pin drop. . . .

1882   This large school continues to exhibit the results of a very efficient superintendence on the part of the Head Master, and hearty co-operation on that of the staff. It is steadily reaching the position aimed at by the Board, namely, one intermediate between an Elementary and a Higher Class School. . . . The ex-sixth pupils amount to 52. This advanced portion of the School is to be further developed by the appointment of another graduate teacher. . . . The work in Specific Subjects is heavy, and generally very good. . . . In Latin, 111 pupils at various stages gave evidence of skilful teaching, the highest Class under Mr Gibson construeing the second Georgics of Virgil with great accuracy. A small class has done an ex-year's work in Greek, and passed a most creditable Examination on a portion of Xenophon. . . . It is rare to find a school with such good discipline, and a Staff so uniformly efficient.

1883   This large and important School. . . . The numbers presented for examination . . . are exceptionally large . . . the quality of instruction generally is very much above average. . . . The presentation in Specific Subjects is the largest I have ever met with in any school. . . . In connection with the secondary branches of instruction generally, it would be difficult to speak in too high terms of praise of the excellent work done by Mr Gibson the Second Master.

And so the reports continue over the years. Yet even the inspector occasionally felt that such perfection was a little too good, and once gently chided the immaculate Infant Department. "Were any improvement possible in the case of a department so highly commended, I might perhaps venture to suggest the infusion of a little more cheery brightness into the present absolutely perfect routine of drill. The unbending now and again of the little bows by even the enormity of an occasional burst of happy laughter might, perhaps, not be much amiss."[1]

However, infants grow up, and then if bright and spirited both need and accept discipline as the necessary means to a desirable end while reserving the right to show their mettle in occasional outbursts of boyish independence. In his reminiscences a pupil of Woodside ungrudgingly admitted of the rival local school, "Woodside was rather overshadowed by Garnethill, where Dr Milligan dealt out learning and punishment to the liveliest lot of pupils in Glasgow. The most stirring of my companions were charges of 'old Milligan', leaders in school fights and in mass plunking."[2]

Less than four years after its establishment Garnethill was making its mark. At the Glasgow University Local Examination in 1883 this school took 21% of the prizes, including four out of the six open bursaries, three of which were won with the highest marks ever gained in the respective examinations.[3] Over the next eighteen months Garnethill pupils won prizes and bursaries to the value of £600, a huge sum for those days.[4]

Already Garnethill had succeeded to an extent beyond anything anticipated by its instigators. Already the Headmaster was using his school's successes to plead that they be capitalised upon by more generous staffing and higher salaries. Already he was able to propose that his school's uniqueness be recognised by a special title—Garnethill Intermediate Public School—recognising that it was something beyond a mere elementary school.

"By their sanction of this proposal the Board will give the School a truly descriptive name. . . . The recognition which the adoption of these proposals would give is a recognition which, I may be permitted to say, the School has won for itself. It is in sympathy with the views recently expressed by the Vice-President of the Committee in Council, in sympathy with the traditions of Scottish Education, in sympathy with the spirit of the present age. The kind of School here indicated, likewise, and of which I hope Garnethill will be the first example, will afford, if not the only, certainly the most

[1] Inspector's Report, 1881.
[2] Wm Power, *Should Auld Acquaintance*, London: Harrap, 1936, p 20.
[3] General Summary of Work: Triennial Reports 1882–1906.
[4] Letter from Milligan to School Board, 6 March 1884.

satisfactory, solution of that urgent educational problem of the day—the supplying of a genuine secondary education to the children of the nation."[1]

Milligan's aspirations were well founded, for his school became the prototype of public secondary schools in Scotland. The chief characteristic of Garnethill and other schools of the type was that they provided a secondary education for the children of parents who were quite unable to pay the fees of the Higher Class schools.[2] "This lower middle class, more, perhaps, than any other section of the people, values the advantages of a sound secondary education, and yet this is the class whose wants have hitherto been the least attended to. They cannot pay high fees, but they willingly deny themselves to keep their children for two or more years beyond the ordinary time of leaving school."[3] Such parents earned between £120 and £350 a year, and managed to pay a fee which was sufficiently high to preclude any need to draw on the rates. From the first, Garnethill paid its way from grants and fees only; the Board was thereby safe from any charge of diverting rate money to the benefit of the better-off classes.

For a while it seemed that the government order limiting fees to ninepence a week might put the work of the school in jeopardy. The continued progress of the school required more money than would come in from grants and a ninepenny fee, but if the fee was raised government money would cease altogether. Then the fee would have to go up to a prohibitive level, equal in fact to that of the High School. There was an alternative: partly to finance the school out of the rates, an extremity to which the Board did not want to be driven. In the end, the Department agreed to permit a fee up to one shilling,[4] and this concession served until new forms of grants for secondary work arrived in the nineties.

In Garnethill the Board had a school whose parents clearly

---

[1] Letter from Milligan to School Board, 6 March 1884.
[2] In 1887 fees for the various schools were:

Glasgow Academy ⎱ Kelvinside Academy ⎰	£12 to £14
High School	£8
Hillhead Public School	£5 to £6
Garnethill Public School	£3 to £4 4/–.

Parker Commission, p 62.
[3] Evidence of Milligan to Elgin Committee, 1892.
[4] Minutes of Board in Committee, 1885, p 220.

E*

desired advanced classes for their children, and because the demand was there the Board, on its part, did its best to make more than ordinary provision for it. The building had unusually good facilities such as physics and chemistry laboratories, an art studio and a dining room. A better staff/pupil ratio was enjoyed,[1] and it seems probable that the quality of the individual teachers was exceptionally good, although they were not yet graduates.[2] The Headmaster was given a special payment of £100 over his normal salary entitlement.

Like the High School, Garnethill drew its pupils from a wide geographic area. Some children travelled in from poorer districts on the strength of Educational Trust bursaries. Fully one third came from outside the Glasgow School Board district altogether.[3]

Academic honours continued to enhance the School's reputation. In the Local Examination of the University in 1890 Garnethill provided one quarter of all successful candidates. It did even better in the list of "Distinguished Candidates", 34% of whom came from the school. Of twenty-one Distinguished Candidates who gained a Senior or Higher Certificate, eleven were Milligan's pupils, and five of these headed the list. That same year a boy was accepted into the Indian Civil Service as his reward for gaining 34th place in that very competitive examination. One girl won an Entrance Scholarship to Royal Holloway College, another an Entrance Scholarship to Girton College, Cambridge. These excursions into England were one of the notable features of Garnethill, especially for girls, as women were not accepted by Glasgow University until 1892.

The outstanding success of Garnethill, and similar schools to a lesser degree, had serious repercussions on private schools— even the best of them. Glasgow Academy and Kelvinside Academy both suffered a serious loss of pupils when parents

[1]

	Teacher/Pupil ratio	
School	Using no of pupils on roll	Using no of pupils in average attendance
Henderson St	1 : 120	1 : 103
Thomson St	1 : 120	1 : 101
Garnethill	1 : 93	1 : 84

School Statistics, 1882

[2] Even by 1885 only the Headmaster and Second Master had degrees.
[3] In 1891 the figure was 32% (School Statistics).

came to believe that just as good an education could be had in some public schools at very much lower fees. Garnethill certainly attracted pupils who would otherwise have gone to the Academies, and the building of Hillhead Public School in 1885 was disastrous for them.[1] Hillhead had been established by the Govan School Board on the model of Garnethill and using the same formula certain to bring success—a well-staffed and well-favoured school placed in a prosperous and interested community.

This competition was bitterly attacked by representatives of the Academies before the Parker Commission. They claimed that the Education Acts had never intended public schools to enter the secondary field, and that they were therefore acting illegally. The Commission did not accept this contention, but its remarks show how these secondary schools had grown up almost incidentally and how important Glasgow was in developing them: ". . . such representations [ie complaints from Glasgow and Kelvinside Academies] forced on our attention a point of great importance, namely, the existence in Scotland of grant-earning schools of a higher grade, attended by the children of prosperous families, and giving to their most advanced pupils an education so high, at least in its profession, as to compete with secondary schools. The chief examples of this are in Glasgow, where it is the avowed policy of the Board, in accordance (they say) with the views of the Education Department, to maintain in each district one school specially adapted for the teaching of higher subjects. . . . The most notable instance of this type of school is the Board School at Garnethill."[2]

An inspector, commenting on the criticisms levelled against Garnethill and the other schools of the type, defended them on the grounds that their case was not new; that schools in the area of the Dick and Milne Bequests had always taught to the secondary stage and yet had continued to receive grants: ". . . the son of the artisan or tradesman in Glasgow should not be denied what is given to the son of the crofter or farmer in Banffshire . . . it is unquestionable that in Glasgow and other

---

[1] The failure of the City of Glasgow Bank in 1879 probably contributed to the troubles of the two Academies.
[2] Parker Commission, p 62.

populous centres the son of the working man now finds within his reach an advanced education in those subjects, which only a few years ago was hopelessly beyond him."[1]

As a corrective to all that has been said about the remarkable emergence of Garnethill as a school of high secondary attainment more than able to hold its own in scholarship with the traditional Higher Class Schools, it should be remembered that it was still mainly an elementary school with a quite small secondary tail. In 1888, out of a roll of 1300, fully 96% were doing the work of the Standards. About 250 were taking one or more specific subject, but a mere 100 or so could be said to be in a proper secondary section.[2] Such a small number taken together with the amazing scholastic successes they achieved and the fame thereby earned is but a measure of how little secondary education existed in Scotland at the time.

Despite the clear evidence of a very high academic standard at Garnethill, a good deal of unease remained in the minds of some critics. There were two main charges. First, that secondary work at Board schools was too serious, too much in the nature of a cram course. Little or no time was available for "education" as opposed to "knowledge". Professor Ramsay felt that although Garnethill was undoubtedly in academic competition with the High School yet he himself would ". . . decidedly prefer the kind of education given in a High school".[3] In the public schools ". . . there is not the general atmosphere of a school life. Garnethill has sent some lady students to England who have highly distinguished themselves. I wish to speak only with praise and respect for the work such schools do; but I repeat that I wish to see the broad all round culture of our high schools, and of secondary schools of a similar character, extended and developed."[4]

Second, and closely connected to the first criticism, was the widely held opinion that secondary education required a quite different form of preparation to that given in the ordinary elementary school. "Educationists in Scotland are aware that the early stages of Elementary Education, however well adapted

---

[1] Committee of Council on Education in Scotland, Annual Report, 1886, pp 197–8.
[2] Inspector's Report, 1886 and Parker Commission, p 62.
[3] Elgin Commission, para 1349.
[4] *ibid*, para 1355.

for the boy or girl whose school life shall end between the ages of 12 and 14, are quite unsuited for the scholar who is laying the foundation of an education that shall extend to his 17th or 18th year."[1] These needed smaller classes, individual attention, an earlier introduction to languages and science, a good teacher able to do his work in a freer and more relaxed atmosphere than the Code made possible. The Glasgow public schools were attacked as falling far short of an adequate conception of secondary education. "It suggests simply a policy of expediency, the tacking on of an advanced curriculum to an elementary course, with the idea of utilising existing materials, an idea based on the assumption that these materials furnish a suitable foundation on which to build up Secondary Education. This position is untenable. Secondary Education to be successful and productive of satisfactory results must start from the commencement on Secondary lines."[2]

So far as Garnethill was concerned these criticisms were shortly to be removed.

Garnethill was admitted to the Leaving Certificate for the first time in 1892, and soon its results were every bit as good as those of the High School, as shown in Table 13.

TABLE 13

LEAVING CERTIFICATE RESULTS, GARNETHILL AND HIGH SCHOOL 1892-7

Year	School	Honours	Grade of Certificate Higher	Lower
1892	Garnethill	17	44	189
	High School	20	103	287
1893	Garnethill	12	86	288
	High School	11	88	255
1896	Garnethill	23	100	175
	High School	11	118	345
1897	Garnethill	10	137	284
	High School	33	123	238

These excellent results, together with the fact that many of Garnethill's brightest stars were girls, enabled the Board to move towards placing Garnethill on an equal footing with the

[1] Mrs E E Anderson, *Secondary Education*, 1891, p 5.
[2] *ibid*, p 1. *cf*, "The instruction in higher branches afforded by the better clss of primary school, such as Garnethill in Glasgow, cannot be regarded as a satisfactory solution of the question of secondary education, but it is a not unimportant contribution towards it." Committee of Council for Education in Scotland, 1885, p 214.

High School, and turning it into a Higher Class School for Girls. It was a development which had been foreshadowed twenty years earlier by the old Board of Education for Scotland: "Probably in course of time it will be found expedient to establish distinct girls' and boys' schools. It is only by doing this that a really first class boys' school can be constituted, or a really first class girls' school, with its own proper distinctive aims and character, set up."[1]

In 1883 the Glasgow Board had declared its ambition; ". . . in Public Higher Class Schools the provision for girls is very restricted compared with that for boys, while in the Private Higher Class it is the reverse. The Board hope to see Higher Class Inspected Schools for Girls erected in different parts of the district."[2]

Now the ambition was realised. With the aid of the Secondary Education Grant the Board turned the upper department of Garnethill into a High School for Girls in 1894. The following year even the Junior School was reserved for girls, except for little boys under eight.[3] Finally, in 1899, the School was declared a Higher Class School for Girls. Besides gaining parity of status with the Boys' High, the School now became outwith the regulations of the Code, enabling an integrated curriculum to be adopted throughout the whole school. Inevitably the loss of grants meant that fees had to be raised, but this had no bad effect on enrolment.

Mr Milligan continued as the School's Headmaster, widely recognised as the outstanding public school teacher of his day. His old university acknowledged his work for education in Glasgow by honouring him with the degree of Doctor of Law, a distinction conferred on no other teacher throughout the period of the School Board. In 1905 ill health forced Dr Milligan to retire from the school he had served so well.

THE LATER YEARS

The pattern of secondary education now set continued unchanged throughout the life of the Board. An additional High

---

[1] Committee of Council on Education in Scotland, Annual Report, 1878, p xviii.

[2] Circular (55) on Higher Education. Reply of School Board of Glasgow to SED, 1883.

[3] The older boys were transferred to Albany Academy, which was purchased in 1895.

School came under the Board's authority in 1911 when Allan Glen's was transferred to it on condition that it would be regarded in all respects as having equal status with the Boys' High. The number of Higher Grade schools was increased to seven shortly after the amalgamation of the Maryhill and Springburn Boards with Glasgow in 1911. North Kelvinside was built to cater for Maryhill, and Albert served Springburn.

The High Schools continued to flourish and the enrolment to rise. By the middle of the Great War both the Girls' and the Boys' High Schools had over a thousand pupils for the first time, and such was the demand for places that many applicants had to be turned away.

The fortunes of the Higher Grade Schools were less certain and less uniform. The Board had carefully placed these schools so as to cater for every area of the city, but merely providing the opportunity for every child to get a secondary education close at hand did not guarantee that each district was capable of providing the essentials necessary to develop a good school. The central district was already dead, commerce having pushed out homes. Consequently, the City Schools (Provanside from 1902) came to nothing. John Street and Kent Road drew on larger populations but were in districts where few parents took advantage of the education available. Whitehill, in a still growing and prosperous part of the town far from the competition of comparable schools, was far and away the most successful of the Higher Grade Schools, while Woodside did only moderately well, which is understandable in view of the several excellent schools with which it was surrounded. These comments can be illustrated by attendance figures (Table 14).

TABLE 14

ROLLS OF THE HIGHER GRADE DEPARTMENTS

Year	City	John St	Kent Rd	Woodside	Whitehill
1900	105	177	175	245	325
1901	114	195	178	295	416
	Provanside				
1902	123	236	255	312	509
1903	145	336	240	298	544
1904	159	326	284	371	550
1905	134	309	301	436	559

Of more importance than total numbers is the proportion which remained at school to complete a full secondary course. It was lamentably small. In 1913–14, the last normal session before the upset of war, the enrolment of the seven Higher Grade Departments was as given in Table 15.

TABLE 15

ROLLS OF SCHOOLS, SEPTEMBER 1914[1]

	John St	Kent Rd	Provanside	Woodside	Whitehill	Albert	Nor Kelvin
1st Year	174	189	147	156	316	66	14
2nd ,,	117	90	85	111	220	36	12
3rd ,,	38	48	39	69	110	17	6
4th ,,				47	54		2
5th ,,				44	57		2
6th ,,				25	31		1
Total*	329	327	271	452	788	119	38

* For comparison, the secondary rolls of the three High Schools were:

Boys' High   551
Girls' High   526
Allan Glen's   443

This early leaving was a nation-wide phenomenon frequently commented on. The Glasgow Board was much concerned by the drop-out rate, on educational grounds of course, but also because it involved them in an expensive provision of staff and equipment which were not fully utilised. The Board tried to ensure that pupils asking for a secondary course gave a written undertaking to complete it. However, many parents failed to keep their promise, and although the Board sought some method of making the pledge more binding they were unable to find a suitable formula.

A more practical measure taken by the Board to encourage longer staying on at school was the progressive lowering of fees. At first a uniform fee of 10/– a quarter was charged; then the first year was freed, the second year paid 7/6d a quarter, third year and above 10/–; eventually fees were completely abolished in one school after another excepting only Whitehill.[2] In view of the large number of bursaries available in Glasgow, and the even more generous provision of free books, it does not seem likely that the actual cost of schooling to a parent was prohibitive. The causes of early leaving must be sought elsewhere.

[1] High School and Secondary Education Committee, 27 October 1914.
[2] See Chapter 8, "Fees, Bursaries and Scholarships".

It soon became apparent that Glasgow had more secondary school places than there were aspirants to fill them. Now, as in the old days of Specific Subjects, the solution was a concentration of the higher work in fewer schools. The City Schools, Provanside, John Street and Albert never developed beyond the third year. Until 1914 Kent Road maintained some pretensions of giving a full course, but then it also declined in status to that of a three-year school. After 1902 these schools prepared pupils only for the new Intermediate Certificate.

TABLE 16

LEAVING CERTIFICATE RESULTS IN SEVEN SCHOOLS, 1896-99[1]

School	Honours	Grade of Pass Higher	Lower	Year
City		1	56	1896
John St		14	75	
Kent Rd	2	14	73	
Whitehill	11	39	143	
Woodside		2	99	
High School	11	118	345	
Garnethill	23	100	175	
City		6	30	1897
John St		17	77	
Kent Rd		16	76	
Whitehill	11	49	121	
Woodside		11	82	
High School	33	123	238	
Garnethill	10	137	284	
City		5	32	1898
John St		9	65	
Kent Rd	1	17	65	
Whitehill	17	66	123	
Woodside	2	11	122	
High School	32	80	231	
Garnethill	19	131	210	
City		7	35	1899
John St		17	116	
Kent Rd	1	19	62	
Whitehill	9	52	144	
Woodside	3	9	182	
Boys' High	16	91	277	
Girls' High	20	125	263	

The original form of the Leaving Certificate was in three grades: the Lower Grade which was equivalent to the Junior Local Examination of the university, the Higher Grade which was equal to the Senior Local, and an Honours Grade which was intended to bear comparison with the most difficult national

[1] Annual Reports of these years.

examinations such as that of the Indian Civil Service. Passes were given on an individual subject basis, a fact which has to be remembered when interpreting the statistics. Ten passes might mean ten children each passing in a single subject, or it might be composed of, say, three or four pupils taking several subjects each.

The figures in Table 16 bring out clearly the relative weakness of John Street, Kent Road and the City schools, a weakness even greater than is apparent, for in these schools a very large proportion of the passes was in one of two of the easier subjects, notably arithmetic. In contrast, Whitehill emerges as the outstanding school of its type, every bit as good academically as the two older high schools. Garnethill and the High School, similar in size, are seen to be equally successful, justifying Garnethill's promotion to Higher Class School status.

From 1902, while the old system of individual passes continued to be used two new and quite different certificates were also awarded. The Intermediate Certificate required a minimum secondary course of two years and a minimum age of fifteen, the Leaving Certificate could not be taken before seventeen and four years of secondary work. An important feature of the new certificates was that they were awarded on a group basis; in the case of the Leaving Certificate four passes on the Higher Grade or three Highers and two Lowers.

TABLE 17

FIRST YEARS OF THE GROUP CERTIFICATES[1]

	Leaving	Inter*	Leaving	Inter*	Leaving	Inter*	Leaving	Inter*	Leaving	Inter*
Kent Rd ⎫ Whitehill ⎬ Woodside ⎭	4	20	5	25	10	32	13	24	13	87
Boys' HS	14	17	9	8	12	11	3	7	9	47
Girls' HS			5	5	2		5		5	28
Year		1902		1903		1904		1905		1906

* Figures for Intermediate Certificates include *all* the Higher Grade schools, not merely the three named in the table.

As shown in Table 17, the Girls' High does not appear to have taken up the new certificates with enthusiasm, although

[1] Annual Reports of these years.

its results of separate passes during these years were consistently superior to those of the Boys' school. Perhaps the reason was that the girls still based their studies on English examination syllabuses, and the school preferred to maintain its scholastic reputation in the South. Certainly in 1902, while ignoring the new Scottish Certificates, girls gained two first division places in the London Matriculation and the top scholarship in classics at the Royal Holloway College.

Of considerable significance is a comparison of the figures for the Higher Grade schools and the Higher Class schools. For the first time the Higher Grade schools can claim to provide their scholars with an equally good chance of success as measured by the new Certificate. It seems likely that the Higher Grade schools adopted the necessary internal reorganisation of classes more readily than the High Schools, and this because they were more susceptible to Government influence and pressure than the more independently minded High Schools. They also had more to gain. The reputations of the High Schools were established and secure; they did not feel an urgent need to prove themselves. But the Higher Grade schools saw the group certificate as a means of showing their mettle, and it had this advantage over the earlier individual subject system, that it acted as an incentive to their pupils to remain at school long enough to gain this hallmark of success.

Twenty years earlier the Glasgow Board had urged that a common standard be set for Higher Class and Public schools in the belief that such an examination would both raise the standard of work in the public schools and force the Higher Class schools to look to their laurels. Now, at last, these desirable ends were brought about by the group leaving certificate.

By the closing years of the School Board there was nothing to choose between the examination results of the High Schools and the others (see graph, page 148).

An important aspect of the Higher Grade Schools was their use for the preliminary training of teachers. In 1912 Glasgow had decided that all her Junior Students (the new name given to pupil teachers in 1906) must undertake the normal secondary course and obtain the Leaving Certificate.[1] The graph shows that over half of all pupils gaining a Leaving Certificate were

[1] See Chapter 10, "The Pupil Teacher".

LEAVING CERTIFICATES GAINED

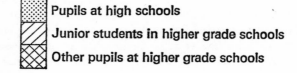

High Schools
Boys' High
Girls' High
Allan Glen's

Higher Grade Schools
Woodside
Whitehill
N Kelvinside

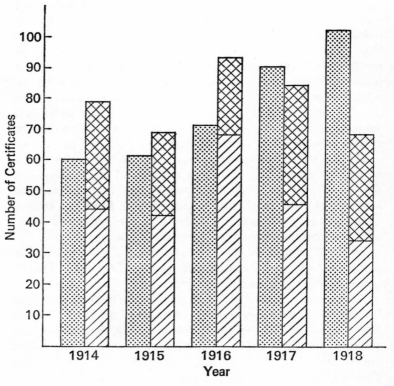

Pupils at high schools

Junior students in higher grade schools

Other pupils at higher grade schools

Annual Reports of these years.

intending teachers. Of this group girls had a near monopoly; in 1916, for example, out of 187 pupils studying under the Junior Student scheme as many as 166 were girls.[1]

Glasgow was proud of her secondary schools and with good reason. Easily the largest School Board in the country, Glasgow was bound to be the most influential in the way Scottish education developed after 1872. In no aspect of schooling was Glasgow's leadership for good more obvious and more telling than in that of secondary work.[2] From the start she had claimed secondary education to be a legitimate province of public schools, and had accepted as a duty the task of making it available to every able and ambitious boy and girl in the city. The proving ground was Garnethill, whose outstanding success in scholarship forced public and government alike to recognise the claims of a public school to parity of esteem with the Higher Class establishments. First bursaries and scholarships of the great educational trusts and then government grants for secondary education steadily cheapened the cost to parents. Eventually the Board was able to offer a completely free schooling for as long as the pupil cared to stay. The Board's early enlightened policy of encouraging teachers to attend university classes in school hours and without forfeiture of pay meant that there were graduates ready to staff the secondary schools as they evolved.

It is hard to see that the School Board of Glasgow could have done more for secondary education. If the numbers coming into the schools remained disappointingly low, and if those completing a full course seem small for so large a town, the blame lay in social and economic conditions beyond the power of any mere school board to determine.

---

[1] Annual Report, 1915–16, p 15.

[2] See, for example, such comments as:

". . . the School Board of Glasgow have done what the Edinburgh School Board have not done; they have fostered in their schools departments for higher education."

Elgin Commission: evidence of Dr Ogilvie, Chief Inspector, para 338.

"Glasgow has a supply of excellent Secondary Schools and Departments of various types. In this great city there is room and scope for the work of all, and there is none of that senseless rivalry and invidious comparison that infests smaller places."

Committee of Council for Education in Scotland, Annual Report, 1897, p 22.

Chapter 8

FEES, BURSARIES AND SCHOLARSHIPS

The sources of income available to a school board were three: the annual government grant, fees paid by the scholars, and the levy placed on ratepayers—the so-called "school rate". There was relatively little a Board such as Glasgow could do to increase the government grant, for this depended on the efficiency of the schools at the annual inspection and Glasgow's schools could hardly be improved upon in this respect. Thus the Board was left to balance its books by deciding in what proportions it should demand fees and school rate.

Of the two, the school rate was the more sensitive. For one thing, it affected far more people, each one of whom was a voter and therefore likely to squeal at any increase in the rate. Not only could this result in Board members suffering defeat at the next election, but it might also threaten laudable and necessary educational improvements by drawing unwelcome attention to their cost, as indeed happened in 1879. On the other hand, the payment of school fees was much more readily accepted by most of the community for it had always been the custom to pay them.

Glasgow decided that the schools should pay their way as far as possible. Consequently the school rate was not yet high, but about in keeping with that of most other boards. A straight comparison of rates charged by school boards is of little value in itself as special circumstances often caused a particular rate to be very high or unusually low. Still, voters seldom stop to question the nicer points, preferring simply to see what is happening to their neighbours, so it is worth while to make the comparison (Table 18, p 151).

A large slice of the Glasgow rate went to paying interest on the loans raised to build the new schools. In 1884, when the rate was still 5d interest repayment used up $3\frac{1}{4}$d of it.[1] The rate

[1] Report of Select Committee on School Board Elections (Voting), 1885. Evidence of Kennedy, paras 3567–8.

reflected Glasgow's huge deficiency of school places. Govan's low rate is probably explainable in the same way, for she had not had to embark on such a large building programme; Govan's problems came only later when her population expanded rapidly.

TABLE 18

SOME SCHOOL RATES IN 1880

Glasgow	5d	Aberdeen	6d
Dundee	2¼d	Greenock	6d
Edinburgh	3d	Paisley	7d
Govan	3d	Falkirk	8d
Stirling	5d	Cadder	10d
Dumfries	5d	Airdrie	1/½d

Throughout Scotland it was the general practice for a school board to set one common fee for all schools under its control. Glasgow was an exception. A great range of charges was set between the schools, and within each school the fee went up according to the seniority of the class. The principle on which the Board worked was that within every district of the city schools should be available at fees which were adjusted to suit the different income groups among parents. Sometimes the distinctions were very fine indeed, as for example that between Campbellfield and Camlachie or Parkhead and Barrowfield (Table 19).

TABLE 19

SCHOOL FEES IN CAMLACHIE DISTRICT IN 1876

Glenpark	2d to 4d per week
Campbellfield	8d to 1/4d per month
Camlachie	9d to 1/4d per month
Parkhead	9d to 1/4d per month
Barrowfield	10d to 1/6d per month
Sister St	1/– to 2/– per month
Thomson St	3/6d to 4/6d per month

Glenpark was only two blocks away from Thomson Street. The exceptionally high fee of Thomson Street was due to its being the nearest school at that time to the select district of Dennistoun, and it consequently recruited pupils of a fairly high social and economic class. Parents were at liberty to pick the school of their choice, and so need not confine themselves even to the list shown but could, if they wished, send their children along to Hozier Street in Bridgeton at a fee of 3/– to 6/– a quarter, or to any other Board school.

A feature of this differential price system was that it differentiated not only in pure money terms but also between weekly, monthly, or quarterly payments. The Board aimed at setting prices which the various markets would bear, and it was just as important to cater for the parent able to pay by the month as by the week. In 1884 a Glasgow parent could choose his child's school from any of the following fee scales:

Weekly fees in 11 schools: 7 schools paid 1d to 5d
2 schools paid 1½d to 4d
2 schools paid 2d to 5d or 6d

An additional advantage was that no charge was made if absent.

Monthly fees in 14 schools where the usual scales were 8d to 1/8, and 10d to 1/6d or 2/–.

No remission was given for absence during the month.

Quarterly fees in 29 schools, also with no remission.

The minimum fee in 3 schools was 2/–
in 5 schools was 2/6d
in 1 school was 2/9d
in 12 schools was 3/–
in 7 schools was 4/–
in 1 school was 5/–

In 4 schools fees rose as high as 12/6d.[1]

There was certainly nothing egalitarian about such a system of fees, and of course there were critics, most notably James Caldwell, a Liberal Parliamentary aspirant. Pointing out that Glasgow fees were much higher than the average for the rest of the country,[2] Caldwell admitted that Glasgow did have cheap schools, ". . . but such schools will not go down with the Scotch people, who will keep their children at home rather than

---

[1] James Caldwell, *Educational Endowments of the City of Glasgow*.
[2] Committee of Council on Education in Scotland, Report, 1882:
Average Fees in England   9/4d
,,   ,,   ,, Scotland   12/8½d
,,   ,,   ,, Glasgow   16/–

for a cheap school fee send them to mix with the lowest classes in the city at the cheaper schools".[1] Caldwell went on to charge the Board with providing the middle classes with cheap but good schools at the expense of the poorer classes. The richer children, being more successful academically, brought in high grants. Therefore their attendance at Board schools was very desirable, and could easily be obtained by public schools being superior in quality to private schools and at a much lower fee. Financed both by central funds and local rates, public schools in Glasgow were able to pay well for the best teachers and to erect buildings more splendid than anything their competitors could offer. Caldwell and his like maintained that the Education Act had never intended such a development; that its whole purpose was to supply public money to provide education for children unable to afford it by themselves. In fact, the Glasgow School Board had filched public money from the poor and applied it to the benefit of the better off. It achieved this end through its policy of a discriminatory fee system. The middle classes were given the benefit of below-cost education by grading the schools socially through fees.

The Board's point of view will be given later. But, whatever some might say, there is no doubt that the fee structure found favour with very many Glasgow parents. The popularity of a school could almost be said to be in direct proportion to the fee charged. There was no scarcity of demand for schools like Garnethill. It was probably more true in 1880 than it still is today that higher fees were ". . . to make the school more select for the sake of shopkeepers and well-to-do artisans, who do not like their children to mix with the very poor".[2]

Was the charging of fees compatible with compulsory attendance? Men of the time were no more agreed on this point than on any other. It was certainly true that bad attendance at school was common in some districts, but it is unlikely that a penny a week was the factor which decided if a boy or girl should stay away from school. General poverty was the more certain reason. In many cases, of course, poverty meant that school fees could not be paid. Such a circumstance was provided for in the Act. The parent had himself registered by the local Parochial

[1] Caldwell, *op cit*, p 35.
[2] *Scotsman*, Editorial, 30 October 1885.

Board[1] as a poor and needy person. The Parochial Board then paid the school fees of the children in the family as part of the poor relief. The School Board of Glasgow came to an arrangement with the parochial boards concerned that the rate for each child would be 4/– for fees plus 1/– for books quarterly.[2] While the Poor Law provided in this way for the desperately indigent, there remained a large group of parents so badly off that they could not scrape together the money for school. A man had his pride; it was better to be skin-and-bone than to go "on the parish". These were bad years for trade and unemployment was common. Moreover, it could strike anyone, not just the lowest paid workers with children attending the cheapest schools.

The problem of what to do with children who came to school without the fee for the current week, or who did not bring the fee owing from previous weeks, was a matter which greatly perplexed headmasters who bombarded the Board for guidance. The Board's reply could not have been over-helpful,[3] as it still left the headmaster with the responsibility of deciding whether or not the parent could in fact afford the fee. If the headmaster thought the case a deserving one he was to admit the child without payment. The parent, being now in arrears of fees, was expected to make good his debt whenever possible. If the headmaster considered a parent could afford to pay his arrears but was not doing so, he was authorised to exclude the child from school and report the case to the Board which then took up the matter directly with the parent. In theory a parent could have been taken to law as a debtor, but this would only happen in a case of wilful and repeated refusal to pay. In practice, exclusion seldom occurred, for headmasters usually acted generously and accepted the plea of poverty. Perhaps, being human and anxious to avoid trouble, they were simply taking the easy way out.

There was a way in which the risk of bad debts could be reduced, but again the onus lay with the headmaster. He was expected to make some inquiry into the financial means of a parent at the time of the child's entrance application, and if it appeared that the fees of his particular school could not be

[1] There were three Parochial Boards within the Glasgow School Board Area: The Barony, the City, and the Govan Parishes.
[2] General Summary of Work, 1873–82, p 23.
[3] *ibid*, p 22. Circular to Headmasters.

met, the headmaster was to refuse to accept the child. Presumably such precautions were inapplicable to the cheapest schools.

Fees were difficult to get out of those who would not pay and impossible from those who could not, and the Board appears to have been resigned to the loss without penalising the children. The average annual arrears of fees amounted to about 3% of the whole, representing between 6000 and 8000 scholars.[1]

1880 was a year of exceptional distress and the Board did not press for payment from 7900 scholars, fully a quarter of the whole in average attendance. Another 3141 children had their fees paid by the Parochial Boards. Together, these figures mean that no less than one third of all the children at school were unable to pay their fees. Headmaster and Board winked at the failure and continued to give the child his lessons.

The Board gave concessions to large families. The eldest of three children paid only half his fee, while the eldest of four children was admitted free.

It is of some interest to see how the children were distributed in the scale of fees.

TABLE 20

NUMBER OF SCHOLARS CHARGED AT EACH RATE, 1880

162 at $1\frac{1}{2}$d (Dovehill)	1,392 at 6d
897 at 2d	114 at $6\frac{1}{2}$d
2,733 at $2\frac{1}{2}$d	348 at 7d
9,067 at 3d	375 at $7\frac{1}{2}$d
3,970 at $3\frac{1}{2}$d	315 at 8d
6,623 at 4d	22 at $8\frac{1}{2}$d
2,331 at $4\frac{1}{2}$d	68 at 9d
3,140 at 5d	77 at 10d
611 at $5\frac{1}{2}$d	436 at $10\frac{1}{2}$d $\Big\}$ (Garnethill)
	50 at $1/\frac{1}{2}$d

Total 32,731

The school fee did not include textbooks or jotters which had to be bought. The old practice had been for the books to be sold by the master, partly for convenience and partly because it brought him a small profit. The School Board did not like this system and tried from the start to alter it. But change came only slowly. It was made clear to teachers that the Board did not

[1] Report of Finance Committee, 1885.

want them to sell books, though it was not absolutely for-bidden.[1] The selling price was, however, laid down, and the Board ". . . made it as clear as possible that they would prefer that parents should supply the Scholars with books directly from the Booksellers".[2]

By 1891 exactly half the schools did not sell books. In the other half, books were kept for sale to the pupils because there was no bookshop nearby, and because children whose books were paid for by the Endowments Boards required to be supplied through the schools. All the headmasters declared they would be glad to be rid of the task of keeping books.

In demanding that books be bought at shops the Board no doubt had the best interest of the pupils at heart. Yet it did not always work in that way. Mr McDonald, Headmaster of Dennistoun, told his pupils that any exercise books would be allowed provided they accorded with the school's form of ruling. So a local stationer, a Mr Perrett, got in a supply of books identical to those in use. "Now, Sir," began his complaint to the Board, "what do you think is the result? Mr McDonald met a boy coming from my shop with one he had bought. He inquired where it was purchased, and told him he would get the right one in 'Robertson's' as got up by the Teachers, and reminded the boy what he would get if he had the wrong one."[3]

On occasion books might be supplied by the Board without charge, as when the inspectors pointed out that the younger Standards were able to complete their reader fairly quickly and then had to spend the rest of the year re-reading the same book over and over again a second set of readers was provided free. In ten of the poorer schools free copy-books, pens and pencils were issued to the children. Even text-books were sometimes supplied. The inspector's report on Greenside Street in 1877 noted that it was attended by ". . . a very poor and hitherto neglected class of children, mostly of the 'Street arab' order." Few had books, and so nothing could be done. He demanded that special provision should be made by the Board and warned, "Unless a good supply of books is immediately provided a deduction may be made next year" (Article 32).

[1] General Summary of Work, 1873–82, p 20.
[2] *ibid*, p 15.
[3] Minutes of Board in Committee, 3 May 1883.

THE EFFECT OF THE NEW ENDOWMENTS SCHEMES

Already work had begun on the difficult and involved matter of reorganising the many educational endowments scattered around the city. Separately they were often too small to be effective, and most of their charters were out of date and inapplicable to the present circumstances. Beginning in 1876 when a Circular was sent to clergymen and Governing Bodies requesting information in connection with contemplated legislation on Educational Endowments, a long succession of Commissions of Enquiry, abortive Bills, and Acts of Parliament followed hard on one another for the next ten years.

Throughout all these deliberations and negotiations the School Board worked hard to have the major part of the funds set aside for two main purposes; to help poor children in their elementary schooling, and to encourage more pupils to remain for secondary education.[1] In its pursuit of these aims the Board had to carry on a long struggle with the trustees of the old endowments, and especially with the richer, and therefore more powerful, trusts. There were two principal matters of contention.

First, many trustees wanted to make secondary education their main province in the future. By itself such an ambition would seem at first to be in keeping with the School Board's own wishes, but unfortunately the trusts saw themselves in the role of an independent body which would supply the Secondary needs of the city almost by itself. If this plan came about public schools would have been confined to the provision of elementary education. The Board was bound to oppose such a development, for its view of the public school system was a much wider one, holding that secondary education was a most important charge laid upon it by the Act and one in keeping with the national tradition. In the event, although Hutchesons' and Allan Glen's retained their separate identities, no new secondary schools were established outwith the public system, and such endowment monies as were allocated for secondary work went largely towards the development of Board Schools.

Second, the Board felt very strongly that the tendency to favour secondary education would lead to too much money being

[1] See Appendix E, Suggestions by representatives of the School Board of Glasgow, pp 238-40.

diverted from the charitable purposes of the original bene-factors.[1] It therefore caused the Educational Endowments Bill of 1880 to be postponed by a motion on the second reading, "That no Act to reorganise the Educational Endowments of Scotland will be satisfactory or just that does not distinctly provide that the founder's intentions shall be respected and secured in the interests of poor children of the class indicated in the Founder's will as regards Elementary Education, and also their maintenance and clothing where provision for such maintenance and clothing is made."[2] Although a safeguard clause in this vein was inserted into the new Act it did not end the affair, for the Board found that the Trustees, while paying lip-service to the clause, were side-stepping it and pressing on instead with their earlier purpose.

> "No prominence has been given to the fact that the great bulk of the funds has been bequeathed in the interests of poor children, variously described in the trusts as 'the most indigent ones of the city', 'poor boys and girls', 'poor orphans and children of poor persons', 'poor deserving boys', 'children of poor but respectable tradesmen', or 'poor but respectable parents', nor to the clause in the Act . . .
>
> "It is no doubt stated in the suggestions of the trustees as to how the funds be administered that the first duty of the governing body would be the provision of free elementary education where such is required to be given by the Endowments Act, and also that due regard must be had to the spirit of the founders' intentions, but while much work is proposed in connection with building and management of schools for secondary and technical education (very proper in their own place), the primary duties of the trusts towards the particular interests of poor children are placed in a very sub-ordinate position."[3]

The Board succeeded to a considerable extent in compelling the educational trusts to devote a fair part of their income to paying the fees of poor scholars in elementary schools. No doubt the School Board had some self-interest in such provision, but its leading members like Connal and Mitchell were moti-vated more by a genuine care for the poor of Glasgow. None better knew that thousands simply could not afford even the

[1] See Appendix F, Objections by Representatives of School Board to suggestions by Committee of Trust Representatives, pp 241-2.
[2] Minutes of Board in Committee, 3 August 1880.
[3] Objections by Representatives of School Board to suggestions by mmittee of Trust Representatives.

smallest school fee, and no one was more aware that without boots on their feet and food in their bellies children gained nothing from the most modern of schools or the best of teachers. The determination and success of the Board in ensuring that endowments were kept for the benefit of the needy make nonsense of Caldwell's charges that the Board was quite happy to ignore their interests in favour of the more well-to-do.

In 1885 the first three endowments schemes affecting Glasgow passed into law. The richest of these was the Hutchesons' Trust with an annual income of about £5130. The School Board was concerned with Hutcheson's only indirectly. Of more importance to the Board were the City Scheme and the General Scheme[1] with incomes of £4500 and £2540.[2] The provisions of the two schemes were virtually identical, the principal difference being in the composition of the trustees. The School Board had three seats on both trusts. The City and General trusts operated as one with a common secretary so the benefits they offered may be taken together:[3]

Free Scholarships for Elementary Education at public or state-aided schools in Glasgow. Free scholars were to be children ". . . whose parents or guardians, not being in receipt of parochial relief, are in such circumstances as to require aid for providing elementary education, and are persons who, in the opinion of the governors, ought not to be required to apply to the Parochial Board for such aid".

If under ten the child was not required to demonstrate any particular scholastic ability, merely prove a record of good attendance, good conduct and satisfactory progress. The scholarship was tenable for one year only, but renewable. Children of ten and over were to be selected by competitive examination. The award was tenable for up to three years, but was forfeit should the recipient win a School Bursary.

School Bursaries were available to children who had passed Standard V or such other standard as might from time to time qualify for exemption from attendance at school. Tenable for two years they were to have an annual value of between £5 and £10, and were won by competitive examination. The parents

[1] See Chapter 7, "The Development of Secondary Education".
[2] Triennial Report, 1882–85; School Attendance Committee, p 14.
[3] See Appendices G, H and I, pp 243–8.

had to be in ". . . such circumstances as to require aid for giving their children a higher education". The intention of the School Bursaries was to encourage children to remain at school after they were legally qualified to leave, and they proved of great value in the growth of secondary education.

Technical and Higher Education Bursaries were to provide for pupils at a technical school or college, and at Higher Class schools.

Evening Class Bursaries, 50 in number, encouraged pupils to continue elementary education after leaving school in Standard VI.

University Bursaries enabled a select few to go to Glasgow University.

The Technical, Higher Education and University Bursaries were at first few in number. Only three university bursaries valued £25 were offered, and a mere seven, worth £20, for technical and higher class schools.

No sooner had the various endowments schemes come into being than elementary education was made free—up to the age of fourteen by 1892. This released all the funds which had been allocated for elementary fees, and these moneys were used instead for secondary schooling.

At first the School Bursaries had a value of £5 a year, but when elementary education became free the value of the bursary was doubled to £10. The competitive examination was based upon Standard VI subjects plus two specific subjects at Stage 1.[1]

By the early nineties a considerable number of bursaries and scholarships were available in the city schools. Each year awards were given as follows.[2]

City and General Endowments Boards

University bursaries	2 value £25	tenable for 4 years
Technical or Higher Education bursaries	44 value £15	tenable for 2 years
School bursaries	131 value £10	tenable for 2 years
Evening Class bursaries	106 value £3	tenable for 2 years
Evening Class bursaries	45 value £5	tenable for 1 year

Free books in Elementary School to about 1850 pupils.

---

[1] Elgin Commission, Evidence of Dr F L Robertson, Secretary to the Combined Trusts, para 1580.
[2] High School and Secondary Committee Report, 1894–7.

Glasgow Highland Society Trust

University Arts bursaries	12 value £20	tenable for 4 years
Technical bursaries	4 value £25	tenable for 4 years
Medical bursaries	7 value £25	tenable for 4 years
Secondary Education scholarships	5 value £10 10/–	tenable for 4 years
Evening Class scholarships	13 value £3	tenable for 4 years

(To be eligible a candidate had to be of Highland descent.)

The Marshall Trust

University bursaries	4 value £30	tenable for 5 years
Secondary bursaries	30 value £10	tenable for 2 years
Secondary bursaries	8 value £15	tenable for 3 years

Maintenance and clothing grants, about 50 value £5 while at elementary school.

Free books and stationery for school	3200 pupils
Fees paid in evening school	1200 students

When the endowment schemes were first published fears had been expressed that the provision that parents had to be ". . . in such circumstances as to require aid for giving their children a higher education" was much too loose a definition and one which would open the door to quite well-off candidates. That success was to be gained through an open competitive examination would, it was thought, give the middle class child a great advantage, and the truly poor boy would be robbed of the birthright intended originally for him and him alone. In fact, these fears proved unfounded for the City and General Board set a £2 per week maximum wage as the normal qualification, while the Marshall Trust awards were available only to the really poor with an annual income of less than £70. The Technical and University bursaries of the Combined Boards were, however, unrestricted as to income.

Other scholarships were available from the Secondary Education Grant, and were allocated among the schools thus:[1]

High School	60 scholarships
Girls' High School	60 scholarships
The 5 Secondary Schools	150 scholarships

[1] High School and Secondary Committee Report, 1894-7.

F

These scholarships were tenable for three years, and one third were competed for annually.

How adequately was Glasgow supplied with financial aid for individual scholars? The answer depends on one's view of who ought to have been helped. The poorer classes were very well supplied. Indeed, virtually every candidate who came within the income limits set by the City and General Boards and who had any sort of pretensions to scholarship could obtain a bursary. The Secretary of the Combined Trusts believed there was a real sense in which it could be said that Glasgow had enough School Bursaries, and he instanced the fact that virtually every candidate who managed to muster half marks in the examination received a bursary.[1] Moreover, a number of these bursars ". . . chucked up their bursary at the end of their first year".[2] It was all further evidence that only a handful of children really wanted, or were able to contemplate, a full secondary education. "According to my experience about three quarters of the secondary education demanded in Glasgow does not really cover more than two years above the Standards."[3] The numbers of children who could go on past this stage was small ". . . and must always be so in a commercial and manufacturing city. Lads going into business cannot afford to remain at school longer than perhaps up to the age of 15, in fact, it is rather a drawback to a lad to begin work later than 15."[4]

This old problem was equally evident when it came to awarding the more valuable Technical and Higher Education Bursaries. These were for pupils who intended to carry on their schooling past the first two years of secondary work which were catered for by the School Bursaries. Although the standard of applicant was high their numbers were few, ". . . and the reason for it is obvious, that it is at the point when we compete for these bursaries the great bulk of young men and even young women leave school to begin work, and we have not the chance of a large competition. It is a very discouraging thing . . . and it is also true with regard to the Hutchesons' Schools, even in regard to bursars who are appointed for four years with an

[1] Elgin Commission, para 1589.
[2] *ibid*, para 1590.
[3] *ibid*, para 1580.
[4] *ibid*, para 1582.

increased money payment, and with the advantage of free education; never a year passes but several of them give up their bursaries because they are drafted into work."[1]

It seems, then, that free education, whether obtained through government decree or by bursaries, did little by itself to enable poorer families to let their children remain at school after the statutory leaving age. For them Glasgow offered plenty of scholarships, but their value was too low to compensate for the wages which could be earned out at work.

The case of the slightly better off family was different. This was the group who were by no means rich, who certainly were unable to pay the fees demanded by the High School, and yet whose income was outside the limiting £104 a year set for bursaries. The only help open to them were the Technical and Higher Bursaries—a mere eighty or so for a school population of about three quarters of a million. "This does not seem an over-supply of bursaries for the children of parents whose incomes exclude them from the benefits of the school bursaries, but are not large enough to enable them to send their children to the secondary schools. The decided majority of the parents of the pupils of these Board Secondary schools, I believe, come under this head, belonging to a class forming the 'back-bone' of the community."[2]

FREE ELEMENTARY EDUCATION AND GLASGOW

It was a Glasgow man, Charles Cameron, who in 1881 introduced a bill in Parliament calling for Free Education. Nothing came of it at the time, though it was not to be long before Cameron and others of like mind got their way.

Cameron, like any good politician, made suitable use of statistics to prove his contention that fees were undesirable and unnecessary.[3] He was especially critical of the high-fee policy pursued by the Glasgow Board. He was able to show that not only was the average of fees throughout Scotland substantially higher than that for England but that the Glasgow fees were well above the normal.

[1] Elgin Commission, para 1590.
[2] *ibid*, para 78.
[3] Charles Cameron, MP, "Free Education". A lecture given to the Glasgow Liberal Workmen's Electoral Union, 1880.

	England	*Scotland*	*Edinburgh*	*Govan*	*Glasgow*
School Rate/child	18/9¾d	13/10½d	17/4d	4/7¾d	10/9d
Average Fee/child	9/3¼d	12/5½d	9/11d	14/1¾d	16/1d

He claimed that the School Board had not considered what fees ought to be in the light of public education as inaugurated by the Act, but had simply based its fees on those formerly existing in private schools. The really poor had been provided for by the establishment of one cheap school in each district.

Cameron's other main point was that so little income was obtained from fees that they might as well be dropped altogether. The legal complications of enforcement and the administrative difficulties involved in their collection simply were not worth the candle. The benefit to the poor would be great, and money would be saved on the enforcement of attendance. Cameron pointed out that fully three quarters of the cost of elementary education was already paid for by the state. He then amused his listeners by working out the following little sum for Glasgow.

	£	
Total fees collected	23,325	
Subtract	1,780	paid by Parochial Boards
	1,233	unpaid fees
	2,300	being fees from children over the compulsory age.
	800	from Garnethill and City Schools Higher Departments
*Net fees collected	17,200	
Subtract about	6,000	for the various costs incurred in the administration of compulsory attendance
*Real income from fees	11,200	

A paltry sum for a government to quibble over!

Cameron received little support at the time, but only a few years later Free Education became a major national issue when in 1885 Joseph Chamberlain included it in his electoral manifesto. Soon the whole Liberal Party, including reluctant luminaries like Gladstone, were committed to the abolition of fees, that "odious and abominable tax".[1]

Many eminent voices in Scotland were raised in defence of fees, among them Sir Francis Standford, Under Secretary of State for Scotland, late Head of the Scotch Education Department, and a Glasgow man.[2] Both the *Scotsman* and *Glasgow Herald* spoke up for fees. Catholic opinion was fearful of the high costs which would fall upon the public as a consequence of abolition, and was sure that free education must inevitably result in Godless schools.[3] Professor S S Laurie, perhaps the most eminent educationist of his day, lectured his university class, "Let them abolish fees, and the child becomes more and more the child of the State, and less and less the child of its own father and mother."[4]

The arguments in favour of fees were less financial than moral. The view that what one paid for one respected was in keeping with the times. To provide education free was to remove responsibility from the parent and deprive him of direct control over the schooling of his child.

While the Glasgow School Board did have one or two members sympathetic to free education the majority were against it. Certainly, the most experienced and influential members, including Cuthbertson and his predecessor in the chair, Connal, all spoke up strongly in favour of retaining some measure of fee-paying. The case was best put by Mitchell, the veteran Vice-Chairman. He published a pamphlet[5] in which he set out the arguments one by one of the Camerons and the Chamberlains and refuted each in turn:

1 Many children kept from school on account of the inability of parents to pay fees

The error in this view was to confuse cause and effect. It was not fees which were wrong but the poverty itself, and that is what should be attacked. In any case, many schools in Glasgow had very low fees, a penny in the earlier stages and never more

[1] Joseph Chamberlain (attributed).
[2] See address by him on "Free Education" on the occasion of the opening of Gorbals School, 1885.
[3] See three articles on "Free Education" by A School Board Catholic Member in the *Glasgow Observer*, 14, 21 and 28 November 1885.
[4] Quoted in *Scotsman*, 30 October 1885.
[5] William Mitchell, *Free Education Considered Practically, Experimentally and Briefly*, 1885.

than threepence. Even the poorest could pay this. Above all, it gave a parent a say: "If he is not satisfied, as occasionally happens, he exercises his privilege and changes the school or the teacher."

2 Free schools would effect an improvement in roll and attendance

Here Mitchell compared attendance statistics in German and American schools. The fee-paying Germans showed an excellent attendance rate, while absence in the free American schools was deplorably high by Glasgow standards. The truth was that absence in Glasgow was not due to fees but to ". . . want of food and clothing, want of stockings and shoes, want of home influence and control, and the urgent need for the small earnings which the children can make".

3 The supposed degradation implied in the necessity of applying to Parochial Boards for payment of fees

This problem would be rectified by the new funds just released by the Endowment Commissioners, especially those of Marshall's Trust.

4 The contention that compulsory education implied free education

The logic of this was denied. It was only tenable if fees were so large that the bulk of the population could not send their children to school. To argue that because a few needed help *all* should be helped was to subsidise the well-to-do.

5 The claim that fees in public schools were an innovation in Scotland

Utter nonsense, said Mitchell. There were innumerable examples of fee-paying right down the ages. And to support his view Mitchell drew on two great figures of the Kirk, one ancient and one modern.

John Knox: "The rich and potent may not be permitted to suffer their children to spend their youth in vane idilness, as hairtofore thei have done. But thei must be exhorted, and by the censure of the churche compelled, to dedicat thair sones, by goode exercise, to the proffit of the churche and to the common-wealth; and that thei must do of thair awin expensses, because thei ar able."

Dr Chalmers: "I stand up most inflexibly on the subject of fees, and I think these persons ought to pay fees for the education of their children. . . . There are three systems of schooling. There is first the gratuitous or wholly endowed system, which is in general a very lax and careless system. The second is the converse of this being wholly unendowed, and which is, I think, very bad too, because it forces people to pay too high fees; it does not meet the people half way. The other system is the parochial or medium system established by the fathers of the Reformation, where the two parties meet each other half way. I would say that the universality of the Scottish education is to be ascribed to the medium system instituted by the fathers of the Reformation."

6 Differential fees in Glasgow maintained class distinction

While all schools in Glasgow provided an equally good education the Board thought it right and proper to charge higher fees in districts where parents could afford them. Undoubtedly this led to a degree of social selection between schools, but to suggest, as one parliamentary candidate in the city was doing, that fees were the root cause of such differences was to blind oneself to the fact that this was what parents wanted. "The School Board cannot prevent the existence of class distinctions in the community. There will be richer and poorer while the world lasts."

And if free education were granted where, asked Mitchell, was the money to come from? The sum required would be great, for it was not simply a matter of making good the lost fees. Much more money would inevitably be necessary. Private schools would be ruined and close down, and then the state would have to undertake the cost of educating all their ex-pupils. In all fairness Roman Catholics would be entitled to an Equivalent Grant which, over and above financial considerations, raised a political issue of great difficulty. Then free books and stationery would need even more money, "He will be a bold man who will propose an additional 9d per £ added to the present 6d for school rate. The unpopularity, if not the impossibility, of such a mode of raising the money has driven certain advocates of free education to suggest two courses; one the endowments of the Established Church; the other an Imperial Grant." The first of these expedients was unthinkable for the Church endowments were given originally for religious education, and to use them for State Education would be barefaced robbery—especially as the advocates of free education tended also to be secularists. As for accepting more money from the Treasury, "The firmer the hold that the State gets on education and the schools, the greater the certainty that secularism pure and simple will prevail."

The School Board feared that free education would mean an education free from parental control, free from religious instruction, and free from economical management. Who today can be sure that they were not right?

Right or wrong, however, a School Board had to submit to the will of parliament, and so in the two years following 1892 all fees were abolished in the elementary schools of Glasgow.

In one respect at least, free education turned out to be no improvement on the bad old days; it made no difference whatever to attendance.[1]

FEES IN SECONDARY SCHOOLS

Although by 1892 education was legally free up to the school leaving age this did not mean that a pupil could pass from primary to secondary school at the age of twelve without any worry about fees. The great majority of children remained in elementary school throughout their careers. The ambitious few who aspired to a secondary course still, in Glasgow, had to pay for the privilege, whether by winning a bursary or through private means.

Fortunately, at this time the government began to give grants for secondary work, and in 1893 the Burgh Committee on Secondary Education began its work. It provided financial aid in two ways: first, by direct subsidies to the School Board enabling it to improve the quality of its schools while reducing fees at the same time; second, by competitive scholarships sufficient to cover the pupils' fees. Ninety such scholarships were available annually which together with the bursaries of the Endowment Boards and another hundred or so awarded by the School Board itself meant that for about one pupil out of every two secondary education was free.[2]

[1] School Board return to SED, 1892 showed that free education had had no effect on attendance. See also Committee of Council on Education in Scotland, 1891, p 5.
[2] In 1897 the total enrolment of the five Secondary Departments was 762 and just over 400 bursaries were available.

The High School especially benefited from the new arrangements. Previously virtually without free places the school now received each year bursars from the Endowments Board, twenty from the Burgh Committee and a further twenty-two through the School Board. Of more general worth was a substantial reduction in fees.[1]

	Form	Fees per quarter Old			New		
1st		£2	5	0	£1	10	0
2nd		£2	10	0			
3rd		£2	15	0	£1	15	0
4th		£3	0	0			
5th		£3	10	0	£2	0	0
6th		£3	10	0			

As the years passed and government money became more generous fees in the Secondary Departments were steadily reduced until, in most of them, tuition was entirely free. But Glasgow never entirely abolished discrimination in her schools.

TABLE 21

FEES IN SECONDARY DEPARTMENT SCHOOLS

School	1893	Per quarter 1900	1906–18
City		1st year free	Free
John Street	All	2nd year 7/6d	Free
Kent Rd	classes 10/–	3rd year 10/–	Free
Whitehill		4th year 10/-	7/6d
Woodside		5th year 10/-	7/6d
Albert			Free
North Kelvinside			Free

The Boys' High and Girls' High charged most highly, and Whitehill and Woodside retained fees to the very end. Their charges were quite low, but were sufficient to mark them off as a cut above the likes of John Street or Kent Road (see Table 21). It should not be thought that the difference was merely one of prestige or snobbery, for it was fully justified by the high quality of education received.

In the fifty years that have passed since the School Boards came to an end little has changed in Glasgow. The Education Department still retains fees—low fees—in a very few schools,

[1] Triennial Report, 1891–94, High Schools and Secondary Education Committee.

F*

and the argument over abolition still continues. As with so many battles, the passage of time often leaves the combatants wondering what the quarrel was all about. For the visitors, victory has not brought about Utopia; for the defeated, defeat has not resulted in the prophesied catastrophe. Mitchell put it well, "Whatever our opinion may formerly have been, I do not think any of us would desire to go back to the old system. I frankly admit that former opponents of the measure of Free Education, of whom I was one, have no special reason to be satisfied with all the arguments advanced by them in opposition. 'All's well that ends well', and while I still believe in fees in the higher classes, I would not desire to see a return to the Fee system in our elementary schools."[1]

[1] William Mitchell, Remarks and Review. Annual Report of School Attendance Committee, 1899.

Chapter 9
ATTENDANCE

The Education Act of 1872 made provision for the compulsory attendance at school of all children between the ages of five and thirteen. Poverty was now no excuse, for the needy parent could apply to the Parochial Board which was bound by law to pay the school fees. It was a great and important step towards the realisation of a wholly literate nation. Yet it was one thing to make the law; it was quite another to put it into effect, and this was the task of the School Board.

In sheer numbers alone the Glasgow Board faced a huge problem, for over 30,000 children in the city were not enrolled in any type of school.[1] The first step was to engage School Attendance Officers,[2] the advertisement for which attracted more than 1100 applicants.[3] The very size of this response was in itself an indicator of what lay before the successful candidates, for the School Board period coincided with the Great Depression, large-scale unemployment, low wages and extreme poverty, and it was the children of such destitute parents who now had to be got into school.

In the machinery of compulsion devised and evolved by the Board can be recognised much that is still used by the Glasgow Education Department today. Little difficulty was found in persuading most of the initial defaulters to enrol in a school, but it was a very different matter to ensure their regular attendance. Once a week teachers prepared a list of children who had been absent for two or more days in the week, and this list was picked up by the Attendance Officer every Friday. Several officers were attached to each of the twelve districts into which the city was divided, and they went round their beats remonstrating with the parents of absentees where necessary. In certain cases

[1] School Attendance Committee Report, 1874.
[2] Mr John McMath was Glasgow's first Attendance Officer. His weekly wage was £1 10 0.
[3] Minutes of Board in Committee, 21 August 1873.

parents were handed a printed form of remonstrance and warning, directing attention to the requirements of the Act.

Parents who after several visits of the officer still continued to neglect the education of their children were classed as defaulters. Special officers were allotted to deal with such cases. After further visit and warning the parents were summoned to appear before the Board. Wholly incorrigibles might find themselves charged before the Sheriff and fined from 2/6d to 10/–.

At least once a week a special operation was mounted against vagrant or truant children to be found in the streets, docks, fairs and markets. Disguised in plain clothes and deployed to districts in which they were not known, the officers swooped down on their prey in a Day Raid. They always got a good bag; 350 was an average figure in 1879. On another day 1034 names were taken—and twenty-three false addresses received![1] The most an attendance officer could do on coming across a child out of school was to take his name and address. The well-known *Illustrated London News* cartoon showing a London School Board officer hauling off two vagrant boys had no counterpart in Scotland, for the law put the responsibility of schooling on the parent, and it was with the parent that the Board dealt.

One of the most demanding tasks facing anyone joining the Board was having to officiate at the meetings of delinquents. These were held regularly about every fortnight, though by the end of the century weekly meetings were quite common. In a school of the district being visited a large room was utilised as a waiting room, and several smaller ones for the hearing of the individual cases. One or two members sat at a plain table in front of which was a bench for the family being interviewed. The local attendance officer, who knew the people well, was also present. We have an account of a typical evening's work.

"The Chairman of the Board[2] has from the first taken a warm interest in these meetings, and has done much by his example to show to the other members how wisely and considerately, yet firmly and kindly, parents and guardians may be dealt with in the way of counsel, remonstrance, and warning. He has an experience which dates far back in connection with the social condition of the poor which enables him so to conduct his inquiries that he instantly

[1] Report on Day Raid, 30 May 1887.
[2] Sir Michael Connal.

secures the confidence of those brought before him. He speedily evokes their varied histories, and does not fail to insist on the whole truth where prevarication is apparent.

"A tidy old women is ushered in accompanied by a sharp bright-looking little fellow of about twelve years old. Anxiety and care are written in indelible lines on the face of granny as she takes her seat with her grandson in front of the Chairman. The record declares that Robert is very irregular in his attendance at school, and the officer supplements the record by the statement that the boy is engaged in casual employment for some part of the week. Old granny tells her story: Robert's mother died when he was only a few weeks old. His father took it so much to heart that he 'listed' and left the country, leaving the infant in her charge. She doesn't know where he is, having only once heard from him during all those years. She is a lone woman now and the little boy is her only comfort. They have never been parted. It is a touching story.

Chairman: 'Come here my wee man, let me hear how you can read.'[1] The boy reads fairly, but not as a boy of twelve ought to do, and his writing and counting are somewhat deficient.

Chairman: 'Would you not like to get the boy into an institution where he would be taken care of and be well fed and clothed and educated, and come to see you very often?'

Upon this granny and the boy fall to sobbing and crying, and all she can say is, 'Oh! don't separate us. Don't take him away. He's all I have.'

Chairman: 'Well, my good woman, what can you do for yourself and the boy?'

Granny: 'He just goes out to the country wi' a man and his cart two days in the week in the afternoons, and he'll go to the school a' the rest o' the time.'

Chairman, referring to the Convener:[2] 'What do you think about that?'

Convener: 'Well, it's perhaps against the strict letter of our regulations, but if Robert will attend an evening school and promise to be at the day school regularly, with the exception of two afternoons in the week, that may perhaps be allowed. It is in accordance with a provision in the Code which gives discretion to managers to act in this way where children are engaged in some beneficial employment.'

Chairman: 'Well, granny, I'm not very sure about it, but I wouldn't like to be the cause of you requiring to go to the poorhouse and far less would I like to separate you from your bright clever boy. You may do as the Convener has suggested. You have acted the

[1] The purpose of this test was to find out if the boy satisfied the minimum educational requirements of the Act which were, in fact, very vague. If the boy could read a little, write a little, and do a few sums he was eligible for exemption from school.

[2] William Mitchell, Convener of the School Attendance Committee.

part of a mother to him, and I think he'll grow up to care for you and be a credit to you.'

Oh! the joy that filled the hearts of granny and boy. Robert went away declaring that he would never leave his granny, and he promised to attend school day and evening as arranged without missing an hour."[1]

The solution might seem too simple and the emotion too open for modern taste, but the description is important as it accurately reflects the attitude of the School Board to compulsion in attendance. In any case, not everything was sweet light and reasonableness.

"There is seldom a meeting without some flagrant exhibition, even in presence of the members, of the drink demon's power in the language and behaviour of some one or other of the company. . . . Stern reproof and warning are as frequently required as advice and sympathy."[2]

WILLIAM MITCHELL

At the first School Board Election the successful candidate with the least votes was a Mr William Mitchell. He served continuously for the next twenty-seven years, and so had the distinction of being the longest serving member of the Glasgow Board. And a right good member he proved. An old High School boy and a self-made businessman, Mitchell, like Connal, was a mid-Victorian with many of the traits so commonly associated with the men of that period. He was deeply religious and a pillar of the Free Church. He believed in Self Help and the moral virtue of having to pay one's way through life (and school!), be it ever so little. He was a social worker among the poor and the maimed. He was a man of deep compassion, though accepting the seemingly immutable nature of social class.

Throughout his period of office Mitchell was Convener of the School Attendance Committee, so it is safe to say that Mitchell's views on this aspect of School Board work were those put into practice in Glasgow. Fortunately very full records of this committee exist for Mitchell was an indefatigable compiler of statistics and a prolific writer of pamphlets. As the years passed his authority within the Board increased, partly thanks to his long experience and partly to his position as Vice-Chairman

[1] William Mitchell, *Rescue the Children*, pp 27–30.
[2] *ibid*, p 34.

from 1888. Only towards the end, when he was over seventy and a man of an earlier age living in a new century, were other voices, critical voices, able to assert themselves. By then, however, Mitchell's stamp on Board policies was indelibly printed and few changes of importance occurred.

It is well known that it was the putting into effect of the compulsory clause of the Act which, both in England and in Scotland, brought to the surface for public gaze the submerged tenth. No longer was it possible to ignore the grinding poverty and revolting living conditions of thousand upon thousand of the population of this country. That Glasgow had one of the worst social problems in the land became apparent from the first day the new attendance officers ventured into the wynds, closes and lands of Anderston, Bridgeton and Calton. From that moment Mitchell spent his life in the alleviation of suffering among the children of the destitute. He never lost an opportunity of publicising their plight in the annual reports of his committee, in lectures to influencial bodies and societies, and in book form. He constantly lobbied Parliament where, although his proposals were never radical for he accepted the inevitability of poverty while being horrified by its effects, he was instrumental in many a Bill being amended to include clauses of a social rather than purely educational nature. The culmination of these efforts was evident in the 1901 Education Act.[1]

William Mitchell, Vice-Chairman of the Glasgow School Board, Justice of the Peace, LL D of Glasgow University, Director of the Juvenile Delinquency Board, Director of the Deaf and Dumb Institute, Director of the Society for Prevention of Cruelty to Children, founder of the East Park Home for Infirm Children, is today one of Glasgow's forgotten men. He deserved better. Let the teachers who served under him have the final word, "To our thinking, Mr Mitchell is the real model of what a School Board member ought to be."[2]

THE RIGOUR OF THE LAW?

How successful was Glasgow in enforcing compulsory attendance? How far did she attempt to do so?

[1] *Glasgow Herald*, 13 August 1910.
[2] *Educational News*, 10 January 1880.

It is impossible to give any very exact answer to these questions. Statistics were never precise and were, in any case, slippery things to handle. Two examples of this problem will illustrate the difficulties.

In January 1884 the *North British Daily Mail* claimed that out of 90,000 Glasgow children 33,000 were absent every day. On the same day Mr Mundella, Vice-President of the Privy Council, visited the city and in a public speech and, using the figures given him by the Board, he admitted the fact but denied the implication, ". . . a statement which is perfectly correct in fact, but I think it tends rather to mislead on the face of it". Both sides then proved their case to their own satisfaction.[1]

A much more serious criticism was made in 1902; more serious because it was an official comment by one of His Majesty's Inspectors[2] and because it was made after nearly thirty years of Board education by which time teething troubles ought to have been overcome. While commending an improvement in attendance over the previous year Mr Scougal questioned the validity of the School Board's figures. These indicated an 84.6% average attendance of children on the school rolls. But what if the numbers on the registers did not accurately represent the total number of school-age children in the city? "It is plain that a Board which, through carelessness or through deliberate neglect, did not have on its rolls the habitual bad attenders might easily be credited with an unfairly high average of attendance in its schools." The inspector, very impressed with Maryhill's figures, and using the Registrar General's estimate of the child population, made a comparison very seriously critical of Glasgow.

	Percentage not accounted for on school rolls of total child population	
	Ages 5–6	*Ages 6–13*
Maryhill	31	18
Glasgow	61	33

The Board sought an explanation from its Chief Attendance Officer. He first pointed out the unreasonableness of comparing suburban Maryhill with the peculiar difficulties facing such a

[1] See J Caldwell, *Educational Endowments of the City of Glasgow*, p 28.
[2] Committee of Council for Education in Scotland, Mr Scougal's Report, 1902.

large city as Glasgow which had a huge itinerant population and where the midnight flitting was one of the most skilled arts possessed by many citizens. "When we remember that in Glasgow we have 20,000 ticketed houses, giving accommodation to 70.000 persons, of whom 14,000 may be taken to be children between 5 and 14; 66 lodging houses giving accommodation to over 9000 persons; between 30 and 40 children of school age lodging nightly in the Night Asylum for the Homeless; over 1000 families living in farmed out houses; and that our officers deal weekly with 450 to 500 removals. When we remember these facts, amongst others, the value of comparison with Maryhill is very much minimised."[1]

Next, the officer dealt with the figures given by the inspector. Little defence was necessary in the case of the five-year-olds as the Board had never attempted to force such young children into school, believing as it did that parents were very much against it. While it was true that of the six to thirteen age group nearly 10% were not on the rolls, almost all of these missing children could be readily accounted for. The six-year-olds accounted for 3.3%, and once again the reluctance of parents to send their younger children to school had never been seriously contested by the Board. Subtracting those in institutions, those physically unfit for school, those educated at home, and nearly a thousand exempted through labour certificates or merit certificates, only about $1\frac{1}{2}$% remained unaccounted for. As for children between thirteen and fourteen, it was well known that very many were able to leave school on certificate before reaching the statutory leaving age. The breakdown of numbers was as follows.

In institutions	900
Physically unfit	100
Educated at home	40
Exempts	230
Certificated (Labour or Merit)	2200
Certificated prior to 1901 being then under 14 years	700

By this reckoning the number of children not on the school rolls who ought to have been was a mere 159.

[1] School Attendance Committee Report, 18 November 1902.

The raw statistics are, therefore, difficult to interpret and dangerous to take at face value. Nevertheless, by using them judiciously and adding other knowledge of the times a fairly accurate picture can be drawn of attendance in the city.

Infants under seven

Although the Act required attendance from the age of five it was never enforced in Glasgow until the child had reached seven. In the early years of the Board it was happy enough to ignore the infants for the problems of accommodation were great and the claims of older children more urgent. Even many years later lack of accommodation was sometimes a problem, though local and temporary, due to an area being newly developed. Such was the position in Dennistoun at the turn of the century when large tenements were sprouting all round existing schools like Dennistoun, Alexandra Parade and Thomson Street whose infant departments were full and unable to cope with over two hundred waiting to get in.

This, however, was a quite exceptional circumstance. The principal reason for only a small proportion of infants being in school was the Scottish custom of keeping the children at home to a later age. It was a common experience of school boards throughout the country that mothers were not prepared to give up their younger children to the school.

The Glasgow Board did its duty up to a point. It distributed encouraging leaflets, it sent round its attendance officers, it reduced fees and, above all, provided attractive accommodation for infants in an attempt to stimulate the attendance of young children. The teaching, too, was first rate as the inspectors' reports testify. Yet the results were not very satisfactory, and the Board was not altogether sorry. As well as being doubtful that such youngsters had much to gain at school the Board feared, from sad experience, that it would simply result in the child leaving school earlier. "Except in so far as it is an advantage to get children from an unwholesome into a wholesome atmosphere, I am not greatly concerned from an educational point of view. . . . It merely means they pass 5th Standard sooner and so are able to leave. . . . It is true that the Factory & Workshops Act stands in the way of their employment in regular trades up to the age of 13, but there is abundance of occupation for such children in ways not controlled by that Act. This desire on the part of parents to get their children to work is forced on your committee every day, and, I fear, is too much lost sight of in this constant outcry to get the infants to school."[1]

So the attendance of infants, while being encouraged, was not actively pressed. After fourteen years of public schools fewer than 12,000 infants were on the Glasgow rolls out of an estimated population at that age of nearly 26,000. At no time during the School Board period did the proportion in attendance ever rise much over 40%.[2]

Unwillingly to School

Naturally, schools in good districts of the City maintained a high attendance, ". . . but there are certain schools in the poorer districts which show, as might be expected, rates of attendance very low and very much in proportion to the poverty of the parents, and the social condition of the families".[3] That Glasgow had a colossal social problem was recognised by the Department. "In the City of Glasgow and its densely populated suburbs there is a large number of vagrant and neglected children that yet puzzle all their well-wishers. It is to be hoped that some effective plan [may be found] by which these infant apprentices to evil may be swept into school and kept there till they are able to earn an honest living. Regarding them, not the least puzzling question is, what sort of school should they be sent to, whether to schools specially established for themselves or to ordinary schools attended by the children of honest well-doing people."[4]

Many of the reasons for irregular attendance will surprise no one; they are the same today. Habitual truancy, want of parental control, fecklessness on the part of parents, girls kept at home to "mind the baby", boys sent messages without any

[1] William Mitchell, Remarks on the Thirteenth Annual Report of the School Attendance Committee, 1886.
[2] School Attendance Committee: Annual Returns.
[3] William Mitchell, Remarks on the Seventeenth Annual Report of the School Attendance Committee, 1890.
[4] Committee of Council for Education in Scotland, Inspector's Report 1877, p 189.

regard to their losing a day or half a day from school.[1] But looming over everything was the crushing poverty of the times, and how to improve the miserable attendance of vagrant, destitute and neglected children was a problem which all but baffled the Board. The truth was that the difficulty was far more of a social nature than an educational one, a fact immediately recognised by Mitchell and his colleagues: "Ah! you say, are they [the 'street gypsies'] not being educated? That will bring them round all right. Will it? I fear not, or at least only partially. Education is the leading spirit of the age, but education is not food; education is not clothing; education cannot take the place of home comforts, home training, home influence. Children must have the natural and material wants of the body supplied ere the benefits and blessings of education can be either received or valued. By the education of the Act, however, light is being thrown in many a dark corner, and attention is being drawn to the miserable condition of a great multitude for whom education will only be a mockery until their untoward circumstances are in some degree amended."[2]

Much of Mitchell's energy over the next thirty years was devoted to bringing these untoward circumstances to the notice of the public and under government action. Glasgow worked conscientiously at enforcing school attendance but its efforts in this direction were outshone by the social welfare work which accompanied it.

The appalling housing conditions of Glasgow at the time are well known. Gross overcrowding was common. As many as 40,820 families were living in single rooms,[3] a common size of room being 12 feet square though some were as small as 8 feet. Nor was the "single end" a relic of the past, "as late as the 1870s when houses were being erected at the rate of 5000 a year much the same relative sizes were maintained".[4] Often the only sanitation for a whole section of tenement was "one earth privy outside, to serve for the hundred people living in the

[1] William Mitchell, Remarks on the Seventeenth Annual Report of the School Attendance Committee, 1890.
[2] William Mitchell, *Rescue the Children*, p 16.
[3] 1881 Census.
[4] *viz*, 30% one apartment
     44% two apartments
     26% three apartments or more
Sir Alex MacGregor, *Public Health in Glasgow, 1905–46*, 1967.

building".[1, 2] A common sink on the stairs was no blessing. "An abominable practice may be observed on the stair landing, where the jawbox[3] is made the receptacle of all the liquid filth from the numerous houses adjoining. This need not be surprising when there is no other cesspool, the jawbox being used alike for the reception of all that will pass through, and at the same time as a scullery for cooking purposes."[4]

Mitchell contrasted the airy, clean, brightly-lit warm schools which the children attended for a few hours each day with the harrowing squalor many returned to at night.

"Let me ask the reader to accompany me while we follow that group of pale-faced, poorly-clad children, who have just left the cheerful playground and the comfortable school. They are returning 'home'.

"We cross several thoroughfares, and at length turn aside along a narrow close or alley, which one may have passed hundreds of times without dreaming that it leads to lands and tenements, largely consisting of innumerable one-roomed houses where many poor families constantly reside. At the foot of the stair a dungstead stands constantly reeking with unwholesome odours. It is being replenished almost without intermission. If the day is sloppy and wet the lower steps get the benefit of the overflow, and a filthy, pig-sty entrance is the result. Up one, two, three, or four stairs, you find long, dark passages with no end of doors, each one opening into the wretched apartment where a whole family dwell, and whither this little group of children are finding their accustomed way.

"If you would follow them into the room, provide yourself with a lump of camphor that you may not run the risk of fainting away after leaving the fresh air of the street.

"The passage is dirty; the house is filthy; no whitewash has come near these walls for many a long day. One miserable bed occupies a dark recess, another made up of some old bedclothes is seen in a corner, and a third—a shakedown—may be found under the first to be drawn out as night approaches.

"The children burst in hungry and full of spirits for their mid-day meal; other little ones, half naked, are toddling about or creeping on the dirty floor. The mother, with an infant at her breast, is outside or in a neighbour's house. The noise of her children attracts her attention, and she enters the miserable room, a loaf of bread is taken

[1] J R Kellett, *Glasgow*, Blond Educational Ltd, 1967, p 58.
[2] Only in 1890 were water closets made compulsory by the Glasgow Police Act.
[3] Glaswegian for a sink.
[4] William Mitchell, Remarks on the Tenth Annual Report of the School Attendance Committee, 1883.

from the shelf; an old brown teapot gets a spoonful of tea, and is filled with boiling water from a rusty kettle on the hob; a lump of salt butter, wrapped in a piece of dirty paper, is produced; two or three broken cups are put on a rickety chair, round which the children cluster, either on stools or squatted on the floor, or on the edge of the iron fender; sugar is cheap; milk a rare commodity; and so, without any kind of order and with a general scramble, they all fall to and quickly consume what is provided for them. This constitutes the principal meal of thousands of poor children day after day. Tea with sugar and bread without butter is very usual fare. Porridge and milk, broth and beef, may be seen in a limited number of houses, but not where the poorest families reside. . . .

"In some rooms may be found a superfluity of articles—old beds, tables, chairs, boxes, pots and dishes, with little regard to order or cleanliness. In others, a shakedown in the corner, a box or barrel for a table, a broken stool, an old pot or pan, with a few dishes. In many rooms no furniture at all; and the families, including men, women, and children, huddled together at night on such straw or rags as they can gather. This barrenness of any kind of furnishing enables the occupants to flit about from one house and one district to another with the greatest possible ease and there is a constant fluctuation going on, enabling the inmates to thwart the School Board officers at every turn."[1]

In the face of such prevalent squalor the Board may be excused if attendance was not all that the law intended it to be. The Board held its frequent defaulters' meetings, employed a large staff of attendance officers, spent much time, money and effort in the uphill task of trying to keep children at school, and regularly hauled a quota of the most flagrant cases before the magistrates for punishment. But it had little faith in the power of the law to coerce recalcitrant parents into sending their children to school. The law was uncertain, the magistrates often unsympathetic to compulsion. Above all, the law was painfully slow to take effect and often lenient in its punishments. It is an axiom that a deterent will only deter if certain to be applied and applied soon after the offence, and neither of these criteria held.

The original Education Act, while requiring attendance to thirteen years of age, permitted exemption to children who could prove their ability to read and write and do some elementary arithmetic. As no definite standard of attainment was laid down it was sometimes difficult to obtain a conviction. In addition, the cost of legal proceedings put off many a school board. As a result, "Soon the parties who need its [the Compulsory Clause] application will come to know this and to stand in as much fear of it as of a potato bogle."[1]

However, these technicalities could easily have been overcome by a really determined school board, but Glasgow's heart was not in it. It was one thing to contemplate legalities in abstraction, it was quite another to face daily the human beings involved. "Too often I have been met with the remark, Why not punish? Why not prosecute? Your philanthropy is only pauperising and demoralising the parents. If punishment only affected a man's own skin he would, in too many cases, be well deserving of it, but what good is it doing his children? The family becomes if possible only more degraded and in a large number of cases the children are little the better for the parents' small fine or short imprisonment. While admitting the necessity, in flagrant cases, for prosecution and punishment, the aim of the Board in all its varied dealing has rather been to rescue the children, to save them from sinking to the same depth as their degraded parents."[2]

Exemption

Many children applied to be exempted from attendance till thirteen. Since no definite educational standard had been laid down in the Act other than the ability to read, write and do arithmetic it took some time to work out what that standard should be. At first the Glasgow practice was to test every applicant individually in the School Board Offices. This, of course, was an exceedingly time-consuming and laborious system, and it was not long before the Board adopted a simpler method. In 1879 the standard for exemption was set at a pass in Standard IV, with the very important proviso that the child must attend evening school until he had managed to pass Standard V. Two years later it became the rule that any child who had passed Standard V could be exempted from attendance at a day school, and any child of twelve years who had passed

---

[1] Rev John Stark, *Suggestions as to the Amendment of the Education (Scotland) Act*, 1872.
[2] William Mitchell, School Attendance Committee Report, 1896.

Standard IV could obtain exemption on condition that he attended an evening school till he had reached thirteen years of age or passed Standard V. Referring to this latter class of child who was granted exemption even although he had not passed the statutory Standard V, Mitchell said, "Here also expediency guides the Board. *Food must come before lessons.* In almost every case of such exemption it has been shown that home circumstances render a child's absence from Day School imperative. In not a few cases, an elder girl must be kept at home where little ones make her help indispensable. The casual employment of newspaper boys, milk boys, shoeblacks, and those who run with parcels brings in food to many a hungry family."[1]

In granting exemption to children who had passed Standard V the Board was but bowing to public opinion that this was as reasonable a standard of education as was needed by the individual and as much as should be demanded by the authorities. Whatever the law said many children left school after completing the Fifth Standard, and it is unlikely that they could have been compelled to remain. Very gradually there came a slight improvement. In 1890 very few left before the age of twelve, but as many as 3000 twelve-year-olds gained exemption.[2] Nearly ten years later Cuthbertson could still claim that the Fifth Standard was regarded by the public generally as enough, and that this feeling was common to all classes of society.[3] This can be seen in the following figures:

Age	Number at School	Percentage left school
10–11	12,685	
11–12	12,000	
12–13	9614	23%
13–14	5668	55%

Nearly a quarter of all children had left school before the leaving age of thirteen, while less than half stayed on after this age. The same trend can be looked at by taking the rolls in the Standards, which is more startling from the educational point of view, revealing, as it does, the very sharp drop after only five years of schooling.

[1] William Mitchell, *Twenty Years of Labour*, 1893.
[2] General Summary of Work: Triennial Reports 1882–1906.
[3] *Glasgow Herald*, 17 October 1898.

Numbers presented for examination	Standard	Percentage defaulting
8641	IV	
7216	V	16%
2725	VI	68%

The effect experienced by one school is shown in Table 22.

TABLE 22

NUMBERS PRESENTED AT KENNEDY STREET IN 1886

Standard I	150 pupils
,, II	175 ,,
,, III	126 ,,
,, IV	150 ,,
,, V	96 ,,
,, VI	26 ,,

In spite of all the difficulties of enforcing attendance the Board in 1898 decided by nine votes to four to press for the raising of the leaving age to fourteen. This was accomplished in the Education Act of 1901. The Act retained provision for exemption but left the power of exemption entirely to the discretion of school boards. Straightway Glasgow decided on a much firmer policy than in the past and agreed "not to grant exemption as heretofore",[1] but to do so only in very exceptional circumstances.

Thereafter, matters seem to have improved remarkably. In 1909 a government inquiry was held into exemption, and when asked if there had been any considerable outcry in Glasgow when the School Board refused to exempt children any longer, an independent witness testified: "In Glasgow there has been none. I have been surprised myself at the extent to which the people in Glasgow kept their children at school until 14 without applying for exemption at 13. In Glasgow last year there were over 100,000 children in the schools . . . and only 104 children were exempted during the year . . . and only 7 were under 13 . . . so exemption of any kind before 14 scarcely exists."[2]

In this respect Glasgow was easily the most progressive of of the major Boards in Scotland as Table 23 (page 186) shows.

[1] Minutes of Board in Committee, 19 August 1901.
[2] Report of Inter-Departmental Committee on Partial Exemption from School Attendance, 1909.

TABLE 23

EXEMPTIONS IN SCOTLAND[1]

	Year	Number on School Roll	Exempted conditionally	Exempted unconditionally	% of number on Roll
Scotland	1906		5875	2322	1·02
Glasgow	1906	100,861	120	None	·12
Govan	1907	37,500	194	None	·51
Paisley	1907	14,149	152	None	1·07
Aberdeen	1907	30,000	256	None	0·83
Dundee	1905	27,584	446	3	1·63

Casual Employment

One of the curses of the times was the extent to which children engaged in part-time employment outside school. The most extreme form of this was the Half-time System where, in reality, work came first and school only a very poor second. There were, however, many other forms of employment which could be undertaken after normal school hours. Street trading of all kinds was common: selling matches, newspapers and similar goods. Delivery carts needed boys and shops wanted message boys.

Within limits no one thought such employment need be condemned—certainly not the School Board—but, of course, moderation was often lacking, and the need of the family for money frequently resulted in the child working far longer and far later than was good for his health, his welfare and his schooling. In 1877 the Board tried to get the government to introduce into the Factory and Workshop Bill clauses regulating the casual employment of children. They failed, but the following year succeeded in having the new Education Act amended to include such provision. Children under ten were not allowed to offer anything for sale on streets, and no child under fourteen was allowed to be casually employed after 7 o'clock in winter or 9 in summer.

The law was difficult to enforce, but a genuine attempt to do so was made. On two nights a week attendance officers in plain clothes patrolled the streets taking the names of offenders. A number of convictions went some way towards bringing about improvement, though 400 to 500 offences continued to be recorded annually. Prosecutions had to be instigated by the

[1] Report of Inter-Departmental Committee on Partial Exemption from School Attendance, 1909, Appendix IV.

School Board under the Education Act, but the Protection of Children Act, 1889, made casual employment at night a direct police offence, and it became the duty of the police to co-operate with the Board in looking after the children. Any hope of improved results proved disappointing. Captain Boyd of the police admitted that he had not dealt very stringently with the matter, and when cases were brought up for prosecution the court often seemed disposed to deal lightly with them, and frequently dismissed the parents with a reprimand and admonition.[1]

While doing all that it could to prevent abuse the Board shared the view of the public at large that it was "... necessary to tolerate such casual employment out of school hours in the case of certain poor children, the circumstances of many families being such that the earnings of the children seem indispensable".[2] It was even possible to see some virtue in the necessity, "The children are better in many cases turning an honest penny in the streets than if they were confined to the unhealthy closes and dwellings where they generally reside."[3]

One of the provisions of the 1878 Act allowed exemption from school during six weeks in any one year. In part, this was designed to enable country children to help with harvesting and other such tasks on the farms. In Glasgow it meant the pantomime season at Christmas.

Child performers were a popular feature of pantomimes of the time. They formed tableaux, sang action songs about the "Jolly, jolly waggoners" or the "Merry, merry, fat boys", were reapers in the fields one moment and transformed the next into harmonious blacksmiths. A major attraction was the drill and maze marching. All this called for a lengthy period of training and rehearsal. It also implied pretty bright children, and so only the well-dressed and pleasant children of the tradesmen and artisan classes had any chance of being selected. Nearly all the performers were girls for they were much more amenable than boys and could easily be made up to take a male part when necessary.

---

[1] William Mitchell, Remarks on the Seventeenth Annual Report of the School Attendance Committee, 1890.

[2] William Mitchell, School Attendance Committee Report, 1891.

[3] William Mitchell, Remarks on Dealing with Neglected Children, School Board Records, 1881.

In certain schools an excited stir among the children began about the middle of November. Soon the lucky ones had been picked by the stage manager and rehearsals begun. They started about five weeks before Christmas and lasted for three or four hours every evening. No wage was given during this training, but the 3/6d a week paid during the theatre season was a godsend to many a family.

Mitchell made it his business to tour the theatres both during rehearsals and performances. He found on the whole that the children were well looked after and kindly treated and that they thoroughly enjoyed the experience. Yet he was perturbed. While admitting that he found little or no evidence that any real harm had come to the children he could not but believe that the world of the peripatetic theatre was potentially dangerous to their morals, especially as so many of them were girls. Bad language was commonplace. The experience of the police confirmed that theatreland provided them with much business. And there was the effect on the children of the unhealthy excitement of the bright lights, the gay dresses and the applause. "The whole tendency of such a life is to unsettle the minds and hearts of children, to turn them aside from any deep interest in the routine of ordinary duties. School becomes more irksome, lessons more neglected. The trades and occupations around them, which they have been intending to follow appear distasteful and insipid, a mirage of bright hopes and vain imaginations flits before their youthful eyes . . . they are petted and encouraged, and it need not be surprising if they imbibe impressions which are not healthful, and long to follow an occupation so seductive."[1]

Mitchell therefore wished to see school boards refuse to grant exemption for pantomime children. Nevertheless, he was not himself to fly in the teeth of established custom, and Glasgow found it served the interests of the children best by permitting the practice while retaining a measure of control. "In dealing with the question it has been the experience of the Board that *some things are expedient though they may not be desirable.* The view taken by the Board has been that it is better to grant certain exemptions, because thereby all children so employed up to 14 years of age are under strict regulations, whereas, by

[1] William Mitchell, *Rescue the Children*, p 71.

refusing to grant exemptions to younger children and abandoning the field, girls from 11 to 14 who had passed the 5th Standard would still be employed without the consent of the Board being required, and would thus be under no regulations whatever."[1]

About a hundred children took part in the pantomimes each year, most of them from Standards IV, V, or VI. The Board gave its reluctant consent only on condition that the theatre managers adhered to the following regulations:

1 The names, ages, and addresses of children proposed to be employed were stated.

2 The date to be specified when such proposed employment, including rehearsals, will begin, and also the date when such employment will terminate.

3 The hours to be defined for which application for exemption on behalf of the children is requested, and in no case will employment be sanctioned later than ten o'clock at night.

4 The children must not be employed during the day till one hour after the close of the afternoon school attendance.

5 A person must be named who shall have special responsibility for the reception, treatment, and dismissal of the children during the period of employment.

6 A meal to be provided for the children during or at the close of their employment each evening.[2]

Cripple Children

There had long existed within and around the City many philanthropic agencies which catered for the blind, the deaf and dumb, the imbecile and the deformed, and with these bodies the School Board co-operated to the fullest possible degree. Soon most of them included representatives of the Board on their own boards of management. Large numbers of hitherto unknown cases were brought to light by the attendance officers, and then passed on to the appropriate society. Only then was it realised that there was a numerous class of infirm

[1] School Attendance Committee Report, 1882.
[2] *ibid.*

children for whom no suitable provision existed—paralytics and children seriously crippled from a variety of diseases. The misfortune of these children was greatly aggravated by the wretched state of their homes since they generally came from families living in abject poverty, a poverty which had often been the actual cause of the disease as in the case of rickets which was tragically common.

As soon as he realised the need Mitchell set about establishing a Home for infirm children. He issued a heartrending appeal for funds, sought and obtained the support of leading citizens, and within a very short time was able to buy a small property on the outskirts of the City. It stood in the garden suburb of Maryhill where its patients, brought from the dingiest slums of the City, could find a more tolerable sickbed amid greenery and in clean western air.

In this way was born the East Park Home.[1] Its foundation was entirely due to the initiative and concern of the School Board and to Mitchell in particular. Alexander Whitelaw, the first Chairman of the School Board, became the first Chairman of East Park Home. Mitchell retained a deep interest in East Park throughout his life, and today the town office of the Home is Mitchell's old business office in Waterloo Street.

Day Industrial Schools

"The problem of how to deal with juvenile delinquency in Glasgow has been a hard one, because of the nature of the people, their habits, and their environment. The City has grown rapidly during the last half century, and those who have come into it have come largely from Ireland and the Highlands. Many have not lived in any very advanced state of civilisation at home, and have had primitive ideas of cleanliness and comfort. When removed from the restraints of home, and lost in a Glasgow slum, they are apt to sink to very low depths indeed. . . . The Irish, the Highlanders, and even the lowland Scots have not been noted in the past for respect for law and order."[2] So said the Chairman of the School Board in 1914.

The more serious cases of juvenile criminal were committed

---

[1] It opened in September 1874 and had 30 beds.
[2] Committee of Enquiry on Reformatory and Industrial Schools in Scotland, 1915. Evidence of Robt S Allan, p 246.

to one of the residential Industrial Schools; boys to Mossbank and girls to Maryhill. These institutions were run by the Glasgow Juvenile Delinquency Board, a quasi-public body, whose members were selected by the Corporation. The School Board was invariably invited to be represented on the Board. Once a child entered an industrial school he was no longer the responsibility of the School Board.

However, the major part of juvenile delinquency consisted of very trifling misdemeanors such as stone-throwing or petty thieving, and it was a great problem to know how to deal with them. They often originated in truancy which, in turn, was usually traceable to inadequate supervision at home. At their Default Meetings the School Board soon realised that there were many homes where the parents simply could not be expected to exercise a proper care and control of their children. A common instance was the home with only one parent. Whether widow or widower they had to go out to work, leaving the children to fend for themselves from 6 o'clock in the morning to 6 or 7 at night. Another example of this class was the deserted wife, a distressingly common feature of Glasgow where it was so easy for a man to take ship abroad. The Scot was well known for his itchy feet, but while his exploratory propensities benefited the outposts of the Empire they as often as not brought disaster to his wife and children.

In England the Day Industrial School system was established by the Education Act of 1876. It had not been put to very great use there, but the Glasgow School Board thought that it saw in the Day Industrial School a device which would admirably suit those neglected and potentially delinquent children. However, it had no wish to enter the field of delinquency itself, but just at this time the Town Council was promoting a new Bill for the better organisation of industrial schools in Glasgow and the Board managed to persuade them to write in a clause permitting the establishment of Day Industrial Schools.[1] The Bill became law in 1878.[2]

---

[1] William Mitchell, *Twelve Years' Experience of Day Industrial Schools in Glasgow*, 1892.

[2] Glasgow Juvenile Delinquency Prevention & Repression Act, 1878. Until the Day Industrial Schools Act (Scotland), 1898 extended the provision to the rest of Scotland, Glasgow remained the only place with such schools.

The first Day Industrial School opened in 1879 in Green Street in the Calton, followed by Rottenrow (1882), Rose Street (1889), William Street and Hopehill Road.[1] The venture was a joint one by the School Board and the Delinquency Board. The buildings, for example, were provided by the School Board and then leased to the Delinquency Board at a nominal rent of 1/– or so.[2] The school was either converted from an old Board school[3] or built specially for the purpose.[4] While the superintendent was appointed and paid by the Delinquency Board the teachers were supplied by the School Board.[5]

The process of committal was normally instigated by the School Board which was well acquainted with the case through its default meetings. The boy or girl was brought to the notice of the Delinquency Board and then taken before a magistrate. The wording of the Act required that the child had been "found wandering", or was out of control or was being neglected by the parents. But in practice the Board used the Day Industrial School less as a form of punishment for, or protection from, some wrong done than as a school where children could be looked after. Usually no difficulty was experienced in getting the magistrates to commit a child, even when no actual offence had been committed, for the parents were only too glad to come forward and ask, "In order that our minds may be at ease, will you commit this child?"[6] This straining of the law led to the suspicion that these schools were being used as a surreptitious means of feeding poor children at public expense (thirty years before the Schools Meals Act) and, although it was denied by the boards, the likelihood must remain.

The schools opened their doors at 6 o'clock in the morning to receive the children as parents went off to work. They were looked after by the janitor until lessons began at 8.30. The child could stay at school till 6 pm, and on Saturday till 1 o'clock.

---

[1] Each school held about 250 children.
[2] Reformatory and Industrial Schools Enquiry: Evidence of Robt S Allan, para 6665.
[3] Green St, Rottenrow and William Street.
[4] Rose St and Hopehill Rd.
[5] William Mitchell, *Twelve Years' Experience of Day Industrial Schools in Glasgow*. Allan, however, says the teachers were provided by the Delinquency Board and, in consequence, were often uncertificated (Reformatory and Industrial Schools Enquiry, para 6719).
[6] Reformatory and Industrial Schools Enquiry, para 6695.

They were given three free meals a day; porridge and milk for breakfast, broth with peas and bread, or cheese and bread and milk for dinner, tea or cocoa with bread and butter or dripping for tea. Such fare was a godsend to poor children, but it sometimes had drawbacks for ". . . it is a curious fact that the children on the day they get pea soup for dinner never do their sums nearly so well".[1] Clothing was regularly provided for the needy by charity organisations. Parents were supposed to contribute about 1/– a week but often were quite unable to do so.

Mitchell was a mighty advocate of the virtues of the Day Industrial Schools. He praised them for being such a help to parents, citing the case of one widower who moved lodgings so that his children could go to Rose Street. He saw it as a place where children for much of the day were removed from squalid and potentially evil environments and placed under the care of kindly women to be trained in regular habits, respectful manners, good conduct, the Bible and moral lessons. A curious feature of the schools was that they were staffed entirely by women, and this as a matter of deliberate policy. "The effect of the female influence upon the boys is marvellous. They have not been much accustomed to the law of kindness. They know something of hard knocks and hard words and hard times, and the new atmosphere into which they are brought is to them like a new life. The most rebellious, stubborn natures are subdued, and truants and vagrants hitherto unmanageable have in most cases become quite reformed."[2]

The Day Industrial Schools served a most useful social purpose. Unfortunately, there was a poverty-stricken class of child which they did not reach at all, the Roman Catholics. By law the Delinquency Board was empowered to deal only with Protestants. The Roman Catholic authorities did nothing to provide such schools themselves, almost certainly because they lacked the money. Many School Board members felt that Catholic children should receive equal treatment with Protestant, and after much discussion it was decided to open Govan Street School as a Day Industrial School for Roman Catholics.[3]

[1] John Morison—in a speech at a Conference of Managers of Reformatories and Industrial Institutions. Glasgow, 1890 (p 78 of Proceedings).
[2] William Mitchell, *Twelve Years' Experience of Day Industrial Schools in Glasgow.*
[3] In 1908.

G

No great religious difficulties appear to have been met with, and the Church authorities seem to have accepted the arrangement gladly, presumably because only Catholic children were present and the staff also were Catholic. However, when the Board proposed to turn over a second of their schools for the same purpose the old religious bigotry of Glasgow burst forth in full fury. Cranstonhill School was one of the old church buildings which had been transferred to the School Board in terms of the original Act. But the congregation had retained certain privileges such as using the buildings for meetings. They refused to allow its use by Catholics, and the affair was only settled by an action in the Court of Session, which the School Board won.[1]

The Catholic Day Industrial Schools are an interesting phenomenon for they were the first Catholic Day Schools to be under the control of a public education authority. It seems probable that the amity which existed between the School Board and the Church in the joint running of these schools helped pave the way to the 1918 Education Act and Roman Catholic Public Schools.

Lack of money had always prevented Catholic children from getting as good facilities as their Protestant contemporaries who drew on public funds, and among the most unfortunate were the physical and mentally defective. When Govan Street and Cranstonhill were opened the opportunity was taken of utilising several of the classrooms in both schools for the education of such handicapped children.[2] Of course, the arrangement was far from ideal but it did fill a great need. It is worth noting that these schools were not a consequence of the 1908 Children's Act. Govan Street was opened, and Cranstonhill planned, by the Board before the Act was passed.

The Truant School

The Day Industrial School catered, among others, for the incipient truant, the type of boy who truanted largely because there was no one at home to get him up in the morning and otherwise look after him. There was another class of truant

---

[1] W Martin Haddow, *My Seventy Years*, p 19.
[2] Cranstonhill had 130 Day Industrial pupils and 80 Defectives.

altogether; the boy who deliberately, systematically, and continually dodged school. Truancy was so prevalent in Glasgow at the turn of the century that the School Board finally decided to take exceptional measures against it by establishing a special short-term residential school.

It is perhaps significant that the decision to build a Truant School coincided with the retiral of Mitchell after close on thirty years' service with the Board. Although the new policy was following a tougher line than before yet the Truant School was, in one sense, intended as a relatively mild form of correction, for previously the only institution available for incorrigible truants was the long-term industrial school to which a child was generally committed until sixteen.

As truant schools had been operating in England for some time the Board sent deputations to London and Liverpool to see how the system worked. They returned to Glasgow convinced of its efficacy, and accordingly a good large site was purchased at Springboig in Shettleston. There was nothing institutional or forbidding about the fine building which was put up, complete with dormitories, classrooms, workshops, dining-room, spray bath, gymnasium and swimming pool. The School had accommodation for 160 boys and it was intended that it should be available to all school boards in the West of Scotland.[1] The School was opened in 1905.[2]

A boy was committed to the Truant School until he reached the age of fourteen. In practice, however, the School Board always let out the boy on licence after three months. Any backsliding in attendance after that would result in recommittals for four and then six months. Thereafter a boy would probably be transferred to Mossbank.

The workday was divided evenly between ordinary classroom subjects and industrial training in the workshops where the boys learned carpentry, tailoring, bootmaking and gardening. All boys followed a half-time regimen, even those as young as seven years of age, although the very small boys helped the sewing maid with darning and such-like tasks.

[1] Reformatory and Industrial Schools Enquiry, Evidence of Haddow, p 275.
[2] After the passing of the Children's Act, 1908, the official title of the school was that of a Short-Term Industrial School. But popularly it continued to be called just the Truant School.

On their visit to Liverpool the Board had found that "When the truant arrived he was sent to an underground room—to all intents a dungeon—for a week or so, fed on bread and water and left there to ruminate over his sins. Such treatment of young boys in Christian England was beyond belief, and needless to say the deputation was determined that such treatment would not form part of our method of reform."[1] On the other hand the School Board did intend to make sure that the new school would act as a deterrent and a form of punishment. "With a rigidly sane appreciation of the fact that truant schools are for the reception of a class of children that have deliberately placed themselves outside the pale of ordinary life . . . discipline is essentially more severe than that practised in ordinary schools."[2] And the erring boy soon discovered that "discipline which is essentially more severe" could mean a strapping on the bare bottom.[3]

And it seems to have produced the desired effect. At any rate, the Board members thought so. "One point I would like to make more strongly than anything else is the good work of, and the absolute necessity of, maintaining our truant school in Glasgow. It deals with the boy who is going to go to the bad, and it sifts him out, and in most of our cases three months at the school is a cure. Another three months cure 50% of the remainder, and it would be an absolute disaster to Glasgow to be deprived of that method of dealing. It acts as a moral tonic, and turns hundreds of boys who would go wrong and prevents the necessity of sending them away to a long-term industrial school."[4] In case it should be thought that Allan, a Chairman of the Board, was a reactionary bourgeois it should be noted that Martin Haddow, a leading socialist and one of the first socialist members of the Board, was equally enthusiastic; ". . . the number of boys absent from school now on account of truancy is much smaller than it was . . . the arrangements by which boys are taken in hand at once, and dealt with by being detained in the short-term school, is most beneficial. It is

---

[1] W Martin Haddow, *My Seventy Years*, p 84.
[2] Allan as reported in the *Glasgow Herald*, 19 November 1901.
[3] General Rules and Regulations for the Management of the Glasgow Short Term Industrial School. Rule XI (b) (i).
[4] Reformatory and Industrial Schools Enquiry, Evidence of Allan, para 6702.

interesting to note that last year in 66% of the cases sent to the school for the first detention proved to be satisfactory . . . in the case of the other 30% two detentions were necessary. It is also found that committing confirmed truants to the school has an excellent effect on a number of other scholars by acting as a deterrent to those who are likely to give trouble by absenting themselves from the ordinary schools."[1]

Liverpool and Glasgow were cities which had much in common, not least their large Irish-Catholic populations and the consequent religious antipathy between Catholic and Protestant. The division between the two groups was nowhere more rigidly maintained than in the separation of their children at school. The Liverpool truant school reflected the whole tragi-comedy. The building consisted of two wings which were divided by a long wall separating Catholic from Protestant. The only place common to both was a washhouse at the end of the building. It had two doors, one opening on the Catholic side, the other on the Protestant side. On the weekly bath night one door was locked while the "other side" used the room.[2] In this way, although within a single building, Catholic and Protestant were kept from contaminating each other.

It was the Glasgow School Board's intention that their new Truant School also should accommodate children of both denominations, but there the resemblence to Liverpool was to end. The Shettleston school had no dividing wall. Indeed, boys of both religions were fully integrated. They wore the same dress, swam together in the same swimming pool, worked together in the same classrooms, played together in the same playground. And in the dining hall they even sang the same grace—one which had been agreed upon by priest and minister. Only at morning prayers and on Sundays did the boys go their separate ways under teachers of their own persuasion.

In the climate of the times the religious integration of the Truant School was a daring and courageous venture, and one that says much for the good sense and mutual confidence of the School Board and the Catholic Authorities. The Board thought it a great success, claiming there had been absolutely no complaints. "There has not been the slightest friction either

[1] Reformatory and Industrial Schools Enquiry, Evidence of Haddow, p 275.
[2] W Martin Haddow, *My Seventy Years*, p 84.

with teachers, pupils, or parents."[1] Perhaps we have regressed: today the old Truant School is St John's Approved School for Roman Catholic boys.[2]

<h2 style="text-align:center">CONCLUSION</h2>

In the beginning there were three parts to the problem of school attendance facing the Board; the physical one of providing enough schools to accommodate the extra thousands of pupils, the wretched and perplexing social conditions which encouraged or even necessitated absenteeism, and the deliberate evaders whether parent or boy.

In due time the rapid school building programme satisfied the need for places.

Unemployment, poverty, slum housing and disease were factors beyond the control of a school board to remedy. But it could and did try to alleviate their effects and, indeed, the way in which the Board was compelled to acknowledge the primary need for social improvements was perhaps more important than the enforcement of attendance in itself. Glasgow, with other boards throughout Britain, acted as a catalyst for much of the social legislation of the time.

That the problem of persuading or forcing antipathetic or incompetent parents to see to the regular attendance of their children was not completely solved need bring no censure, for it is doubtful if we succeed any better today. Some schools still expend much time and energy in curbing truancy, Glasgow still has to employ over one hundred attendance officers, parents still aid and abet their children to absent themselves on the flimsiest excuses, it still takes months before a prosecution is made, boys still get up at 3 o'clock in the morning to deliver milk.

Commenting on the general improvement in attendance throughout Scotland an inspector said, "Of the Glasgow Board this is certainly true, and few, if any, Boards in Scotland have such a Herculean labour to face. One who has visited the fine

---

[1] Reformatory and Industrial Schools Enquiry, Evidence of Haddow, para 7377.

[2] Glasgow's Truant School was the only one in Scotland.

schools in those grim streets that fringe the great arteries of traffic, and has seen the pale, pinched, and joyless faces of the children can form some idea of the difficulties of the situation."[1] Glasgow's responses to the situation were firm yet kindly and largely successful.

[1] Committee of Council for Education in Scotland, 1897, p 6.

Chapter 10

THE PUPIL TEACHER

The importance of the pupil-teacher system inherited by the school boards was twofold; it was virtually the only source of recruitment for the teaching profession, and without pupil teachers the schools could scarcely have been run at all. Until standards of entry into teaching had become much higher, and until the size of classes had become much smaller, the pupil teacher remained an indispensable part of the educational scene.

In Glasgow there were as many pupil teachers as there were all other teachers put together.[1] Their value is most easily appreciated by looking at their place within a school and then within one classroom. When Thomson Street had 1029 pupils on its register and an average attendance of 900, the adult staff comprised five women and five men including the headmaster.[2] Each teacher therefore had a hundred or more children to cope with. Clearly it was an almost impossible task. It was in circumstances like this that the pupil teacher proved such an asset. A fourteen-year-old boy or girl could help in all sorts of useful ways; give out books, hear the reading round a section of the class, write up work on the blackboard, correct exercises and so on. Thomson Street had fourteen pupil teachers for such necessary work.

Of course, as the pupil teacher was often little or no older than other children at the top end of the school, he was less useful

[1] eg, in 1880 the number of teachers was 319 and the number of pupil teachers 3 *School Statistics*, 1880.

[2] *School Statistics*, 1880.
There was nothing unusual about Thomson Street in this matter.
Other typical examples were:

School	Adult Staff		Pupil Teachers		On register	Average attendance
	Men	Women	Boys	Girls		
Rockvilla	4	1	4	4	658	507
Kennedy St	4	4	3	4	869	602
Garnethill	6	5	1	7	1220	850

there, for his own knowledge was scarcely greater and discipline much more difficult. For these and other reasons pupil teachers tended to be concentrated in the younger classes, a practice continually deplored by both Education Department and School Board, but it went on just the same. It was especially prevalent in the infant classes. That stage in school life which is thought so important today was then little regarded. Little was expected and little was demanded. In Grove Street School Standard I had an average attendance of 164 six- and seven-year-olds.[1] No doubt the sole mistress was glad enough of her three pupil teachers.

The pupil teacher led a hard life and many did not stay the course. In Glasgow they went to school before 8 o'clock, "and were taught and crammed with subjects for the yearly examinations by the second master or senior teachers of the school".[2] Then after their normal working day at school they remained behind for further instruction until about 5 o'clock.

In 1881 the Board instituted a Committee on Pupil Teachers which investigated all aspects of the system and brought in some improvements. The standard of entry was raised to a pass in Standard VI and one or more specific subjects. Glasgow, always having more applicants than it needed, was thus able to move ahead of national qualification requirements, and was thereafter always the leader in improvements and developments within the pupil-teacher system.[3]

Recognising that too much was being demanded of the pupil teacher the Board now abandoned the extra instruction of pupil teachers immediately before and after school hours. Instead they attended Central Classes[4] on two evenings a week and on Saturday mornings. Besides easing the strain somewhat on the boys and girls, concentration of instruction had other advantages; many teachers in the ordinary schools were relieved of the task of tutoring their pupil teachers, the Central Classes enabled the Board to exercise a firmer control of the curriculum and to select teachers best qualified to instruct the advanced subjects of mathematics, analysis, Latin and French. It became possible, too, to organise special courses in the more

[1] *School Statistics*, 1881.
[2] W Martin Haddow, *My Seventy Years*, p 14.
[3] *cf* Scotch Code.
[4] Girls attended at the City School, boys at Kay School.

G*

"professional" subjects, such as elocution and geography, which would be helpful when teaching.

The scheme was thought a grand success and was highly commended to other boards by the Department. Soon Glasgow was placing less and less emphasis on the pupil teacher as a cheap source of teaching power. She[1] taught only half the day, either in the morning or the afternoon, and joined the ordinary classes at other times. Sixteen became the minimum age of acceptance,[2] although this limitation was not always adhered to.

Of course, not everyone was pleased with the new system. A very sour article in *The School Monthly* warned parents against putting their child into teaching. True, the prospects might seem attractive at first sight—long holidays, a steady job, light and clean work—but years of drudgery had first to be suffered, for although the girl got out of school at 4 o'clock, she then had to go home and prepare lessons for the Central Classes three times[3] a week from 6–8 pm, ". . . getting as much work as keeps her busy after school hours each day until lesson night, when the same is repeated".[4] But even before this article appeared, the system it criticised had been replaced by a much better one.

The pupil teacher system in earlier days had been able to work reasonably well because the general level of education was very low. In the days when most children left school by the time they were twelve it was easy enough for the apprentice teacher, who of course stayed on, to outshine the other scholars in knowledge. In addition, the free instruction and the wage, however small, enabled her to finance her longer schooling. Throughout the eighties, however, the steady development of secondary education together with the bursaries which became available through the Educational Trusts meant that there was a new kind of scholar at school. Even if the pupil teacher did not actually teach in the secondary department the presence of other students there, perhaps better informed students, necessarily placed the pupil teacher in an awkward position. What was more, the boy or girl who had previously chosen

[1] In referring to pupil teachers I use the pronoun "she" as there were always about four times as many girls as boys. But in this context "she" includes "he".

[2] Committee of Council for Education in Scotland. Inspector's Report.

[3] By now a third evening had been added to enable the pupil teacher to take Science classes.

[4] *The School Monthly*, February 1893.

teaching as the only possible route to some degree of higher education, now found an alternative avenue opening up, one which might well offer a far better prize in the end.

Other forces also were operating to push up the standard of scholarship required by the pupil teacher; competition for entry into a training college was becoming fiercer, higher subjects were being added to the curriculum, and in 1892 the Leaving Certificate was thrown open to public schools. Finally the Code of the same year forced a reconsideration of prevailing methods of training.

From the beginning of the new school session in 1892 Glasgow's pupil teachers received all their lessons during the day instead of at night. The apprentice teacher was thus the first to move away from the weariness of evening school to the relative ease of day-release, a boon not enjoyed by apprentices in most other trades until after the second world war. The instruction was given in part of the City School which was set aside for the purpose and designated the " Pupil Teachers' Institute ".[1] Henceforth the pupil spent half her time on her duties at school and half her time on her lessons at the Institute. Her pay remained unaffected.

The Institute was well staffed. The Headmaster was assisted by two Mistresses, five Masters, three Teachers of Drawing, four of Science, three of Needlework and visiting Masters for Drawing, Elocution and Singing.[2] The table shows how classes were organised.[3]

| | Numbers in 1897 | | Number of | | Saturday |
Pupils	Boys	Girls	Hours/Week	Week days	Morning
Monitors	26	78	15	Every forenoon	No
1st Year	27	100	15	,, ,,	,,
2nd Year	32	107	12	3 forenoons	Yes
3rd Year	23	106	12	3 forenoons	,,
4th Year	19	94	9	2 half-days	,,

Glasgow's establishment of the Pupil Teachers' Institute was a most progressive measure. It caused considerable upset within the schools, and it was fairly costly as it meant the

[1] This accommodation soon proved inadequate and the Institute moved next door into the Highland Society School. When this building was demolished in 1902 to make way for the Technical College, Albany Academy became the Pupil Teachers' Institute.

[2] Triennial Report, 1897. Report of Committee on Pupil Teachers.

[3] *ibid.*

employment of many more pupil teachers to replace those no longer in the schools all day.[1] Yet the Board was glad to face these drawbacks in the conviction of having better trained teachers for the future. "This step marks an epoch in the training of teachers,"[2] said the inspector; "The Glasgow Board further lead the way in the action they have taken towards providing for the instruction of Pupil Teachers during the day, and, as a consequence, shortening to a proportionate extent their wearisome hours of teaching. This movement initiates a fundamental reform of the whole Pupil Teacher system. . . . It gives scholarship a chance alongside of training . . . and cannot fail to be an ultimate gain to education."[3]

And so it proved, as examination results were to show. "The Pupil Teachers' Institute in Glasgow is a splendid success. . . . The successes of the pupils attending this institute, both at the University and at the Queen's Scholarship Examination,[4] are certainly most striking and remarkable."[5] Year after year a Glasgow pupil, both among the male and female candidates, was placed first in the order of merit for the whole of Scotland at the Queen's Scholarship Examination. In 1896 Glasgow boys obtained nine out of the first twelve places. The girls got six out of the first ten.[6]

A number of other enlightened Boards followed Glasgow's example. Govan built a Pupil Teachers' Institute in the grounds of Bellahouston Academy and opened it in 1899. Several towns in Fife adopted the system, followed by Bo'ness and Linlithgow.[7] Edinburgh was tardy, not centralising her pupil teachers till 1904.[8]

One of the drawbacks of the scheme arose out of the need to recruit far more pupil teachers than formerly. As there were simply not enough candidates forthcoming the Board found it necessary to take the retrograde step of reducing the minimum age of entry for girls to fourteen. Previously a girl had not been

[1] See Appendix J, p 249.
[2] Committee of Council for Education in Scotland, 1892.
[3] *ibid*, 1893.
[4] ie, the entrance examination for the Training Colleges.
[5] Committee of Council for Education in Scotland, 1897–98. Report of Dr Stewart.
[6] Triennial Report, 1894. Pupil Teacher Committee.
[7] J D Wilson, "The Junior Student System", p 18. An EdB thesis, Glasgow University, 1964.
[8] *ibid*.

accepted until fifteen and unless she was able to pass the examination set for the end of the first year of training. However, this temporary expedient in no way lowered the scholastic standard demanded of the pupil teacher as the Board insisted on the maximum four years period of apprenticeship. Better qualified, and therefore older, pupil-teacher candidates were allowed to shorten their course. The possession of a Lower Grade Leaving Certificate lopped off a year, and a two-year course was possible on the strength of a Higher Grade Certificate,[1] but ". . . only candidates of exceptional ability will be admitted for the shortened periods".[2]

While some Theory of Teaching was undertaken in the Institute, training in the practical aspects of teaching continued to be done within the schools and was the responsibility of the headmaster. Not all headmasters found the time or had the inclination to give much attention to the pupil teachers, and in consequence methodical training often was neglected and the student had to get by merely on what he picked up by watching other teachers in action. And the models were not always of the best. In an attempt to improve matters the Board laid down a set of Regulations on the Practical Training of Pupil Teachers:[3]

> "1 *Notes of Lessons:* Pupil Teachers in their third and fourth years shall write out once a fortnight, in a book provided for that purpose, Notes of a Lesson to be prescribed by the Headmaster. These should be examined by the Headmaster, who will sign and date each exercise.
>
> 2 *Direction & Supervision of Methods of Teaching:* The Headmaster should carefully direct and supervise their methods of teaching. He should devote at least half-an-hour per week to each Pupil Teacher. This may be done either individually or collectively. On suitable occasions the Pupil Teachers should be collected together and a lesson given by one of them, which the others should afterwards be asked to criticise.
>
> 3 *Theory:* At the annual examination by H.M. Inspector and at the admission examination to Normal Schools questions are set in Knowledge of Method to Pupil Teachers. . . . The Board regret that so many of their Pupil Teachers are marked defective in

[1] These standards were considerably higher than those laid down in the Scotch Code.

[2] Report of Pupil Teacher Committee, 1894.

[3] Regulations for the Practical Training of Pupil Teachers, 1 September 1893.

this subject, and that so few of the boys gain the mark (S) at the admission examination. They do not think it is from want of ability on the part of the Pupil Teachers, but rather from want of practice in answering questions on the subject in writing.

4 *Report by Headmaster*: The Headmaster will be asked to furnish a report on the Pupil Teacher's ability as a teacher at the end of each year of the apprenticeship.

"The Board take this opportunity of impressing upon Headmasters the importance of seeing that Pupil Teachers have experience of the working of several departments of the School. Complaints have frequently been made that during their apprenticeship Pupil Teachers are almost entirely confined to the Infant Department, and they cannot be said to have had a thorough training if this has been the case."

Clearly, these regulations were directed at the headmaster to force him to pay some attention to his responsibility as the master craftsman training the apprentice. Generally, he found the pupil teachers rather a nuisance. Probably so did most of the class teachers, an attitude which might do much to explain why the pupil teachers were so often bundled down to the infants; there they were out of most people's way. For by now the pupil teacher was less of an asset in the classroom. At best he was only a half-timer, and classes were beginning to become a little smaller and more manageable, and public schools had settled down into a routine, a steady discipline and an accepted pattern. Classroom life was calm. The teacher could cope by herself. The pupil teacher then became just another extraneous bother. Indeed, the pupil teacher was already on her way out for she was not valued by the teachers.

In 1894 the Board petitioned the Department to make certain changes in the annual examination of pupil teachers. The examinations at the end of the first and third years should be abolished because they now served little useful purpose and tended to hold back the steady progress of teaching in order to revise and specially prepare for the examination. The second year examination should be more rigorous and a failure in it should bar a pupil teacher from continuing her course. Until now they could go on until failing twice to pass the Queen's Scholarship. The most important of the Board's recommendations was that pupil teachers should be permitted to take the

Leaving Certificate Examinations, a privilege which had been extended to all schools in 1892 but not to pupil teachers.

These proposals were incorporated in the Code of 1895, and in the following year pupil teachers took Leaving Certificates for the first time. The opening of the Leaving Certificate proved to be the greatest contribution to the standard of the work of pupil teachers and, "Now that the first and third years' examinations have been abolished, and the second year's papers are comparatively easy, the preparation for the Leaving Certificate examinations, which goes forward *pari passu* . . . gives the needed stimulus throughout the whole course of the apprenticeship".[1]

The Code now allowed for exemptions from the normal pupil teacher examinations: three Lower Grade passes (in main subjects) in the Leaving Certificate exempted from the second year apprenticeship examination; three Higher Grade passes were regarded as having passed the Queen's Scholarship examination in the First Class and so entitled a pupil teacher to enter straight into training college under Article 95.

From now on the Glasgow pupil teacher moved away from the old established path through her apprenticeship and concentrated more and more on the Leaving Certificate—while, of course, keeping up her professional subjects as well. Increasingly the pupil teachers' efforts and time were directed towards study. More time was spent at the Institute where all, and not only the younger pupil teachers, now spent half of *every* day. By 1900 a change in the Code limiting the number of hours a pupil teacher might spend in the day schools to twenty resulted in her not having to report into school until 10 o'clock. Thus she was devoting only a couple of hours a day to teaching duties. In fact, the Institute was really acting as a Secondary School, and its students followed a normal secondary course but with rather more subjects and with rather less time in which to do it all than was enjoyed by the general secondary school pupil.

These developments were bound to raise the questions, Is there any point in having a separate pupil teacher system at all? Would it not be just as well—or better—to put the boy or girl through the secondary school and only then take up the

[1] A Glasgow headmaster, quoted in Committee of Council on Education in Scotland, Report of Dr Stewart, Appendix A, 1898.

matter of professional training? Certainly neither the schools nor the pupil teachers were gaining much advantage from the present arrangements. Relays of pupil teachers for only two hours at a time did not delight a class teacher's heart. The pupil teacher, for her part, gained nothing in monetary terms, for her free tuition and wages were little more than she would have received from a School Bursary from the Educational Trusts.[2] Already there was a definite trend in Glasgow towards a longer school career followed by a shorter apprenticeship. In 1897, for example, forty-three pupil-teacher candidates, eleven of whom were boys, entered on a Two-Year Course, and forty-one of them had already obtained the Leaving Certificate.[3]

TABLE 24

LEAVING CERTIFICATE PASSES[1]

	Honours	Higher	Lower	Total
1896		108	185	293
1899	5	171	296	472
1902	6	269	207	482

The efficiency and excellence of Glasgow's pupil teacher training is readily seen from the figures in Table 24. The figures show a clear increase in absolute terms, and this increase is in fact greater than it appears as the number of pupil teachers in the city in 1902 was almost 200 fewer than in 1896. Then, too, the proportion of Higher passes has improved markedly.

TABLE 25

QUEEN'S (KING'S) SCHOLARSHIP RESULTS[4]

	Young Men				Young Women			
	1st	Passed 2nd	3rd		1st	Passed 2nd	3rd	
Year	Class	Class	Class	Failed	Class	Class	Class	Failed
1893	7	9	10	4	37	57	35	10
1895	9	6	1	1	27	44	21	8
1897	20	1			60	49	6	
1899	25	4			71	50	7	
1901	26	1			43	25	7	
1903	19	6			85	8		

[1] Committee on Pupil Teachers: Annual Reports.
[2] Always provided that her father's income was low enough.
[3] Committee of Council on Education in Scotland, Appendix A, 1898.
[4] Committee on Pupil Teachers: Annual Reports.

Similarly good results were won at the Queen's (after 1901 the King's) Scholarship Examination, and particularly noticeable is the beneficial effect of Day Instruction once it had had a year or two to work its magic (Table 25).

The Code of 1906 completely recast the whole system of teacher training. Pupil teachers were to be phased out and replaced in the schools by a new breed—the Junior Student.

The new regulations were a recognition that the old system had largely failed to produce teachers of suitable calibre in sufficient numbers, and were an attempt by the Department to force backward Boards into appropriate action for the better. "In 1904 14% of all the teachers in Scotland . . . were uncertificated, their number varying with the area and its attractiveness—from 11% of the school staff in Edinburgh to 24% in Linlithgow, and even more in Berwickshire and the Highlands."[1] Many of the uncertificated, and therefore untrained, were ex-pupil teachers who, for one reason or another, had failed to gain entry to the training college. These people, being cheap, were readily employed by impecunious or thoughtless Boards.

None of these strictures applied to Glasgow. From the very first it had set its face against employing ex-pupil teachers except on a very brief and temporary basis, and even that concession was purely out of consideration for the pupil teacher so that he might have another chance at the College examination. The uncertificated teacher simply did not exist in the Glasgow Board schools. That this was to the credit of the Board rather than to any magnetic attractiveness of the area is clear from the remarks of an inspector. "The School Board of Glasgow shows wise restraint in using untrained teachers. In its schools in my district there are only eight untrained teachers as against two hundred and eight who have attended a training college. In the suburban parishes[2] in the public schools there are seventeen untrained and forty-eight trained teachers. In the Roman Catholic schools I find twenty-four untrained and fourteen trained teachers."[3] There can be no doubt that

[1] J D Wilson, "The Junior Student System", p 37.
[2] The parishes are not named, but probably were Maryhill and Springburn, and perhaps Shettleston.
[3] Committee of Council on Education in Scotland, Inspector's Report, 1903.

Glasgow's fine pupil-teacher training methods were a major factor in enabling the city to recruit fully qualified teachers, and the new Code regulations introduced little that was new for Glasgow in practical terms.

The junior student had first to obtain the Intermediate Certificate, after which she would follow a two and a half year course at a recognised centre, which would usually be a secondary school registered as such by the Department. Teaching practice and her own studies were to continue concurrently, but greater emphasis than before was to be placed on the junior student's own schooling. The student would receive her certificate at the end of her course provided her record was satisfactory. She then proceeded to training college. After a necessary period for adjustment no uncertificated teacher would be allowed in schools.[1]

For Glasgow the transition from pupil teacher to junior student scarcely caused a ripple. Some pupil teachers worked out their indentures in the old way, the others changed their title and moved into the secondary departments. The Pupil Teachers' Institute closed in 1908.

Not all Boards accepted the Code so readily. In particular, Edinburgh, already angry with the Department for having been compelled to centralise its pupil-teacher training, voted against the proposals and organised a protest meeting. Edinburgh thought the pupil-teacher system served well enough.[2]

Inevitably the junior student scheme had its teething troubles. The most serious was a difference of view between the Department and some of the Boards as to the exact relationship between a junior student and an ordinary secondary pupil. The Department regarded the junior student as first and foremost a budding elementary school teacher. As such there was no need for her to spend a great deal of time on the higher reaches of languages, mathematics or even English. On the other hand, a fair proportion of her time-table ought to include singing, needlework, science and nature study as well as the theory and practice of teaching. Many Boards, led by Glasgow, did not accept that the junior students were marked out for teaching at

---

[1] Code of 1906.
[2] For a full account of Edinburgh's attitude see J D Wilson, *op cit*, pp 58–68.

the elementary stage only. Rather they should be encouraged and assisted to go on to university if possible, and even those proceeding straight to training college certainly ought not to do so with an inferior academic background, thereby lowering the status of primary teachers in particular and the teaching profession in general. In this view junior students should pass through the secondary school in the ordinary way and complete their course with a Leaving Certificate. This, of course, required a heavy emphasis on languages and mathematics. The Boards had two strong allies; the Educational Institute of Scotland, which was already pressing for an all-graduate profession, and the students themselves, especially the boys, whose ambitions stretched as far as their talents might conceivably take them.

For a few years many junior students struggled to satisfy both the requirements of the Department and the demanding syllabus of the Leaving Certificate. The result often was exhaustion. While it was clear to all parties that such over-pressure of work was bad, neither side in the dispute was prepared to alter its stand. The Department continued to demand conformity with the regulations; the antagonistic Boards never ceased to press for some suitable form of amendment.

A special committee of the Glasgow School Board was set up to consider Circular 437 which gave effect to the new regulations. The report of the committee was wholly uncompromising.

"It is inexpedient that anything should be done to lower the standard of scholarship of Junior Students, or to segregate them from other Secondary pupils. This standard should continue to be such as to enable Junior Students to enter the University at the end of their course should they so desire. Even where they do not aim at a University course, and where it is their intention to proceed to Elementary School teaching, there is not any adequate reason for their preliminary education being on a lower level than that required for other professions.

"It is not possible to maintain the present standards on the condition laid down in Section 2 of the Circular, which, moreover, is contrary to the spirit of the Junior Student system in respect that it differentiates between the Junior Student and other secondary pupils."[1]

[1] High School and Secondary Education Committee minutes, 14 December 1910.

Six months later the Board was still petitioning the Department: "I am directed to impress strongly upon the Department the desirability of withdrawing Circular 437",[1] but officialdom continued to demand the submission of the Board's proposed curriculum for junior students based on the recommendations of the Circular. Failure to offer an acceptable syllabus would result in the withdrawal of the grant.

Yet another special committee, the Sub-Committee on the Junior Student Curriculum, spent several months preparing the Board's answer without conceding anything to the Department. The outcome of these deliberations was the submission of a time-table which was as traditionally academic as could be.[2] Out of a thirty-five period week no less than thirty would go to English and history, mathematics, French and a secondary language. It was, in fact, a more extreme expression of the Board's view than proposals it had accepted only eighteen months earlier.

The Department's reply made it quite clear that the time-table was unacceptable,[3] and the point had now been reached where Glasgow must either bow to the Government's wishes or sacrifice the Junior Student grant. There was, however, an alternative course by which the Board could adopt its own curriculum at the cost of a lower grant rate.[4] This was to train the junior students under Article 15(b) of the Code which provided for entry to the training colleges by way of a full group Leaving Certificate followed by six months teaching practice.

To Glasgow the principle of insisting on scholarly teachers seemed worth the financial sacrifice involved, and it was resolved "that the Board should adhere to curricula sent up to the Department, adopt Article 15(b) of Regulations for Training of Teachers, and suggest that Headmasters communicate with pupils regarding the change".[5] A few months later the Glasgow lead was followed by Govan.

And so from 1912 nothing remained in Glasgow of the

[1] High School and Secondary Education Committee minutes, 28 June 1911.
[2] Appendix K, p 250.
[3] Letter to Board from Scotch Education Department, 16 August 1912.
[4] Junior students would receive the grant of an ordinary secondary pupil instead of the higher rate normally paid for junior students.
[5] Sub-Committee on the Junior Student Curriculum minutes, 4 September 1912.

pupil-teacher system. The city had made great use of pupil teachers in the earlier years but, as it built up a good supply of qualified teachers (a substantial number of these graduates), as classes gradually became smaller, and as secondary education developed, the Board turned more and more to providing its pupil teachers with an ever sounder basic schooling. The monetary cost was readily borne, as was the upset to school routine when pupil teachers were sent to the Institute during the daytime. Glasgow's enlightened attitude to pupil teachers was in keeping with the policy of teacher training which had been formulated by the very first Board: that all teachers must be trained, that as many as possible be graduates, that non-graduates be encouraged to attend university during the day without any loss of pay, and that Glasgow salaries should be high enough to attract the ablest teachers. Even the "Economist" Board of 1879 provided but a temporary check to the belief that schools could only be as good as the teachers who staffed them.

When Glasgow opted out of the system by which junior students were in danger of becoming an inferior class within the teaching profession, and insisted on their completing a school career equivalent to that of future university entrants, it performed a valuable service to Scottish education. In time the Glasgow standard became the nation's standard, and Scotland's teacher training the envy of all.

THE PUPIL TEACHER'S PAY

The wages of pupil teachers changed little throughout the whole of the period. The earlier salary scale[1] was revised under the "Economist" Board in common with the salary of other teachers, as follows.[2]

	Boys	Girls
1st year	£15	
2nd year	£19	£12
3rd year	£23	£19
4th year	£27	£22

[1] See Chapter 3, "Teachers' Salaries".
[2] Report of Pupil Teachers' Committee in General Summary of Work, 1888–91.

So popular was teaching for girls that a higher entrance standard could be demanded thus saving the first year of apprenticeship. Indeed, ". . . the number of Girl Candidates is so great that the friends of many were very anxious that, to secure places in the schools, they should be employed as Monitors without pay".[1] Although the Board did not take advantage of this source of cheap labour for more than three months at a time it had as many as sixty-eight unpaid monitors in 1885.[2]

TABLE 26

THE SCALE OF 1893[3]

	Boys	Girls
1st year	£10	£8
2nd year	£15	£12
3rd year	£20	£16
4th year	£25	£20

A new scale was introduced in 1893 (Table 26). The payments were lower than before, and the Board probably felt justified in this as the pupil teacher was now getting her tuition at the Institute during the day and was therefore giving less service in the schools. Moreover, the Board was having to spend more than ever before on pupil teachers because of the need to double their number.

In addition to these basic rates a pupil teacher could earn herself another pound each year by doing well in the annual examination, and even £3 if gaining a First Class entrance pass into the Normal School.

The pay of a pupil teacher might, at first sight, seem deplorably low. But when it is remembered that the average pay of a fully trained and experienced Assistant Mistress was £75 13s 7d,[4] the schoolgirl of seventeen or eighteen may be thought to have been relatively well-off. After all, she served the school only half-time.

---

[1] Report of Pupil Teachers' Committee, 1885.
[2] ibid.
[3] General Summary of Work, 1894, p 49.
[4] ibid, p 44.

Chapter 11
POLITICS

THE COMPOSITION OF BOARDS

A criticism often heard today from older men who remember the school boards, and more especially if they served under a school board as a teacher, is that they were dominated by churchmen. Why was this so? How far was it true? Was it detrimental to the organisation and improvement of the public schools?

In quite large measure it was a fact that most boards throughout both England and Scotland were elected on religious tickets, and it was inevitable that this should be so—at least in the early years—for education had always been the province of the churches. Therefore it seemed natural that the question of who should control the new public schools was really a question of which church should have the control. In Scotland the problem was a relatively small one for apart from Roman Catholics, who tended in any case to be concentrated in a few well-defined areas, the community was fairly homogeneous in doctrinal matters. Established Churchmen and Free Churchmen were both happy to see their children nurtured on the Bible and the shorter Catechism. In England, Anglican and Non-Conformist were deeply and bitterly divided. It was a rift which might easily have seriously jeopardised the working of the Education Act but for an alteration to the original Bill.

Forster's first Bill proposed that the new school boards be appointed by the town councils in boroughs and by vestries in rural parishes. It was not intended nor expected that appointees would be confined to members of either councils or vestries, but simply that these authorities would choose men from any walk of life who they felt would make good school board members. However, in Committee this indirect method of election was challenged by Sir Charles Dilke who proposed instead that election should be direct by the ratepayers.

Although Dilke's amendment was defeated it lost by such a very narrow margin—five votes—that Forster felt that the feeling of the House favoured an *ad hoc* authority, and he accepted the idea in principle. Later in the debate the proposal was made to adopt the cumulative vote system and it was agreed to without a division.[1] Under cumulative voting each elector had as many votes as there were seats on the board, and he could distribute his votes among the candidates as he pleased, perhaps giving all to one candidate or even, if somewhat eccentric, favouring every candidate with a single vote. The purpose of this unusual device was to give minority groups a good chance of winning representation on the boards, a result which they could achieve by good organisation and skilful distribution of their multiple votes between their own candidates. The question of the control of education was potentially so explosive that it was felt to be essential that all substantial minorities share that control. Once they were on the board they would, it was hoped, gain confidence in its work for education. In Gladstone's words, "The representation on the local board of every shade of opinion would tend to divest the elections of acrimony and animosity."[2]

When the Scottish Bill came up for debate a year or two later no particular discussion took place on the method of electing board members. The cumulative vote was written into the Act simply because it was already the practice in England.[3]

Cumulative voting certainly succeeded in its main purpose in that it did, broadly speaking, bring minorities on to the boards. These were not always religious parties. A man might be voted in to bring pressure to bear on an unsympathetic board over some particular issue of public excitement at the time, or to look after the interests of a district within a board. Such a case was Cumbernauld where the board did not want to put up a school in one part of the parish but was forced to do so when that district pooled its votes to get their own man on the board.[4]

Unfortunately, the system could lead to abuses by letting in men who had only a very small following indeed. Sometimes it

---

[1] Report from the Select Committee on School Board Elections (Voting), W E Forster, 1885, paras 417–18.
[2] *ibid*, para 444.
[3] *ibid*, para 443.
[4] *ibid*, paras 574, 846.

was a man with an axe to grind which had little or nothing to do with education, such as an anti-vaccinationist. Sometimes the effect of such misuse of the school board could be serious, as when a Walthamstow member set out deliberately to wreck the board by obstructing all business and keeping the board up all night long.[1] Sometimes it was merely frivolous: "There was one case in Scotland I am told of, in a very small parish. There was a man who was a habitual attendant of public houses, and so one day some labourers who had votes met this man; he happened to be sober, so they offered to put him on the board as a kind of joke if he kept sober for a week, and he did so, and he was elected."[2]

In 1885 a committee of inquiry set out to report on the best method of voting in School Board elections.[3] Inevitably the greater part of its investigation was taken up with learning how successful was the present cumulative voting system. On the whole most witnesses were fairly content with the cumulative vote. While it was true that it sometimes resulted in rather odd men getting on boards yet it did succeed in bringing in minorities, it had become accepted by the public, and the progress which had been achieved under many boards proved that good men had been elected to them. However, the chairman of the London Board, the largest board in the country, was strongly opposed to the cumulative vote. Not so Glasgow, second in size only to London itself.

THE COMPOSITION OF THE GLASGOW BOARD

Glasgow's witness before the Forster Commission was the Clerk to the School Board, William Kennedy. A teacher of long experience Kennedy had served as Clerk since the Board's inception, and was therefore well qualified to testify as to its efficiency and operation. Kennedy advocated certain changes in the composition of the electoral role, but when asked if the cumulative vote had worked well in Glasgow he replied, "Yes, I think it has."[4]

Setting aside the Roman Catholics, the first election had

[1] Report from the Select Committee on School Board Elections (Voting), 1885, para 568.
[2] ibid, para 571.
[3] ibid.
[4] ibid, para 3492.

been fought over the issue of use and wont. The traditionalists won a comfortable victory and only two secularists gained seats on the Board. After an early debate on whether or not to teach the Catechism the Board put aside religious controversy and gave all its energies to improving the tragic educational condition of the city. Indeed, once use and wont had been decided on as the method of religious instruction to be adopted not one other motion had to be put to the vote throughout the first Board's term of office. Said Kennedy, "I started a book in which to record the divisions, but for the first three years it was a failure.[1] . . . I think that in 1873 when the figures were produced, and Members saw the bad state of Glasgow educationally, it had a very decided effect in getting them to work harmoniously. All through it has been harmonious."[2] In later years the only occasions on which contentious religious questions intruded on to the Board was when a member had been elected on a particular promise, such as to abolish the Catechism. Then he felt obliged to move for such action, but its certain defeat was more of a ritual than a serious issue. Now and again differences would arise between Catholic and Protestant, notably on the matter of free books for Catholic children, but generally relations were amicable and Catholic members often gave considerable active service on the Board.

In considering alternative forms of voting Kennedy did not much like the idea of proportional representation. For one thing it tended to produce too great a fragmentation of the vote. For another it was awkward to administer and too difficult for the ordinary voter to comprehend. Kennedy was not even sure that he understood it himself.[3]

A much more likely suggestion was to divide the area into wards as was done at parliamentary elections, for this offered some real advantages. It would permit local prides and prejudices to get a voice on the Board, as already happened in Govan. More importantly, perhaps, a much closer relationship between the public and their representative could be expected. As things were it was quite impossible at election time for Board members to canvas all the districts of the city to put

---

[1] Report from the Select Committee on School Board Elections (Voting), 1885, para 3578.
[2] *ibid*, para 3579.
[3] *ibid*, paras 3514–20.

their views before the electorate and to be challenged on them. Consequently, the members often seemed remote figures and interest in the affairs of the Board languished.

But while a ward system had advantages it also had its dangers and these, in Kennedy's view, were serious enough to rule it out. For it threatened the Roman Catholic interests. The Catholic population of Glasgow was then about one-fifth of the whole.[1] Catholic representation on the Board was always three members; that is, exactly one-fifth, and so the cumulative vote clearly ensured that Catholics were fairly dealt with. Under a ward system such a just result was far from certain, even although the Catholic population tended to be massed in certain districts, for it was a curious fact that no Roman Catholic had been able to win election to the Town Council,[2] and this might well happen with the School Board were it elected in the same way.

Yet there was a general feeling that wards should be introduced, and Kennedy believed that this method might still give Catholics an adequate voice provided that there were three divisions only instead of the parliamentary sixteen. This was, in fact, the ultimate solution but it did not come about for another thirty years.

Catholic representation on the School Board was absolutely essential, not merely because they too were ratepayers but because some aspects of the Board's work could not have been carried on effectively without the whole-hearted backing of the Roman Catholic authorities. This was especially evident in the matter of attendance. School Boards were the bodies responsible in law for the enforcement of attendance irrespective of the child's religious persuasion. Just as in Protestant schools the Catholic schools furnished weekly lists of absentees to the Board and the Board's attendance officers visited Protestant and Catholic homes alike. Catholic defaulters were brought up before Members at Defaulters' Meetings and, if necessary, prosecuted by the School Board. All of this would have been quite unworkable without full co-operation from the Roman Church, and it is very doubtful if that would have been forthcoming had Catholics not had confidence in the Board, a

[1] Report from the Select Committee on School Board Elections (Voting), 1885, para 3570.   [2] *ibid*, para 3729.

confidence born out of their inner knowledge of its methods and motives through their direct membership of it.

Except for an occasional sectarian clash over some particular religious issue, direction of education by the churches in the case of the School Board of Glasgow was more apparent than real. The first Board was heavy with clerical luminaries of the time, but most of them soon died off. Thereafter they were never so numerous and certainly not so distinguished. No minister ever became Chairman, only one was Vice-Chairman. What gave the Board such a strong religious flavour, in respect both of clergymen and lay brethren, was the absence of any parties other than the churches with any sort of educational platform. The two great political parties of the nineteenth century did not attempt to control local education by direct participation in its affairs, while in Glasgow it took the Socialists a long time to make any headway. Only with the election of Martin Haddow in 1903 did Socialism gain a strong voice on the Board. Failing the presence of alternative loyalties people voted for their churches. "To a certain extent." said Kennedy, "the churches come in more as a convenient machinery for electing members than because of any church question that is involved. It has become almost a proverb in Scotland that the men with the best chance to get into the School Board are those that have either a Kirk or a work; that is to say, either a clergyman or an employer of labour. Church organisations are used for the purpose; even those who will work together on the Board have used the church organisation in canvassing, the members of one church working in one organisation and the members of another in another; but I think that on the whole there is a desire to get the men and women who are most suitable for the work."[1]

Writing many years later Haddow pointed out that, ". . . it was an almost unwritten law that three candidates were furnished by the 'Auld Kirk', three by the Free Church, three by the Catholic Church, and Labour also put forward three. The remaining three seats were left to independent candidates."[2] Throughout there seems to have been no desire on the

[1] Report from the Select Committee on School Board Elections (Voting), 1885, para 3580.
[2] W Martin Haddow, *My Seventy Years*, p 60.

part of any one party to monopolise the power but, on the contrary, a genuine belief in the rightness of giving the whole community an effective say in the running of their schools. This sense of balance and fair play all round extended into many fields. For example, newly qualified teachers were recruited by Glasgow in equal numbers from the two local Normal Schools.[1] It seems very likely that staff promotions were made on a similar basis of equal shares. It is very questionable whether today's system of virtually giving monopoly power to one political party is a better one.

Any criticism of the churches' hold on the School Board of Glasgow must prove both that it was detrimental to the education of the city's children and that it was not in tune with the public feeling of the times. Neither contention can be upheld.

AMALGAMATION WITH OTHER BOARDS

During the whole period of the School Board the population of the metropolitan area around Glasgow was growing rapidly, and difficulties soon arose from the existence of too many parishes and burghs sharing the control of what was geographically and economically one large region. Inexorably Glasgow extended her municipal boundaries to include many surrounding districts. Great fights took place over every proposed annexation, but bit by bit Glasgow's neighbours were forced to give ground. These changes were bound to have repercussions on the school boards.

As early as 1874, and outwith any question of a change in municipal areas, the Springburn School Board instigated negotiations with the Glasgow Board for some form of cooperation. It had not yet reached the stage of proposing amalgamation, but Springburn was already aware that she was too small a board to cater adequately for her children. The outcome of the discussions was that Glasgow was to build a new school, Rosemount, and that it would accept a hundred children from the Springburn parish which would pay Glasgow £100 per annum for the privilege.[2] Within a few months the two

---

[1] Second Report of Committee to Inquire into Education in Scotland. C S Parker, 1888, p 3.
[2] Minutes of Board in Committee, 8 June 1874 and 8 July 1874.

Boards were meeting with a view to combining in terms of Section 42 of the Act,[1] though nothing came of it.

A few months later the Govan Board wrote to say that it wanted to keep the old boundaries even if part of her territory was lost to the City of Glasgow as was now threatened.[2] The Glasgow Board would not agree to such a proposal. It was "unanimously and very strongly of the opinion" that the School Board district should include the extended municipality. Otherwise many difficulties would arise out of the confusion of boundaries.[3] Glasgow therefore pressed her case before the Scotch Education Department and Parliament. The Bill passed the Commons with Glasgow's clauses intact, but the Board was warned that strong opposition was to be expected from the Lords, and in fact the Lords refused to sanction any change in school board areas. So although several outlying districts were absorbed by Glasgow under the Municipal Act of 1878 the School Board remained unaltered.

As the years passed the difficulties of some of the smaller boards became more and more pressing and the advantages of amalgamation more and more apparent. Maryhill and Springburn especially were keen to join Glasgow but several attempts to do so proved abortive. The probability of eventual amalgamation had detrimental effects on education in these areas as they put off building new schools and extending facilities in order to save themselves the expense. Maryhill, for example, was said by the inspector to have ". . . for a series of years been laying hall after hall under contribution".[4]

Efforts at amalgamation were renewed in 1902 in preparation for the impending Education Bill. Representatives of Glasgow, Govan, Eastwood, Maryhill, Springburn and Shettleston all met and agreed to approach the Secretary of State on the matter. There were good grounds for supposing that he would be sympathetic to amalgamation as he had recently spoken in Greenock in favour of elementary and higher education being placed under one education authority and of extension of educational areas.[5] When the deputation met Lord Balfour,

---

[1] Letter from Glasgow School Board to Scotch Education Department, 31 December 1874.
[2] Minutes of Board in Committee, Feb 1875, p 120.
[3] Letter to Scotch Education Department, 12 February 1878.
[4] Committee of Council for Education in Scotland, Report, 1896.
[5] Minutes of Board in Committee, 11 December 1902.

however, Govan and Cathcart were missing as they opposed any change.[1] Once again nothing came of it as the 1904 Education Bill fell through. A merger between Glasgow and Rutherglen was at first approved by Parliament but collapsed at the committee stage, yet, "The Rutherglen Board still was determined to sink back on to Glasgow's broad bosom, but the 1908 Act, when it came, offered no chance."[2]

At long last, in 1911 Maryhill and Springburn achieved their ambition and were incorporated into the Glasgow School Board,[3] the only amalgamation which was effected in the area. Govan had always fought for her independence tooth and nail, Shettleston had wavered from time to time, Rutherglen had been keen to combine but was eventually frightened off by the threat of total annexation which it did *not* want.

Besides adding twelve schools to Glasgow and involving her in building in the annexed territories, opportunity was taken at the amalgamation of making changes in the structure of the Board and in the method of voting.

From quite early in its career it had become clear that fifteen members were really too few to cope with all the work which had to be undertaken by the Glasgow Board. A vast amount of time was demanded of any member who did the job conscientiously. Apart from public meetings and meetings of the Board in committee, he was expected to attend sub-committees, take his part at defaulters' meetings, perhaps act as the Board representative on such bodies at the Delinquency Board, the Secondary Education Committee, or the Buchanan Trust, visit schools regularly, attend Edinburgh or London on an occasional deputation, and many other time-consuming duties of one kind and another. Few men could afford to give so much of their time. Many very good men were deterred from offering themselves for election. Now, with the addition of Maryhill and Springburn, the Board membership was increased to twenty-five which went some way towards easing the situation.

And it was only now that Kennedy's proposal in regard to a ward system of voting was put into effect. The City was divided into three electoral areas; North-East, North-West and South

---

[1] Minutes of Board in Committee, 12 February 1902.
[2] G Paton, "The Development of Education in Rutherglen, 1872–1918", Unpublished EdB Thesis, Glasgow University, 1960.
[3] For details see *Edinburgh Gazette*, 17 January 1911.

with eight or nine seats each. It was hoped that greater interest in the Board's affairs would result from the more local connection, but the results of the first election under the new system in 1914 scarcely bore this out. In the North-East section there was not even a contest. The poll in the other two areas was only 30%. In 1911 36% had voted. The intention of wards had failed.

Chapter 12
CONCLUSIONS

The purpose of school boards was to see that ". . . efficient education for their children may be furnished and made available to the whole people of Scotland".[1] The purpose of the School Board of Glasgow was to furnish efficient education for the people of Glasgow. And this it did.

At the outset it was faced by the worst social and educational conditions of anywhere in Scotland. Long before the School Board was extinguished by the Act of 1918, the public educational facilities of Glasgow exceeded the demand made on them by her citizens and even catered for a substantial number of children from other areas.

Most work on the history of Scottish education has been written from a study of government records, and this has led to an impression that the Scotch Education Department was the initiating force behind the educational advances of the period and that by its authority it was able to impose its enlightened will on school boards generally reluctant and indifferent. This view must be considerably modified in the light of the history of the Glasgow Board, and of some other large Boards when they come to be studied. It seems probable that the true function of the Department was to force on the country at large reforms already pioneered and proved by enlightened and progressive Boards like those of Glasgow and Govan. By using their example and by having their support the Department was able to extend their work across the nation.

Glasgow was, of course, a key city. Its size and its wealth made it so. Fortunately for Scotland it had a forward-looking Board. Other progressive Boards looked to Glasgow for leadership and generally found it.

Glasgow eliminated the half-timer long before Parliament acted; it set a high standard for teachers by taking only those

[1] Preamble to Education (Scotland) Act, 1872.

properly trained and by encouraging them to attend university and so improve their scholarship; by progressively relieving the pupil teacher of her teaching duties, and by making her spend more and more time on her own studies, Glasgow paved the way for the abolition of the pupil teacher system, and further indicated future national practice by refusing to accept the Department's limited view of the junior student's function; almost alone Glasgow laid the foundations of a type of public school which was truly secondary in character; she called for the national establishment of a Leaving Certificate of uniform and high standard many years before its adoption; Glasgow long urged the Department to help improve the work of Higher Class Schools by taking over their inspection from the locally appointed examiners.

In social services, too, the School Board did what it could to help the needy. Boots and clothing from charity organisations were distributed through the schools, including Catholic schools; free or cheap dinners reached hundreds of children through the day industrial schools; and an imaginative stretching of government grant provisions sometimes enabled the Board to go beyond what was intended as, for example, when it supplied free spectacles.[1]

No philosophy or ideology of education guided the Board. It sought simply to improve the lot of the children of the City as seemed best at any given moment. Policy was directed by the recognition of an obvious need or modified as experience dictated. Such pragmatic methods were sometimes slow and always unspectacular. They were also solidly sane and they served Glasgow well.

Stability and continuity of purpose were among the Board's chief merits. Throughout the school board period virtually only four Chairman led the Glasgow Board:

Sir Michael Connal	1874–1885[2]
Sir John Neilson Cuthbertson	1885–1903
Robert S Allan	1903–1914
Dr Henry Dyer	1914–1918

[1] W Martin Haddow, *My Seventy Years*, pp 67–8.
[2] Nominally, the Chairman from 1873–6 was Alexander Whitelaw, but he left for Westminster within a year and Connal took over in his absence.

As each of these men had previously filled the office of Vice-Chairman the degree of continuity was very strong indeed. To these names must be added that of William Mitchell, Vice-Chairman from 1885 to 1900, who served under Cuthbertson in a long and fruitful pàrtnership.

The Education Act of 1918 ended the school boards and merged all the boards in the Glasgow region in a greater unit. The *Glasgow Herald* epitaph read, "The extinction of the Glasgow School Board as a separate education authority closes a chapter of outstanding importance in the annals of the city. Under the Board the development of education has been continuous and progressive, and in the domain of higher education especially it has played a leading part."[1]

---

[1] *Glasgow Herald*, 15 March 1919.

Appendix A

TEACHERS' EMOLUMENTS—REASON OF DISSENT BY MR KIDSTON

Mr Kidston gave in the following reasons of dissent and protest against the decision of the Board in regard to Teachers' Emoluments, which were adhered to by the Rev Dr Dodds and Mr Long:

1. Because the Report on Teachers' Emoluments is not founded on the remit, and is inconsistent with it.

2. Because the argument on which the remit was based, viz., that the fees and grant should pay not only the current expenses of the Schools but also the salaries of the teaching staff, is wrong in principle and contrary to the spirit of the Act; and because before publicly enunciating such a theory, the possibility of carrying it out in practice ought to have been carefully considered and clearly demonstrated.

3. Because the injudiciousness and impropriety of promulgating the principle aimed at was clearly shown by the fact that, after consideration, the Committee discovered, that as a principle, it was impracticable, being applicable only to 13 Schools out of 40.

4. Because this inconsiderate remit was carried by a majority of one vote only, and was of a character which prevented many members of the Board from acting upon the Committee; and as only members of the Committee who had voted with the minority did not approve of the Report, but submitted proposals of their own, the Report was necessarily of a one-sided character; and because each and every amendment suggested by those members of the Board who disagreed with the Report was summarily rejected.

5. Because, while a salary of £500 is declared to be within the reach of teachers, as a maximum, regulations have been passed which render it impossible for even one teacher to reach this sum; and because delusive calculations have been made, upon the supposition that the Schools shall be full all the year round—a result which, except in very rare instances, cannot be attained.

6. Because the carrying out of the scheme adopted by the Board will reduce the salaries of some of the teachers of the Board below the amounts they received before entering the service.

7. Because, while higher qualifications than formerly are required from candidates for the teaching profession, so that now only a limited number obtain first class marks, the lowering of the

Head Masters' salaries has not been accompanied by a corresponding increase in the salaries of assistant masters; and because a payment of £70 as an entrance salary for young men, with the prospect of reaching only £100 as a maximum, in 4 or 5 years, is not sufficient inducement to secure or retain for the School Board of Glasgow the services of men certified by Government as first-class, who will easily obtain larger salaries in provincial Schools; and because, while the Report provides that no assistant-master shall receive more than £100, the minimum salary of a Head Master is fixed at £200, thus shutting up the Board to the alternatives of either never promoting assistants or *per saltum* of doubling their salaries—a policy on either supposition hardly creditable to the Board.

8. Because, in a central and populous city, such as Glasgow, it is desirable that first-class men should be attracted to the teaching profession, whereas the immediate and necessary effect of lowering the salaries to the extent proposed, will be to discourage candidates, especially able young men, from entering on the teaching profession; and because the disastrous results caused by the lowering of incomes under the influence of the Revised Code of 1863, from which the Country took a long time to recover, will in all likelihood be repeated.

9. Because, while the changes will deteriorate the quality of the teaching staff, the scheme will be all the more disastrous as one of its principal features is unduly to reduce the Staff; and because, in the arrangements generally, efficiency has been sacrificed to mere pecuniary saving—saving which to the ratepayer will be very small, while the educational results will be disastrous.

10. Because it is extremely undesirable that the current expenses of the Schools should be deducted from the fees and grants before the teachers' salaries are calculated, thereby placing their pecuniary interests in conflict with the due maintenance of the Schools in cleanliness, furnishings, and repairs, and making their salaries dependent on expenditure over which they have no control, and which the Board alone can regulate.

11. Because, while the calculations of the Report are based on the high grants at present obtained from Government, there is no security that these grants will be maintained at their present rates, but, on the contrary, the policy of the Board is likely to be used as an argument for seriously reducing them; and because, even if the large grants are maintained, the employment of less qualified assistants, of a large proportion of pupil-teachers, and of unsuccessful Normal School Candidates renders it very doubtful whether the amounts hitherto obtained will be earned in future.

12. Because the lowering of salaries in Glasgow will operate prejudicially as regards teachers and the cause of education, throughout the country, and place an arrest on a most beneficial movement.

13. Because the Report makes no distinction in dealing with the salaries of teachers in Schools where the property (in some gratuitously transferred to the Board) on the stipulation specially sanctioned by the Act, that the services of the masters shall be retained; and because the dissentients believe that, to reduce the salaries of such masters while the income of the School and the number of scholars have not been reduced, is illegal, and they hold themselves exonerated from any consequences which the reduction of such salaries may involve.

14. Because, while the past policy of the Board has been to provide very highly-qualified teachers for Schools in poor localities, on the ground that poor children, being least regular in attendance, and leaving school at an early age, it is of paramount importance that the highest quality of instruction should be given them, the scheme now approved will tend to degrade such Schools and to deteriorate the instruction given in them.

15. Because, while the action of the Board hitherto has been one of friendly co-operation with the masters, the changes introduced will tend to develop a different spirit on the part of teachers, and even tempt them to regard their scholars rather through the medium of what can be made out of them in pecuniary results, than of what knowledge and instruction can be imparted to them.

For the above reasons they decidedly dissent from, and protest against the one-sided and mischievous Report on Teachers' Emoluments.

Appendix B

MEMORIAL FROM HEADMASTERS ON SALARIES

To The School Board of Glasgow, City Public Schools, Glasgow, 15th Sept., 1879.

Gentlemen,

At a meeting of Headmasters under your Board, held on Friday evening, the 12th currt., to consider the proposal now before you for the reduction of our salaries, it was unanimously resolved, most respectfully to submit the following statements for your consideration:

1. We would desire, at the outset, to express our sympathy with every effort to reduce the expenditure of the Board, consistent with the efficient management of the schools. At the same time, we think that a reduction of salaries on the lines, and to the extent contemplated, will be neither fair to us, nor satisfactory in its ultimate results to the cause of education.

2. In the scheme proposed no adequate notice is taken of the difference existing between Schools in respect of locality and date of inspection, both of which exercise an important influence in determining the income of a School.

3. While the scheme proposed fixes the *maximum* salary at £500, it offers little likelihood of this sum being ever realised, and, as the average attendance ought never to reach the limit of accommodation, it makes it impossible for a teacher to earn the maximum fixed for his School. The average salary, in the present circumstances of the Schools, would be £200 less than the maximum indicated; and, in view of the responsibilities and necessary qualifications of a Head Master, the proposed minimum is unduly low.

4. In any scheme that may be adopted it is not desirable that our salaries should be affected by such indefinite and variable deductions as cleaning, repairs, school requisites etc.

5. While, of late years, there has been an increase in the Teachers' salaries, it must be borne in mind that this has arisen mainly from an increase in the Government Grant, and not from local sources.

6. In Glasgow the attained salaries in other professions are, as a rule, larger than elsewhere in Scotland, and it is not unreasonable to expect that the same should hold in the case of Teachers.

7. Several of our number had higher salaries under their former management than are paid them now.

8. We understand that higher salaries are at present earned in Glasgow in state-aided Schools, with attendances similar to our own than are attainable under the scheme proposed.

9. We would be sorry if any proposal to limit Assistant-Teachers' Salaries to £100 were approved by the Board, as the natural results would be that the less efficient would remain in your service, while the more active and aspiring would seek appointments elsewhere. We would also regret the adoption of any proposal to reduce the payments to Female Pupil Teachers—a most deserving class.

10. After the work of organising Schools of the size and character of these under the Board, and after having gradually secured, by long and earnest application to labour of a somewhat heavy and complicated nature, a generous recognition of our services at your hands, we cannot conceal the fact that such an abrupt and serious reduction of our salaries as is at present contemplated, would have a most depressing effect on the minds and activities of the whole of your teaching staff.

11. In a matter so deeply affecting not only our personal interest, but the efficiency of so large a number of Schools, we have respectfully to ask if the Board, before coming to a final decision on any scheme, will be pleased to allow us the opportunity, through a deputation of our number, of laying before them a full statement of our views.

Signed in name and by appointment of the Meeting,

Alex F McBean
Chairman

I

Appendix C
NEW SCHOOLS BUILT BY
THE GLASGOW SCHOOL BOARD

Date of Opening	School	Fate in 1970
1874	Rose St	Building demolished
1875	Barrowfield	Still in use
	Crookston St	Building demolished
	Kennedy St	Now Nursery School, Secondary School annexe and Technical Maintenance Section
	Oatlands	Demolished for housing development
	Sister St	Demolished for Bridgeton Cross Station 1889
	Springburn	Still in use
	Thomson St	Still in use
1876	Centre St	Now an Immigrant Centre
	Rumford St	Closed—building used as store
	Camden St	Closed—building used as store
	Greenside St	Building demolished
	Henderson St	Closed—building used as store
	Tureen St	Presently Occupational Centre—to be used as extension to David Dale College Annexe
	Rockvilla	Now Occupational Centre
1877	Dovehill	Still in use
	Bishop St	Demolished for road development purposes
	Overnewton	Now Occupational Centre
1878	Camlachie	Still in use
	Garnethill	Still in use
	Oakbank	Still in use
	Keppochhill	Still in use
1879	Parkhead	Now used by Visual Aids and Youth Employment Services
	Mathieson St	Demolished
	Campbellfield	Used as Occupational Centre
	Abbotsford	Still in use

Date of Opening	School	Fate in 1970
1882	Woodside	Still in use
1883	John St	Demolished
	Dennistoun	Now St Denis's Primary School
	Springfield	Now Our Lady of Fatima Primary School
	Shields Rd	Now used as Occupational Centre
	St George's Rd	Still in use
1884	Springbank	Now St Columba's Primary and Nursery School
	Townhead	Still in use
1885	Wolseley St	Still in use
	Gorbals	Still in use
1886	Kent Rd	Still in use
1887	Dobbie's Loan	Annexe to Stow College of Engineering
1888	Grove St	Still in use
	Kelvinhaugh	Still in use
	Petershill	Annexe to Albert Secondary
1890	Washington St	Still in use
	Napiershall St	Still in use
	Calton (Kerr St)	To be used as Further Education Centre
1891	Whitehill	Still in use
1892	Annfield	Still in use
1893	Queen Mary St	Annexe to Dalmarnock School
	Dalmarnock	Still in use
1894	Adelphi Terrace	Annexe to Glasgow College of Building
1895	Newlands	Still in use
	St James'	Still in use
1897	Rosemount	Still in use
	Alexandra Parade	Still in use
	Martyrs	Annexe to St Mungo's Academy
1898	Finnieston	Closed December 1970
1900	Dunard St	Still in use
1901	Willowbank	Still in use
1902	Provanside	Now City Public Secondary
1903	Elmvale	Still in use
	Golfhill	Still in use

Date of Opening	School	Fate in 1970
1904	Quarry Brae	Still in use
	Haghill	Still in use
	Strathclyde	Still in use
1905	Garnetbank	Still in use
	Hayfield	Still in use
1906	Sir John Neilson	
	Cuthbertson	Still in use
	Scotland St	Still in use
	St Rollox	Now Royston Primary
1909	Hyde Park	Still in use
1913	Bluevale	Still in use
1914	Onslow Drive	Still in use
1915	North Kelvinside HG	Still in use
	Shakespeare	Still in use
1916	Bernard St	Now St Mary's Secondary

NOTE: (a) Special Schools and Industrial Schools are not included.

(b) Although the pre-Board Dobbie's Loan had always been used by the Board before 1887 the new addition was so large as to justify its inclusion in this list.

(c) The old St Rollox had been demolished to make way for the new building.

Appendix D

SCHOOL BOARD LETTER TO EMPLOYERS, 1874 REGULATIONS FOR HALF-TIMERS SCHOOL BOARD OF GLASGOW

Sir,

I have to inform you that Half-timers will be admitted to this school on the following conditions:

1st. The fees for beginners shall be   a week, and for those writing on copy books   a week, payable by the employer.

2nd. The School Board must receive evidence that each pupil is of the age required by the Act of Parliament.

3rd. The employer will be expected to see that the pupils provide themselves with books and copybooks. The School Board will supply the use of pens, ink and slates.

4th. The fees shall be paid for each pupil enrolled, whether in attendance or not, until the employer requests the teacher to withdraw the name from the school roll.

5th. The employer will be expected to use his utmost exertions to secure that the pupils are cleanly in person and dress.

The school Board will consider themselves entitled to modify these conditions of admission as experience shall suggest. And it must be distinctly understood that Half-Time pupils will be continued only where they do not interfere with the instruction and discipline of the school.

I am, Sir,

Appendix E

EDUCATIONAL ENDOWMENTS ACT

SUGGESTIONS BY REPRESENTATIVES OF THE SCHOOL BOARD OF GLASGOW

THE Representatives of the School Board, while reserving to themselves and to the Board entire freedom to take such action as the Endowment Act secures regarding any Scheme which may be before the Commissioners, desire to make the following suggestions on two points, viz.:—*First*, What would be the best plan of grouping the several Trusts, so far as the Governing Bodies are concerned? and, *Second*, What are the best means of administering the Trusts, so as to secure the ends aimed at by the Act?

With regard to the first of these, while there appear to be advantages in one managing body for all the Trusts, it is doubtful whether such a plan is practicable. If proposed, however, the representatives believe that such an arrangement would receive the favourable consideration of the Board. As a more practicable plan it is suggested that some of the larger Trusts, such as Hutchesons', Allan Glen's, Alexander's, and Buchanan's, which are in active operation and have certain well-marked peculiarities, might, with advantage, remain separate as at present, with such alterations as would bring them into harmony with the "New Act". The first and second of these were quite recently constituted under special Acts of Parliament, and they will probably desire to continue as far as possible on lines with which they are familiar, and which are similar to those on which they are already moving. The first of these has sufficiently large Endowments, inclusive of the Trusts already incorporated with it, to stand by itself. The other three, not being very large Trusts, might have one or two other Trusts of a kindred nature grouped with them, not with the view of separating the Trusts into groups or classes with different or conflicting interests, but with the view of enabling those special Trusts to carry out their work more effectively on lines which to some extent have been already approved. It is suggested that, for all the Trusts other than these, or those grouped with them, there should be created one Governing Body, and that Governing Body should consist of probably about 30 Members, of whom at least one-third might be chosen by the Town Council, and one-third by the School Board. This would not exclude gentlemen who are now taking, or may be found inclined to take, an interest in special departments of work. The Town Council and School Board, apart from the certainty of such gentlemen being found

238

in the remaining third, would naturally look for such men, and would be glad to secure their services.

With regard to the administration—

A. Every scheme should, first of all, as far as possible and requisite, carry out the spirit of the founder's intention in regard to the education, clothing, and maintenance of poor children "or otherwise for their benefit."

B. Every scheme should provide that any funds not required under the previous head should be applied, to use the words of the preamble, "for affording to boys and girls of promise opportunities for obtaining higher education of the kind best suited to aid their advancement in life."

C. Every scheme should, to use the words of the seventh section, "have special regard to making provision for secondary or higher or technical education, in public schools [1] or otherwise," The functions of the School Board are not limited to primary or elementary education. Such a view is against the letter and the spirit of both the Education Acts, whereby School Boards are not only bound to promote higher education, but to take charge of all High schools existing at the passing of the Act of 1872. In point of fact, the School Board are at present largely supplying secondary education in their Schools, and are engaged in further developing this object by constructing several Schools specially adapted for the purpose. The Endowment Commissioners are instructed, in consistency with the Education Acts, to have special regard to making provision for higher education in connection with public schools. The Board are therefore the natural and proper parties to erect new schools where these may be required, and to manage them. The funds might also be applied to the erection and equipment of laboratories and the providing of suitable apparatus, &c.

D. After providing as above in public schools and otherwise for secondary or higher or technical education, the best means of further promoting these objects would be the creation of a large number of bursaries, granted, after competition, to children of parents whose circumstances were ascertained to be such that without aid of this kind their children would not be likely to obtain higher education. A portion of the endowments might be made available for providing teachers with special qualifications, so that the fees for higher education might be made sufficiently moderate to attract scholars not able to pay high fees.

[1] A Public School is defined by the Act of 1872 as any School under the management of a School Board. That this is the meaning of the term in the Endowments Act is clear from the section quoted above, as also from Sections 19, 33, and 45.

E. The Board have no desire that any of the Endowment Funds should pass directly into their hands for administration. They desire to have the power of nominating and recommending poor children to the benefits under Pars. A and D, and of harmoniously co-operating with the new Governing Bodies in carrying into effect the purposes indicated in Pars. B and C.

WILLIAM MITCHELL,
THOMAS RUSSELL,
Representative Members of School Board.

SCHOOL BOARD OFFICES,
GLASGOW, *26th December,* 1882.

Appendix F

SCHOOL BOARD OF GLASGOW
EDUCATIONAL ENDOWMENTS

OBJECTIONS BY REPRESENTATIVES OF SCHOOL
BOARD TO SUGGESTIONS BY COMMITTEE OF TRUST
REPRESENTATIVES

The grouping is defective, and the constitution of the governing bodies unsatisfactory.—But passing to objections of a more serious character it may be noticed that the suggestions for administration are neither in accordance with the spirit of the founders' intentions nor with the letter or spirit of the Act. In particular—

First—No prominence has been given to the fact that the great bulk of the funds has been bequeathed in the interests of poor children, variously described in the trusts as the "most indigent young ones of the City," "poor boys and girls," "poor orphans and children of poor persons," "poor deserving boys," "children of poor but respectable tradesmen," or "poor but respectable parents;" nor to the clause in the Act, Section 15, which says, "provided always that where the founder of any educational endowment has expressly provided for the education of children belonging to the poorer classes, or otherwise for their benefit, such endowment shall continue so far as requisite to be applied for the benefit of such children," and that not only for the elementary, but also for the higher education of the children of promise of these classes.

It is no doubt stated in the suggestions that the first duty of the governing body would be the provision of free elementary education where such is required to be given by the Endowments Act, and also that due regard must be had to the spirit of the founders' intentions, but while much work is proposed connected with building and management of schools for secondary and technical education (very proper in their own place), the primary duties of the trusts towards the particular interests of poor children are placed in a very subordinate position. With reference to poor children it may be well to state, That the Board are quite in accordance with what they believe to be the spirit of the Endowment Act that, as a rule no part of the Endowment funds should be expended on children of parents in receipt of parochial relief; and it is always necessary to be kept in mind, That the School Board have no power of granting free education, or of paying school fees from the school fund or any other source.

1*   241

Second—Instead of suggesting how best, after the foregoing duties are fulfilled "so far as may be to make an adequate portion of such Endowments available for affording to boys and girls of promise opportunities for obtaining higher education of the kind best suited to aid their advancement in life," by "making provision for secondary or higher or technical education in Public Schools," the chief work proposed by the Trust Representatives for the largest governing body (comprising about three-fourths of all the Trusts) is to provide school accommodation, or, in other words, to build new schools beyond what may be provided by the School Board and to take the management of them. Certain prominent Trust Representatives do not disguise, as was brought out in the discussion, that they propose to charge the principal governing body to a large extent with the secondary education of the city, leaving the School Board to deal with elementary education alone, which is not only contrary to the Education Acts, but which would undoubtedly have the effect of deteriorating and lowering the tone of the whole education of our ordinary schools.

The strongest possible objections are taken by your representatives to this course. Two reasons may be stated:

(1.) The Endowment funds are not sufficient, even if they were available, for building large new secondary schools and endowing them. Supposing that out of the funds of the principal group, which are stated at £138,000, only two schools were built and endowed, this would take away more than two-thirds of the capital sum, leaving a ridiculously small proportion for bursaries and other purposes.

(2.) The suggestion to build new schools for secondary education, and to take the management of them outside and apart from the School Board is founded on an entire misapprehension of one of the principal functions of the School Board as may be seen in the Education Acts and from the official communications of the Scotch Education Department.

WILLIAM MITCHELL,
THOMAS RUSSELL,
Representative Members of School Board.

The above was laid before the Board at their Monthly Meeting, on *Monday, the 15th inst.* The Board approved of it generally, and ordered it to be made public.

WM. KENNEDY, *Clerk.*

SCHOOL BOARD OFFICES, 129 BATH STREET,
    11th *January*, 1883.

Appendix G

THE GLASGOW CITY
EDUCATIONAL ENDOWMENTS BOARD

FREE SCHOLARSHIPS

The Governors are prepared to appoint 90 Free Scholars under Ten years of age: and 185 above Ten years of age.

The area of selection is not restricted, but the Scholarships must be held "*at Public or State-aided Schools in Glasgow.*"

TENURE OF SCHOLARSHIPS

(*a*) Children under Ten will have their fees paid for them, with books and stationery, for one or more years as the circumstances of each case may seem to require, effect being always given to the provision of the Scheme that the fees "in respect of children under Ten years of age shall not be paid for more than one school year without re-appointment."

(*b*) Free Scholars above Ten years of age will have their fees paid for three years with books and stationery, provided always that their conduct and progress is satisfactory to the Governors.

FREE SCHOLARS UNDER TEN YEARS OF AGE

The grounds of selection of Free Scholars will be: (1) as regards parents and guardians, that they, "*not being in receipt of parochial* "*relief, are in such circumstances as to require aid for providing elementary* "*education, and are persons who, in the opinion of the Governors, ought* "*not to be required to apply to the Parochial Board for such aid*"; and (2) as regards the candidates, applicants will be dealt with according to whether they have or have not been at school.

(*a*) The merit of children who *have not been at school* will be ascertained by such examination as the Governors may prescribe, and by evidence that they "*possess such qualifications as to justify their selection.*"

(*b*) With respect to children *who have been at school*, "*special weight* "*shall be given to good conduct, attendance, and progress at school* "*during the previous year, as reported on by the teacher.*"

FREE SCHOLARS ABOVE TEN YEARS OF AGE

These Scholars will be selected by Competition, and that "*whether they have or have not previously been beneficiaries,*" Section 27.

ELIGIBILITY OF CANDIDATES

The sole test of eligibility is whether or not their parents or guardians possess the qualifications prescribed in Section 27. The eligibility of candidates, as ascertained by the facts stated in the Schedules, or by inquiry otherwise, will be determined finally *before they are admitted to compete.* Thereafter the Scholarships will be awarded in order of merit as appearing on the competition.

Regard will be had to the provision of the Scheme, that *"in the "event of equality between candidates, preference shall be given to "candidates who have been constantly resident for three years in the "High Church, College, St. John's, and Calton Parishes."*

Notice will be given to applicants for Scholarships of both classes, whose applications are entertained of the day and place of examination, and the lines on which it will be conducted.

Forms of application to be filled up by Parents or Guardians may be had at the Office, 1 South Frederick Street, Glasgow.

F. LOCKHART ROBERTSON, D.D.

All Applicants must be lodged on or before January 18th, 1886.

Appendix H

THE GLASGOW CITY EDUCATIONAL ENDOWMENTS BOARD

(Constituted by Scheme No. 10, under the Educational Endowments (Scotland) Act, 1882)

BURSARY COMPETITION, 1886

I.—SCHOOL BURSARIES

The Governors will offer ONE HUNDRED School Bursaries for competition in the month of April. They are of the yearly value of *Five Pounds*, and are tenable for two years.

The Governors will select, "as the Schools at which these Bursaries "may be held, certain Schools in each quarter of the city, whether "Schools maintained under a Scheme by the Commissioners under "the Educational Endowments (Scotland) Act, 1882, or Public or "State aided, in which efficient instruction is given in the higher "branches." (Minute of Board, dated 1st December, 1885).

ELIGIBILITY OF COMPETITORS

Competitors must be (*a*) Children "whose parents or guardians are "in such circumstances as to require aid for giving their children a "higher education;" (*b*) They must be attending "Public or State-"aided Schools in Glasgow, and have passed the Fifth Standard of "the present Scotch Code."

Seventy-five Bursaries will be allotted to children who have passed the Fifth Standard, and *twenty-five* to those who have passed the Sixth Standard.

The eligibility of Candidates, as ascertained by Schedules, or otherwise, *will be determined finally before they are admitted to compete.*

The Bursaries will be awarded strictly in the order of merit.

The competition is open to girls as well as boys.

Regard will be had to the provision of the Scheme, that "*in the event* "*of equality between Candidates, preference shall be given to Candidates* "*who have been constantly resident for three years in High Church,* "*College, St. John's and Calton Parishes.*"

II.—BURSARIES FOR TECHNICAL AND HIGHER EDUCATION

The Governors will offer SEVEN of these Bursaries for Competition in April. They are of the yearly value of Twenty Pounds. They are tenable for two years. They must be held at (*a*) a Technical School or College or place of professional training; or (*b*) at such Higher-class Schools as the Governors may hereafter select. The successful competitors shall elect whether they will hold their Bursaries at a Technical or Higher-class School; and they will give attendance at the day classes at such Technical or Higher-class School.

ELIGIBILITY OF COMPETITORS

"These Bursaries shall be awarded by competitive examination "among pupils of Public or State-aided Schools in Glasgow, or of any "School maintained under this Scheme" (Section 30).

Competitors must have passed the Sixth Standard, with special subjects.

The competition is open to girls as well as young men.

III.—UNIVERSITY BURSARIES

THREE Bursaries of the yearly value of Twenty-five Pounds, will be offered for competition. They are tenable for four years, at the University of Glasgow.

ELIGIBILITY OF COMPETITORS

They will be awarded "by competitive examination among those "who have attended Public or State-aided Schools in Glasgow, or a "School established under the Thirty-ninth Section of the Scheme, "and require aid in obtaining a University education."

"The names of Candidates who are found to possess the qualifica- "tions prescribed in the Section will be sent to the Clerk of Senate, "that they may be entered at the University competition for Bursaries "for the first year.

"The Bursaries will then be awarded to the candidates highest in "the order of merit who fail to win a Bursary at the general competi- "tion."

Forms of application for the several classes of Bursaries may be had by parents or guardians, or by the Candidates themselves, at the Office, 1 South Frederick Street.

Notice will be given to *accepted* Candidates of the day, place, and subjects of examination, and the lines on which it will be conducted.

"If, in the judgment of the Governors, the holder of any Bursary "shall be guilty of serious misconduct, or fail to make reasonable "progress, they may withdraw such Bursary, and their determination "in such case shall be final." (Section 36.)

F. LOCKHART ROBERTSON, D.D.,
Secretary.

1 South Frederick Street, *January*, 1886.

Forms of application must be filled up and returned on or before the 15th March, 1886.

Appendix I

THE GLASGOW GENERAL EDUCATIONAL ENDOWMENTS BOARD

(Constituted by Scheme No. 11, under the Educational Endowments (Scotland) Act, 1882).

BURSARY COMPETITION, 1886

I.—SCHOOL BURSARIES

The Governors will offer FIFTY School Bursaries for competition in the month of April. They are of the value of *Five Pounds* for the first year and *Seven Pounds Ten Shillings* for the second year. They are tenable for two years.

The Governors will select, "as the Schools at which these Bursaries "may be held, certain Schools in each quarter of the City, whether "Schools maintained under a Scheme by the Commissioners under the "Educational Endowments (Scotland) Act, 1882, or Public or State-"aided, in which efficient instruction is given in the higher branches." (Minute of Board, 6th November, 1885.)

ELIGIBILITY OF COMPETITORS

Competitors must be, (*a*) Children "whose parents or guardians are "in such circumstances as to require aid for giving their children a "higher education;" (*b*) They must be attending "Public or State-"aided Schools in Glasgow, or Public or State-aided Schools in the "district of the School Board of Cathcart, or of any School Board "contiguous to and immediately adjoining the district of the School "Board of the Burgh of Glasgow, and have passed the Fifth Standard "of the present Scotch Code."

The eligibility of Candidates, as ascertained by Schedules, or otherwise, *will be determined finally before they are admitted to compete.*

The Bursaries will be awarded strictly in the order of merit.

The competition is open to girls as well as boys.

II.—BURSARIES FOR TECHNICAL AND HIGHER EDUCATION

The Governors will offer TWELVE of these Bursaries for competition in April. They are of the yearly value of *Twenty Pounds*. They are tenable for two years. They must be held at (*a*) a Technical School or College or place of professional training; or (*b*) at such Higher-class Schools as the Governors may hereafter select. The successful competitors shall elect whether they will hold their Bursaries at a Technical or Higher-class School; and they will give attendance at the day classes at such Technical or Higher-class School.

ELIGIBILITY OF COMPETITORS

"These Bursaries shall be awarded by competitive examination, "among pupils of Public or State-aided Schools in Glasgow, or "Public or State-aided Schools in the district of the School Board of "Cathcart, or of any School Board contiguous to and immediately "adjoining the district of the School Board of the Burgh of Glasgow, "or of any School maintained by the Glasgow City Educational "Endowments Board." (Section 29.)

Competitors must have passed the Sixth Standard, with special subjects.

The competition is open to girls as well as young men.

III.—BURSARIES FOR EVENING CLASSES

The Governors will offer FIFTY of these Bursaries for competition in April. They are of the yearly value of *Three Pounds*, and may be held for *two* years. *The second year's appointment being dependent upon the progress and diligence of the Bursar during the first Session.*

The Governors will fix and give due intimation of the Evening Classes for Technical or Higher Education at which these Bursaries may be held.

ELIGIBILITY OF COMPETITORS

These Bursaries "shall be awarded by competitive examination "among Children attending, or who have attended, Public or State-"aided Schools in Glasgow, or Public or State-aided Schools in the "district of the School Board of Cathcart, or of any School Board "contiguous to and immediately adjoining the district of the School "Board of the Burgh of Glasgow." (Section 30.)

The competition is open to girls as well as young men.

Forms of application for the several classes of Bursaries may be had by parents or guardians, or by the candidates themselves, at the Office, 1 South Frederick Street.

Notice will be given to *accepted* Candidates of the day, place, and subjects of examination, and the lines on which it will be conducted.

"If, in the judgment of the Governors, the holder of any Bursary "shall be guilty of serious misconduct, or fail to make reasonable "progress, they may withdraw such Bursary, and their determination "shall in that case be final." (Section 36.)

F. LOCKHART ROBERTSON, D.D.,
Secretary.

1 South Frederick Street, *January*, 1886.

Forms of application must be filled up and returned on or before the 15th March, 1886.

Appendix J

NUMBERS OF PUPIL TEACHERS IN GLASGOW SCHOOLS

DATE	NUMBER	REMARKS
1882	330	
1885	307	
1888	393	
1891	406	
1894	462	From 1892 pupil teachers serve only half-time in schools, necessitating the numbers employed to be doubled.
		In 1896 pupil teachers take Leaving Certificate for the first time. Henceforth numbers diminish as emphasis passes to a full secondary schooling.
1897	620	
1900	551	
1903	431	
1906	335	

Appendix K

20th JUNE, 1912

HIGHER GRADE SCHOOLS (INCLUDING JUNIOR STUDENT CENTRES),
CURRICULA BASED ON A WEEK OF 35 PERIODS OF 45 MINUTES' DURATION.

SUBJECT	I. No. of Periods per Week	II. No. of Periods per Week	III. No. of Periods per Week (a)	III. (b)	IV. No. of Periods per Week (a)	IV. (b)
English, including History	8	8	8	8	8	8
Latin, or	} 8 = 8	} 8 = 8	} 8 = 8	—‡	} 8 = 8§	—
Greek, or						
German						
French	7	7	—	7‡	—	7§
Mathematics	7	3†	7	7	3	3
Physical Exercises	1	1	1	1	1	1
Additional Subjects:						
Science	2*	2*	2*	2*	2*	2*
Drawing	2* } = 4	2* } = 4	2* } = 4	2*	2* } = 4	2*
Needlework or Handwork	2*	2*	2*	2*	2*	2*
Geography	2*	2*	2*	2*	2*	2*
		4†	7‡	8‡	11§	12§
	35	35	35	35	35	35

Unless in exceptional cases provision will be made for Music as a recreative subject.

* Two of these as may be arranged by the School Authorities.

† The four periods set free can be distributed over the additional subjects or devoted to Drawing (HG) or History (HG).

‡ Where only one language is taken with Higher Mathematics, the seven or eight periods set free can be allocated to Science (HG) or distributed between (a) History or Geography; and (b) the additional subjects.

§ Where only one language with Lower Mathematics is taken, pupils would specialise in Drawing or History and take all the additional subjects.

Note.—For Junior Students, practice in the art of Teaching will be given by devoting one period per week from the beginning of session to the date of the Leaving Certificate Examination at Easter, and twelve periods per week from the Leaving Certificate Examination at Easter to end of school session in June.

SELECT BIBLIOGRAPHY

Records of the School Board of Glasgow

Minutes of Public Meetings, 1873–1919
Minutes of Board in Committee, 1873–1919
General Summary of Work, 1873–82
General Summary of Work, Triennial Reports, 1882–1906
Annual Reports, 1907–18
School Statistics, 1876–1907
Album of the School Board of Glasgow, 1876
Letter Books, 1873–1919
Report of Progress in preparations for providing new Public Schools, 1874–81
Glasgow Short-Term Industrial School: General Rules and Regulations, 1910
Govan Street Day Industrial School: General Rules and Regulations, 1908
Prospectuses of Higher Grade Schools, 1900–16
Log Books of individual schools

Newspapers and Periodicals

Glasgow Herald
North British Daily Mail
The Bailie
The School Monthly, 1892–93
The Educational News

Parliamentary Papers

Reports of Children's Employment Commission, 1862
Returns showing Children under 13 in Factories and Workshops (House of Commons), 1871
Reports of Committee of Council on Education in Scotland, 1873–1919
Report of Factory and Workshops Commission, 1876
First Report of Commissioners on Endowed Institutions in Scotland (Lord Moncrieff), 1881
Report of Departmental Committee on Factory Statistics, 1895
Summary of Returns of Persons Employed in:
  Textile Factories (Home Office), 1907
  Non-Textile Factories, 1910
  Workshops, 1911
Report of Reformatory and Industrial Schools Commission, 1896

Report of Departmental Committee on Reformatory and Industrial Schools in Scotland, 1915

Report of Departmental Committee on Partial Exemption from School Attendance, 1909

Reports of Royal Commission on Schools in Scotland (Duke of Argyll), 1865–68

First Report of the Educational Endowments (Scotland) Commission (Lord Balfour of Burleigh), 1884

Report from the Select Committee on School Board Elections (Voting) (W E Forster), 1885

Reports of the Committee appointed to enquire into certain questions relating to Education in Scotland (C S Parker), 1888

Minutes of Evidence taken by the Committee appointed to inquire as to the best means of distributing the Grant in Aid of Secondary Education in Scotland (Earl of Elgin and Kincardine), 1892

Report of Physical Condition of Children in Glasgow, 1907

Books[1]

CALDWELL, JAMES *Educational Endowments of the City of Glasgow: a Review of School Board Education in Glasgow*, Glasgow, Robert Forrester, 1884

B   CONNAL, M *Diary of Sir Michael Connal*, Glasgow, Maclehose, 1895

Dow, H A *History of St Rollox School*, Edinburgh, Murray & Gibb, 1876

GILLESPIE, A *Sir Michael Connal and His Young Men's Institute*, Glasgow, Morison Bros, 1898

B   HADDOW, W M *My Seventy Years*, Glasgow, Robert Gibson, 1943

HENDERSON, G *Some Personal Recollections of School Days in the Calton Forty Years ago*, Glasgow, Harry Hobbs, 1914

KELLY, J (ed) *University Pamphlets*, Glasgow, Robert L Holmes, 1885

B   MITCHELL, W *Rescue the Children*, London, Wm Isbister, 1886

MUIR, T *Sketch of the History of the High School of Glasgow* 1825–77, Glasgow, David Bryce & Sons, 1878

WADE, N A *Post-Primary Education in the Primary Schools of Scotland, 1872–1936*, London, University of London Press, 1939

Pamphlets and Speeches

B   ANDERSON, Mrs E E *Secondary Education*, Glasgow, Robert Maclehose, 1891

BALFOUR OF BURLEIGH, LORD *Secondary Education in Scotland: an address at the opening of Glasgow High School Extension*, Glasgow, Morison Bros, 1887

[1] In this list and that which follows, authors marked "B" were Members, Teachers, or Servants of the Glasgow School Board, though not necessarily at the time of writing.

BLACKIE, W G *Commercial Education*, Glasgow, Blackie & Son, 1888

B BUCHANAN, REV ROBERT *The Schoolmaster in the Wynds*, Glasgow, Blackie & Sons, 1850

CAMERON, C *Free Education*, Glasgow, Wm Munro, 1880

B CAMPBELL, J A *The Education Question*, 1871

B CAMPBELL, J A *General Culture*, 1884

B CAMPBELL, J A *Secondary Education and the State: The Present Position of the Question in Scotland*, Glasgow, James Maclehose, 1891

B COLLINS, A G *Policy and Operations of the Glasgow School Board*, 1879

CRICHTON, G *An Educational Address delivered at the opening of the enlargement to Kinning Park School*, Govan School Board, 1887

B CUTHBERTSON, J N *Secondary Education from the School Board Point of View*, Glasgow, Aird & Coghill, 1887

DICKSON, W P *Recent methods of Educational and University Legislation*, Glasgow: James Maclehose, 1889

B DYER, H *The Technical Schools (Scotland) Act, 1887, and some of its relations to Elementary and Higher Education*, Proceedings of Philosophical Society of Glasgow, 1887

GUTHRIE, W *Recollections of Bridgeton*, Glasgow, R Robertson, 1905

HUTCHISON, J *Secondary Education*, 1876

IRWIN, MARY H *Women's Industries in Scotland*, Proceedings of Royal Philosophical Society, 1896

B KENNEDY, W *Large Schools: Their Educational and Economic Advantages*, 1879

B KENNEDY, W *On Examinations*, Glasgow, Wm Collins & Sons, 1884

B KERR, J G *Educational Experiments*, Proceedings of Philosophical Society of Glasgow, 1897

LAURIE, S S *On the Educational Wants of Scotland*, 1881

LAURIE, S S *Free Education*, 1884

LAURIE, S S *On the Parliamentary Grants to Schools*, Edinburgh, John Lindsay, 1889

LAURIE, S S *The Scottish Code of 1899 and Other Matters*, Edinburgh, Oliver & Boyd, 1899

LAURIE, S S *The Equivalent Grant*, Edinburgh, Neill & Co, 1892

B LONG, H A *Glasgow School Board Elections: How the Roman Catholics Capture the Vote*, Glasgow, John Menzies, 1873

B LONG, H A *How the Glasgow Knoxites can capture the poll head at all future elections while the cumulative vote is legal*, Glasgow, John Menzies, 1900

B MACEWAN, A R *The Dangers of Professional Training*, Glasgow, Robert Maclehose, 1889

McKail, D *Extrinsic and Intrinsic Conditions Affecting School Children: a study of some schools and schoolchildren in Glasgow*, Glasgow, Alex Macdougal, 1909

B   McMath, J *Progress of School Building in Glasgow*, 1873–92, Proceedings of the Philosophical Society of Glasgow, 1892

Miller, J F *Ruchazie: A District and a School in the Provan*, Glasgow, Maclehose, Jackson, 1920

B   Milligan, J *Is Teaching a Profession?* Glasgow, David Bryce & Son, 1889

B   Mitchell, W *Free Education Considered Practically, Experimentally and Briefly*, Glasgow, David Bryce & Son, 1885

B   Mitchell, W *Neglected Children in our Towns and Cities*, Glasgow, Bell & Bain, 1891

B   Mitchell, W *Free Education*, Glasgow, David Bryce & Son, 1885

B   Mitchell, W *Twelve Years' Experience of Day Industrial Schools in Glasgow*, Glasgow, Bell & Bain, 1892

B   Mitchell, W *Twenty Years' Work of the School Attendance Committee*, School Board of Glasgow, 1893

B   Mitchell, W and Munro, A B *The Evening Schools of the School Board of Glasgow: a sketch of their origin and development from 1874–91*, Glasgow, Aird & Coghill, 1898

B   Mitchell, W and Others *Remarks on Commercial Education made at a meeting in the Chamber of Commerce*, Glasgow, Aird & Coghill, 1888

Moir, J *Secondary Education*, Edinburgh, Robert Anderson & Son, 1889

Moncrieff, Lord *An Educational Retrospect: an address at the opening of Kent Road School*, Glasgow, Morison Bros, 1886

Ramsay, G G *A Summary of Entrance Standards and the Practicality of Introducing an Entrance Examination*, Report to the Senate of Glasgow University, 1876

Ramsay, G G *Allan Glen's School and Technical Education*, Glasgow, Robert Anderson, 1888

Ramsay, G G *Report of the Association of Teachers in the Secondary Schools of Scotland*, 1889

Somers, R *Enquiry into the State of Schools and Education in Glasgow*, Richard Griffin, 1857

Stark, J *Suggestions as to the Amendment of the Education (Scotland) Act*, 1872, Glasgow, James Bruce, 1872

Tait, M S *Opposition to a Scheme Affecting the Ferguson Bequest Fund*, issued by the Educational Endowments Commission, 1896

Tulloch, Principal J *Educational Progress and University Reform*, 1882

Theses of Glasgow University

Dobie, T B *The Scottish Leaving Certificate*, 1888–1908, EdB, 1964

MACROBERT, A E *A Study of the Finances of School Boards in the Area of Glasgow*, MEd, 1967

MORRISON, J L *The Implementation of Compulsory Scottish Education from 1883 to 1914*, EdB, 1966

PATON, G *Development of Education in Rutherglen, 1872–1918*, EdB, 1960

SKINNIDER, MARTHA M *Catholic Elementary Education in Glasgow, 1818–1918*, EdB, 1962

WILSON, J D *The Junior Student System*, EdB, 1964

INDEX

Publications of the Scottish Council for Research in Education

**60 A BIBLIOGRAPHY OF SCOTTISH EDUCATION BEFORE
    1872**
    By JAMES CRAIGIE, OBE, MA, PhD, FEIS £4·50 net

**61 A HISTORY OF THE TRAINING OF TEACHERS IN
    SCOTLAND**
    By MARJORIE CRUICKSHANK, MA, PhD £2·50 net

62 A STUDY OF FIFTEEN-YEAR-OLDS   £2·10 net

63 THE SCHOOL BOARD OF GLASGOW, 1873-1919
    By JAMES M ROXBURGH, MA, BSc (Econ), MLitt
    £2·50 net

THE SCOTTISH PUPIL'S SPELLING BOOK
Parts I-V 10p each   **Teacher's Book 75p** each

**MANUAL FOR THE SCOTTISH STANDARDISATION OF
THE WECHSLER INTELLIGENCE SCALE FOR CHILD-
REN**   **25p** net
    (Available only to users of the Wechsler Scale and on
    application to the Council)

**SCHOLASTIC SURVEY TESTS IN ENGLISH AND
ARITHMETIC** (as used in Publications No XLVIII, L and 56)
    20 tests £1